helena čapková / kōichi kitazawa (eds.)
チャプコヴァー・ヘレナ / 北澤興一 編

日本における アントニン レーモンド 1948—1976

ANTONÍN RAYMOND IN JAPAN 1948—1976

知人たちの回想

recollections of friends

karolinum press · prague 2023

謝辞

阿部 賢一
土屋 重文
稲岡 鈴木・由香
石井 麻理亜
叶谷 渥子
川上 純子
河上 春香
松岡 温彦・玲子
長瀬 海
須藤 輝彦
杉田 真珠
高嶺 エヴァ
富重 聡子
ヤクブ・ヴァーレク
レーモンド家
北澤アーカイブ

Thanks

Abe Kenichi
Tsuchiya Shigefumi
Suzuki Inaoka Yuka
Ishii Maria
Kanaya Atsuko
Kawakami Junko
Kawakami Haruka
Matsuoka Atsuhiko and Reiko
Nagase Kai
Sudo Teruhiko
Sugita Shinjū
Eva Takamine
Tomishige Satoko
Jakub Válek
The Raymond family (USA)
Kitazawa Archives

ISBN 978-80-246-5330-3

目次

Contents

Note: Japanese names and titles are presented in English transcription, with the exception of bibliographic data. Names are written in the established order of surname followed by first name.

建設技術と工業が全面的に発展した1921年に、33歳のアントニン・レーモンドが初めての建築設計事務所を日本に構える決断をしたのは偶然ではなかった。近代化の猛烈な勢いはますますダイナミックなものになりつつあり、古い家屋の建て直しにも、最新技術を駆使した新しく都会的なあらゆる展示会にも、それが表れていた。好戦的な大日本帝国の経済と工業の飛躍的な成長と並行して、大正時代（1912〜1926年）および昭和の最初の10年にはコスモポリタン的な社会層が育ち、現代的な生活スタイルへの渇望が生まれた。こうした社会層では、贅沢品や特別な娯楽（社交クラブなど）に加え、各国の大都市への旅行や、人気の高い夏の別荘、国際的企業のある街への滞在などが好まれた。レーモンドは自身のキャリア発展の機会を感じ取り、突然、師である世界的な建築家フランク・ロイド・ライト（1867〜1959年）のもとを離れることに決めた。レーモンドはライトと共に、まさに東京で、近代都市の象徴である帝国ホテルの建築（1914〜1923年）に携わっていた。日本美術の愛好家であり、浮世絵や屏風を収集し、伝統建築を愛していたライトは、日本で様々なプロジェクトに関わっていたものの、そこでキャリアを発展させるには至らなかった。彼は後にアメリカで、さらなる代表作となる建築を生み出す[1]。日本では、帝国ホテル以外は小さな仕事をいくつか請け負ったに過ぎなかったが、日本近代建築という広い文脈から見ると、ライトの重要性は親交のあった日本の建築家のグループ、特に遠藤新（1927〜2003年）や同じく建築家であった土浦夫妻[2]に対する直接的な影響に見ることができる。日本はフランク・ロイド・ライトではなくアントニン・レーモンドとそのフランス系アメリカ人の妻ノエミ・ペルネッサン・レーモンド（1889〜1980年）に手を差し伸べ、生涯にわたるキャリアの成功の機会を提供した。

　1920年代のレーモンドのキャリアは、外国人や外交関係のコミュニティと強く結びついたものだった。帝国ホテルのプロジェクトで共に働いた同僚を通じ、レーモンドはこうした界隈に簡単に出入りできた。ライトが新たに建て替える前から、国内外の要人は伝統的に帝国ホテルで会合を持っていた。こうして続いていた交流の中でも、特にレーモンドを助けたのが同時期（1920年）に

01 ライトの日本への情熱については、以下の論文に詳しい。Julia Meech, Frank Lloyd Wright and the art of Japan: the architect's other passion. New York; London: Harry N. Abrams, 2001.

02 Karen Severns, Arata Endo, Wright Collaborator and Iconoclast to the Last. (SaveWright, Frank Lloyd Wright Bldg Conservancy – Spring 2015 (Published semi-annually by the Frank Lloyd Wright Bldg Conservancy, Chicago), pp. 8–13. 土浦信子（1900〜1998年）とその夫亀城（1897〜1996年）は、1924年から25年まで、タリアセンのライトのスタジオで学んだ。東京のソヴィエト大使館（1931年完成）のプロジェクトなどで、レーモンドとは仕事上で緊密な関わりを続けていた。詳しくは以下を参照。Helena Čapková, Bedřich Feuerstein: Cesta do nejvýtvarnější země světa (Praha: Aula a Kant, 2014), (章題) "Japonská moderní architektura a Feuersteinovo přátelství s Cučiurovými", pp. 55〜69.

The Raymond Studio – Between Japan and America

It is no coincidence that the thirty-three year old Antonín Raymond decided to establish his first architectural enterprise in Japan in 1921, when a boom was under way in construction and industry in general. The rapacious tendency to modernise presupposed increased activity, which found its expression both in the renovation of outmoded buildings and in the construction of new urban planning complexes with the aid of the latest technologies. In parallel with the commercial and industrial conjuncture of the aggressive Japanese empire of the Taishō period (1912–1926), as well as in the first decade of the subsequent Shōwa era, there was a proliferation of a cosmopolitan social stratum, which demanded a corresponding modern lifestyle. This social group developed a taste for luxury and a specific kind of entertainment (in society clubs etc.) on trips to international metropolises, during residences in popular summer resorts and within the commercial environment of international firms. Raymond sensed an opportunity for his own professional advancement, and made a sudden decision to abandon his mentor, the internationally renowned architect Frank Lloyd Wright (1867–1959), with whom he had worked precisely in Tokyo on an iconic structure of the modern city, the Imperial Hotel (1914–1923). Although Wright, a lover of Japanese art, a collector of woodcuts and screens and an admirer of traditional architecture, obtained a prestigious project in Japan, he did not succeed in developing his career further here – he reached his next architectural milestones in America.[1] He did manage to realise a number of subsequent smaller orders in Japan, but within the broader context of Japanese modern architecture his significance consists in his direct influence on the work of a narrow circle of Japanese architects, in particular his close co-worker Endō Arata (1889–1951), or on the married couple of architects Tsuchiura Nobuko and Kameki.[2] Instead of Frank Lloyd Wright, Japan chose Antonín Raymond and his French-American wife, the designer Noémi Pernessin Raymond (1889–1980), providing the couple with an opportunity to pursue a lifelong successful career.

01 For a detailed account of Wright's passion for Japan, see: Julia Meech, *Frank Lloyd Wright and the art of Japan: the architect's other passion*. New York; London: Harry N. Abrams, 2001.

02 See Karen Severns, Arata Endo: *Wright Collaborator and Iconoclast to the Last*. (SaveWright, Frank Lloyd Wright Bldg Conservancy – Spring 2015 (Published semi-annually by the Frank Lloyd Wright Bldg Conservancy, Chicago), pp. 8–13. The architects Nobuko Tsuchiura (1900–1998) and her husband Kameki (1897–1996) studied at Wright's Taliesin studio in the years 1924–1925. They maintained close working contacts with Wright, e.g. in the project for the Soviet embassy in Tokyo (completed 1931). For further details see Helena Čapková, *Bedřich Feuerstein: Cesta do nejvýtvarnější země světa* (Praha: Aula a Kant, 2014), subchapter Japonská moderní architektura a Feuersteinovo přátelství s Cučiurovými, pp. 55–69.

設置されたチェコスロヴァキア大使館や、いくつかの特別なサークルでのつながりだった。この時期のレーモンドは頻繁に旅行し、アメリカでの人脈の利用しようと試みつつ、同時に合衆国でのキャリアの基盤を固めようともしていた[3]。レーモンドが始めるビジネスは、特定の人物との協力関係で特徴づけられる。彼は常に何らかの形でアメリカに関係した同僚と会社を設立した。不和が起こると、また同じ戦略をとり、新しい共同経営者を探した。建築家を確保する場合でも同じように行動しており、1920年代のこの時期にはヨーロッパ系アメリカ人を雇用している。レーモンドの共同経営者の中にはレオン・ウィテカー・スラック（1887〜1970年）がおり、2人は「アメリカン・アーキテクチュラル・アンド・エンジニアリング・カンパニー」を設立した。1925年から27年の間には、スラックよりも若い建築家のアレック・R・サイクスと共に「レーモンド・アンド・サイクス・アーキテクツ」を設立している。その後の10年は自分の名前で会社を設立し、特に1926年から1930年の間は、ベドジフ・フォイエルシュタイン（1892〜1936年）[4]をはじめとする重要な人物と共に仕事をしている。レーモンドが日本からの引き上げを検討していた1930年には、日本人建築家との協力関係が強くなりはじめ、1937年7月20日には日本で彼らと「レーモンド建築設計事務所」を設立した。この会社は今日まで存続している[5]。戦時中、正確には1942年から45年までの間には、レーモンドはニューヨークの建築設計事務所「タトル・シーリー・プレイス・アンド・レーモンド」の共同経営者だった。戦後間もない1946年には、スロヴァキア系建築家のラジスラフ・レランド・ラド（1909〜1993年）と共同で「レーモンド・アンド・ラド」を設立した。この会社は1980年代まで、ニューヨークのパーク・アベニュー101番地でにあった。

大陸をまたいだ休みない活動の間に、レーモンドはチェコスロヴァキアに何度か足を運び、家族のもとへも訪れていた。父のアロイス、兄弟のヴィクトル、フランチシェク、エゴン、エルサ、イルマとは非常に親しかった。レーモンドはチェコでも建築家として有名になり仕事を受けたいと考えていたが、上手くいかなかった。1925年、プラハでマーネス芸術家連盟のために「アメリカの建築について」をはじめとする連続公演を行った。この1年後、人気の高かった芸術月刊誌『ヴォルネー・スムニェリ』に、アントニン・レーモンド＝レイマンの署名と共に何枚かの日本建築の写真が掲載された。レーモンドは主に若い世代の建築家に影響力を持つことに成功した[6]。1935年には再度、日本の建築に関する講演を行った[7]。弟のヴィクトルのおかげで、レーモンドはプラハの芸術界とのつながりを失うことはなく、元チェコ軍団員であり外交官、また作家でもあるヴラジミール・ヴァニェック（1895〜1965年）をはじめとした良い友人に恵まれた。彫刻家オト・グットフロインドの高名なアトリエでは、自分の胸像を作らせた[8]。父のアロイスが1936年に死去し、他の家族はレーモンドの必死の努力にもかかわらず、ナチスの強制収容所で殺害された[9]。それでもレーモンドとチェコスロヴァキアのつながりが失われなかったのは、本書の結論部に収められた研究、すなわち現在まで残っている書簡からも明らかである。アントニン・レーモンドと故郷との関係には、1968年8月のワルシャワ条約機構軍による侵攻も根源的な影響を与えた。レーモンドは自らの作品の回顧展を準

03 A・レーモンドの絶え間ない旅行と、日本だけでなく特にアメリカ、そしてまた出来ればチェコスロヴァキアや他の国々でも名声を確立し維持したいという野心は、レーモンド夫妻の間で交わされた書簡に記されている。2人が離れて暮らしているとき、特に戦間期には、非常に頻繁に手紙のやりとりがあった。書簡はペンシルベニア大学建築アーカイブ（以下AA UPENN）に所蔵されているアントニン・レーモンドの資料から取得されたものである。

04 B・フォイエルシュタインとの仕事については以下を参照。Helena Čapková, Bedřich Feuerstein: Cesta do nejvýtvarnější země světa (Praha: Aula a Kant, 2014), pp. 35〜129.

05 友人である外交官・劇作家のポール・クローデル（1868〜1955年）に宛てた1930年2月19日の手紙の中で、ノエミ・レーモンドは次のように記している。「［...］アントニンはますます（日本から）去ろうかと考えるようになっています。外国人建築家の仕事は減るばかりです。アメリカ大使館と聖路加病院の仕事が終わったら、出ていきたがっています。疲れた時には、ヨーロッパのどこか人里離れたところに引きこもりたいと考え、他の時にはまた大都市を恋しがっています」。手紙からのチェコ語訳は抜き書きを基にし、W・ウィテカー氏 (AA UPENN) の厚意による許可を得て行った。

06 Volné směry XXIV (1926), no. 2, p. 46, pp. 52〜56. ヤロミール・クレイツェルのコメントが1924年5月のPestrý týdenに掲載されている。

07 Antonín Raymond, „O architektuře japonského domu“, Volné směry XXXI (1935), pp. 168〜174.

08 グットフロインドのアトリエを訪れたことは、ノエミと習慣的にやりとりしていた手紙のうち、1925年9月19日にプラハで投函されたものから読み取れる。この手紙は以下の書籍で公刊されている。Kurt Gerard Frederick Helfrich and William Whitaker (eds.), Crafting a Modern World: The Architecture and Design of Antonin and Noémi Raymond (New York: Princeton Architectural Press, 2006) p. 323. レーモンドの胸像は、グットフロインドの作品リストの中では所在不明と記録されている（例えば Jiří Šetlík – Václav Erben, Otto Gutfreund, Národní galerie, Praha 1995)。しかし本書では、アメリカの家族のコレクションの中にあることが確認できる。

09 父親に死をもたらした病気の状況については、兄弟からの、特に姉妹のイルマ・ロハティ

In the 1920s, Raymond's professional strategy was strongly linked with foreign and diplomatic circles, to which he had easy access thanks to his colleagues from the Imperial Hotel project. Both local and foreign dignitaries had met together in the old hotel building, which was replaced with Wright's new construction. Furthermore, Raymond was also helped in establishing contacts by the then newly-opened Czechoslovak embassy (1920), as well as by his membership of a number of exclusive clubs. Raymond travelled extensively during this time, and also attempted to make use of his American contacts in order to concurrently lay the foundations for a career in the United States.[3] His beginnings as an entrepreneur are characterised by a certain type of co-operation: he always established a company together with an American colleague. Following disagreements, he repeated this strategy and sought a new partner. He employed a similar approach also in the case of the artists he recruited during that period, i.e. the 1920s, from the ranks of Euro-Americans. His partners included Leon Whittaker Slack (1887–1970), with whom he established the American Architectural and Engineering Company. Between 1925 and 1927 he was in business with the young American architect Alec R. Sykes, operating under the name of Raymond and Sykes, Architects. For the next ten years he ran a company under his own name, though in the period of 1926–1930 this was in co-operation with such a distinctive figure as Bedřich Feuerstein (1892–1936).[4] In the 1930s, when he was considering whether to pull out of Japan, he began to increase his co-operation with Japanese architects. On 20 July 1937, together with these architects, he eventually opened the Japanese firm Reimondo kenchiku sekkei jimusho (Raymond Architectural Design Office), which is still operating to this day.[5] During the Second World War, specifically in the years 1942–1945, he was a partner in the Tuttle, Seelye, Place and Raymond office in New York. Immediately after the war, in 1946, he established a partnership with the architect of Slovak origin Ladislav Leland Rado (1909–1993). The Raymond and Rado company had its headquarters at 101 Park Avenue in New York until the 1980s.

On his frequent intercontinental travels he visited his family in Czechoslovakia several times. He was very close to his father Alois and his siblings Viktor, František, Egon, Elsa and Irma. He was also keen to further his professional reputation in the Czech lands and if possible obtain an order, but did not succeed in this. He delivered a number of lectures in Prague, for example *On American Architecture* for the Mánes Union of Fine Arts in 1925. One year later, the popular monthly arts journal *Volné směry* published a number of Japanese realisations, signed Antonín Raymond-Rejman. Raymond thus succeeded in making an impact especially upon the younger generation of architects.[6] In 1935 he also published the lecture *On the Architecture of the Japanese House.*[7] Thanks to the efforts of his brother Viktor he did not lose contact with the Prague arts scene, where he had a number of good friends, above all the legionnaire, diplomat and writer Vladimír Vaněk (1895–1965). He had a bust of himself made in the renowned studio of the sculptor Otto Gutfreund (1889–1927).[8] Antonín Raymond's father Alois died in 1936, and despite Raymond's intense efforts the re-

03 Antonín Raymond's constant travels and his ambitions to establish himself and maintain a career not only in Japan but primarily in the United States and if possible also elsewhere, for example in Czechoslovakia, are documented by correspondence between Antonín and his wife, which was very intense during the time of their separation, thus primarily in the inter-war period. The letters are stored in the Antonín Raymond resource at the Architecture Archives of the University of Pennsylvania (hereinafter referred to as AA UPENN).

04 On his co-operation with Bedřich Feuerstein see Helena Čapková, *Bedřich Feuerstein: Cesta do nejvýtvarnější země světa* (Praha: Aula a Kant, 2014), pp. 35–129.

05 In a letter dated 19 February 1930 to her friend, the diplomat and dramatist Paul Claudel (1868–1955), Noémi Raymond wrote: "…Antonín is thinking ever more of leaving (Japan). There is increasingly less work here for foreign architects. He would like to leave once he finishes the US embassy and St. Luke's Hospital. When he feels exhausted, he thinks of how he'd like to disappear somewhere in Europe, in isolation, while at other times he yearns for the big city." Excerpt from letter translated according to excerpts and with the kind permission of Mr. W. Whitaker (AA UPENN)

06 *Volné směry,* no. 2, annual 24, 1926, pp. 46, 52–56. In particular Jaromír Krejcar, see his note in *Pestrý týden, 1 May 1927*

07 Antonín Raymond. O architektuře japonského domu. *Volné směry XXXI*, 1935, pp. 168–174.

08 We learn about his visits to Gutfreund's studio from the obligatory correspondence of Noémi Raymond sent from Prague on 19 September 1925, published in Kurt Gerard Frederick Helfrich and William Whitaker, eds., *Crafting a Modern World: The Architecture and Design of Antonin and Noémi Raymond* (New York: Princeton Architectural Press, 2006) p. 323. Raymond's bust is listed as missing in the inventory of Gutfreund's work (e.g. in Jiří Šetlík and Václav Erben, *Otto Gutfreund*, Národní galerie Praha 1995). However, here we can confirm that it is housed in the family collection in the USA.

備していたが[10]、チェコスロヴァキア侵攻のために叶わなかった。その代わり、彼はアメリカでこの悲劇を周知する活動に積極的にかかわった。例えばカレル・フイェルによる「ソヴィエトの科学者への公開書簡」にも反応している。フイェルの妻に向けて、レーモンドは次のように書き送っている。「私は、チェコ民族に向けて行われたこのような暴虐に私たち皆が大きな衝撃を受けていると確信していますし、同じくらいに、議論の余地もないと思っています。私たちは本当に深く打ちのめされたのです。フイェル博士の文章は非常に重要なものです。可能な限り大部分が刊行されるよう、私はあらゆる手立てを講じます。うまくいくことを願っています。私は今年、30年ぶりにチェコスロヴァキアを訪れる予定でした。なのにこんな恐ろしいことが起こったのです…」[11]。この年の12月にレーモンドは、建築家ヴィクトル・ルディシュ（1927年生）が設計した大阪万博のチェコスロヴァキア館建設の補佐を要請する手紙を、ブルノの著名な建築家ボフスラフ・フックスから受け取っている[12]。後の1971年には、チェコスロヴァキア大使館の建設が始まる。レーモンドが長年力を入れていたプロジェクトで、最終的にいくつかの提案を出したものの、採用は叶わなかった。コンペで勝利したのは建築家のイヴァン・スカーラとイジー・ロウダ（M・クヴィーズとK・コトルボヴァーの協力による）だったが、建築監督はレーモンド建築設計事務所の建築士が務めた（本書180～190ページ）。

だが今は1920年代の日本に戻ろう。この時レーモンドは数多くのプロジェクトを成功させ、国内の建築界で名声を確立していた。しかし困難な生活上の状況、「若者からの敵意」や共同経営者との対立により、1930年代に入ると会社の構造や運営を大きく変えることになった[13]。1920年代にレーモンドを見舞った悲しい出来事の中には、第一子の死亡も含まれる。翌年には、２人目にして唯一の子となったジャン・フランソワ、通称クロードが生まれた[14]。

日本との関係、そして日本の伝統的な建築技法や芸術との関係を深めていく中で、レーモンドは日本人同業者との協力関係を深めるという新しい方策も手にした。彼は世界的な潮流と同時代の建築に関する言説を常に取り入れていた（これはル・コルビュジェから着想を得ていたことからも見て取れる。コルビュジェによる未完のマティアス・エラズリス邸の設計（1929～1930年）は、レーモンドの軽井沢の別荘（1933～1935年）に驚くほど似ている）が、そのうえで独自のスタイルと自律性を保っていた[15]。こうしたレーモンドの成長は、*Antonin Raymond: His Work in Japan 1920–1935*（アントニン・レーモンド：日本での作品、1920～1935年）と*Architectural Details*（建築の細部、1938年） という2つの書籍に収められている。レーモンドは日本で、伝統的な建築技法と近代建築の技術を統合することに自らの独自性を見出したのだ。レーモンドのアトリエに見られるこうした独自路線の建築が、多かれ少なかれクライアントの希望に沿って作られるもう1つの中心的業務たる住宅建築と並んで行われていたということは指摘しておかねばならない。さらに会社に関わる人員にも重要な変化があった。下流工程に携わる技師や設計士に限らず、建築家に関しても、日本人と協力することがますます多くなった。レーモンドは若い、後に名を成すことになる建築家たちと共に働いた。その中には前川國男（1905～1986年）や吉村順三（1908～1997年）も含まれている。本書に収め

ーノヴァーからの手紙に克明に記されている。書簡からは、アントニン・レーモンドが家族と父親の葬儀を金銭面で惜しみなく支援したことが明らかに見て取れる。例えばイルマ・ロハティーノヴァーからアントニン・レーモンドへの1935年9月6日の手紙（AA UPENN)、Irena Veverková, Antonín Raymond a Reimannové: osud židovské rodiny ve XX. století. (Společnost Patria, Slaný 2006) を参照。

10 クラドノ地区教育センター所長、A・シンデラーシュへの手紙より。1965年11月22日 (AA UPENN)。

11 アントニン・レーモンドが1968年10月に東京から出したH・フイェロヴァー夫人宛ての手紙より (AA UPENN)。カレル・フイェルの“An Open Letter To a Soviet Scientist“が初めて公開されたのは1968年10月8日のThe Chatanooga Times、p. 10。

12 ボフスラフ・フフスの手紙、1968年12月6日、ブルノ (AA UPENN)。

13 1920年のチェコスロヴァキア大使館設立後、1910年以来2度目となるレーモンドの横領に関する訴訟が起こされる。レーモンドには国際令状が手配され、元の金額を大幅に超える多額の支払いが命じられた。レーモンドは即座にそれを支払い、訴訟は正式に決着を見た。Helena Čapková, Bedřich Feuerstein (2014), pp. 46～47を参照。

14 レーモンド夫妻の最初の子供は、1925年2月19日に東京の聖路加病院で生まれ、同年の3月23日に死亡した。ジャン・フランソワ・レーモンドは1926年の3月24日に誕生した。Helfrich and Whitaker (eds.), *Crafting a Modern World* (2006), p. 269.

15 この事例についての詳細は以下を参照。Helena Čapková, “Influence of Spirit and Not of Form: Antonín Raymond, Le Corbusier, and Architectural Piracy in the Transwar Era”. In: Shigemi Inaga (ed.), A Pirate’s View of World History, A Reversed Perception of the Order of Things From a Global Perspective, International Symposium proceedings No. 50 (Kyoto: International Research Center for Japanese Studies, 2017) pp. 85～93.

maining members of his family were murdered in Nazi concentration camps.[9] Nevertheless, Raymond did not lose contact with Czechoslovakia, as documented by the study in the conclusion of this book, or his preserved correspondence. However, a devastating impact on Antonín Raymond's relationship towards his homeland was made by the invasion of the Warsaw Pact armies in August 1968. Despite having prepared a retrospective exhibition of his work,[10] he never returned to occupied Czechoslovakia. Instead, in America he fervently disseminated reports of the Soviet aggression, responding for example to Karel Hujer's "Open Letter to a Soviet Scientist". Raymond wrote to Karel Hujer's wife: "I am convinced that we are all wholly shaken by this horror inflicted on the Czech nation, even to the extent that we are incapable of discussion – it has affected us very deeply. Dr. Hujer's article is genuinely very important, and I will do everything to ensure that it is published as widely as possible. I hope I shall succeed. For the first time in thirty years I had been planning to visit Czechoslovakia this year – and then something so appalling happens..."[11] In December that year he received a letter from the renowned Brno architect Bohuslav Fuchs (1895–1972), with a request for his assistance on the construction of the Czechoslovak pavilion at Expo in Osaka, which was designed by the architect Viktor Rudiš (born 1927).[12] One year later, in 1971, the construction of the Czechoslovak embassy began, a project that Raymond had long been attempting to secure, even creating a number of designs, but the realisation eluded him: the competition was won by the architects Ivan Skála and Jiří Louda (in co-operation with M. Kvíz and K. Kotrbová) – although the construction supervision was provided by Raymond's architects (see pp. 181–195).

However, let us return to the Japan of the 1920s, when Raymond succeeded in realising a considerable number of projects, thereby establishing himself on the local architectural scene, although a number of complex life situations, a certain "misadventure from his youth" and disagreements with his colleagues caused Raymond to implement fundamental changes in the mechanisms and activities of the company in the 1930s.[13] One of the unfortunate, tragic events of the 1920s was the death of the Raymonds' first child. One year later their second son was born in New York – Jean-Francois, known as Claude.[14]

Raymond's deepening relationship towards Japan, as well as its local traditional construction approaches and art, led him to a new modus operandi: to closer co-operation with Japanese colleagues. Although Raymond continued to keep pace with international trends and the contemporary architectural discourse – which is illustrated also by the case of his inspiration by Le Corbusier, specifically his unrealised design of the house of Mattias Errazuris (1929–1930), which bears a conspicuous resemblance to the architecture of Raymond's summer villa in Karuizawa (1933–1935) – his style took on greater autonomy.[15] Raymond himself documented this development in two publications: *Antonin Raymond: His Work in Japan 1920–1935* (1935) and Architectural Details (1938). In Japan he found his own distinctive style, consisting in a synthesis of elements of Japanese aesthetics and traditional construction methods with the approaches of modern architecture. It is necessary to point out that this distinctive, autono-

09 The circumstances of his father's illness, which led to his death, are recorded in detail in letters from his siblings, in particular for his sister Irma Rohatýnová. It clearly ensues from the correspondence that Antonín Raymond generously supported his family and contributed to his father's funeral. See e.g. Irma Rohatýnová to Antonín Raymond, 6.9.1935 (AA UPENN). Irena Veverková, *Antonin Raymond a Reimannove: osud židovské rodiny ve XX. století.* (Slaný: Společnost Patria, 2006).

10 Letter to A. Šindelář, director of the District House of Education in Kladno, Kladno, 22 November 1965 (AA UPENN).

11 From a letter from Antonín Raymond to Harriet H. Hujer sent from Tokyo, dated 17 October 1968 (AA UPENN). Karel Hujer's article "An Open Letter To a Soviet Scientist" was first published in *The Chatanooga Times* on 8 October 1968, p. 10.

12 Letter from Bohuslav Fuchs, Brno, 6 December 1968 (AA UPENN).

13 After the establishment of the Czechoslovak embassy in 1920, the case of Raymond's defrauding from 1910 was reopened. An international warrant was issued for Raymond's arrest, and a large sum was demanded from him, several times the original amount. Raymond immediately paid the money and the case was thus formally closed. See Helena Čapková, *Bedřich Feuerstein* (2014), pp. 16–47.

14 The Raymonds' first child was born in St. Luke's Hospital in Tokyo on 19 February 1925, and died on 23 March the same year. Jean François Raymond was born on 24 March 1926. See Helfrich and Whitaker (eds.), *Crafting a Modern World* (2006), p. 269.

15 For further details see e.g. Helena Čapková, Influence of Spirit and Not of Form: Antonín Raymond, Le Corbusier, and Architectural Piracy in the Transwar Era. In: Shigemi Inaga (ed.), *A Pirate's View of World History, A Reversed Perception of the Order of Things From a Global Perspective, International Symposium proceedings no. 50* (Kyoto: International Research Center for Japanese Studies, 2017) pp. 85–93.

た関係者の証言からもわかるように、彼らとレーモンドは生涯にわたる協働関係と友情を築いた。前川は比較的すぐにレーモンドのもとを去って独立した。レーモンドを、一部の歴史家が日本の近代建築の実質的な創始者と呼ぶほど重要な作家にしたのは、逆説的にもこのわずか3年の協働関係（1932〜1935年）だった[16]。1930年代におけるレーモンドのアトリエでの最後の大変化は、妻のノエミ・レーモンドがより積極的に関与するようになったことである。ノエミはクロードの誕生後日本に戻っており、この国に深く触発され、関係者の証言によると、とても健やかな気分で暮らしていたそうだ。

ノエミ・レーモンドの作品にはいくつかの非常に際立った特徴がある。初期の作品には、先進的な美術学校であったティーチャーズ・カレッジからの極めて深い影響が表れている。ノエミ・レーモンドに根本的な影響を与えたのは、著名な教育家で、教育学の改革者であり、日本愛好家でもあったアーサー・ウェズリー・ダウ（1857〜1922年）である。ノエミは未完に終わった自伝の中で、ダウについて次のように表現している。「彼は何年か日本で勉強し、私たちみんなにその芸術を紹介してくれた。非常に才能のある画家というわけではなかったが、天賦の才を与えられなかったすべての人たちがそうであるように、素晴らしい教師だった」[17]。卒業後、ノエミは気鋭のグラフィックデザイナー・イラストレーターとして活躍した。アントニン・レーモンドとの長い結婚生活の初期、特に夫がキャリアの危機に瀕し、自由な芸術の創作のみに打ち込もうと真剣に考えていた時期には、ノエミが家計を支えていた[18]。レーモンド夫妻のキャリアの初期を支えたもう一人の重要人物は、ノエミとその母の親友マリー・カーチャー・ブルックスだった。長期にわたる彼らの友情は、仕事の面だけではなく、精神生活の面でも良い影響を与えた。同時代の「人脈」は方々につながり、例えばパリのグランド・ショミエール芸術学校時代からノエミの友人だった画家のサン・クレア・ブレコンは、後にフランク・ロイド・ライトの二番目の妻となるモード・ミリアム・ノエル（1869〜1930年）の友人でもあった[19]。これがきっかけとなって、レーモンド夫妻はウィスコンシン州タリアセンにあるライトのアトリエを訪れることになり、後の日本への旅にもつながった。

精神生活の探求と、自らの存在を豊かにすることを目指した生涯にわたる霊的な実践、さらに近しい人々の精神を慮る姿勢が、ノエミをニューヨークの神智学協会へと向かわせた（1919年から会員だった）。この協会の国際的なつながり、さらに日本とインドにあった関連団体も、ノエミの役に立った。ノエミが神智学協会に参加していたのは戦間期に限られていたようだが、友人たち、特にフランス人のフィリップ・サン・イレール（1894〜1969年）、通称パヴィトラとの書簡からは、人間存在の霊的側面とヒューマニティに関する問題が、ノエミの生涯を通じたテーマであったことが見て取れる[20]。パヴィトラは東京のスピリチュアリズム関係の会が開いた講座でノエミと親しくなった。彼はインドのポンディシェリに渡り、シュリー・オーロビンド・アーシュラムに参加して運営に携わり、「マザー」と呼ばれた精神的指導者でフランス人のミラ・アルファッサ（1878〜1973年）と親交を持ち共に働いた[21]。神秘主義と精神世界に対するノエミの関心は、オカルトの分野にとどまることはなかった。例えば

16 こうした表現が最初に登場したのは、レーモンドの死に寄せて1976年10月28日の毎日新聞に掲載された記事「現代建築の父、アントニン・レーモンドの死」であり、次いで1976年11月22日のTimes誌（ロンドン）に「ミスター・アントニン・レーモンド」のタイトルで掲載された記事にも見られる。詳細はHelfrich and Whitaker (eds.), Crafting a Modern World (2006), p. 29, イントロダクションの注47を参照。

17 ノエミ・レーモンドの自伝原稿から抜粋、ページ番号なし（AA UPENN）。

18 Helfrich and Whitaker (eds.), Crafting a Modern World (2006), p.16.

19 同書、p. 21。

20 AA UPENNから取得した書簡にはパヴィトラとの手紙は含まれていないが、神智学協会の他の会員、例えばシーク教徒のグルチャラン・シン、ヘンリー・ベディンガー・ミッチェルやブレッコンズ夫妻との書簡が含まれている。「連絡」の取り合いは1970年代まで続き、これも精神的価値に対するノエミの長期間にわたる関心を示している。

21 以下を参照。Helena Čapková, “Theosofie jako síť: Metodologické zamyšlení v kontextu meziválečného Japonska”. In: Rostislav Švácha – Sabina Soušková – Anna Šubrtová (eds.), Věda a umění; Sborník z 5. sjezdu historiků umění (Artefactum, Praha 2017) pp. 216〜〜224。

mous line of Raymond's studio existed concurrently with his other, in fact predominant production, which to a greater or lesser extent accommodated the wishes of his clients. Another striking change was in the personnel composition of the firm: Raymond started to incline more towards his Japanese co-workers; these were no longer merely engineers and designers on lower levels, but also architects. He collaborated with a series of young and later very famous designers, including Maekawa Kunio (1905–1986) and also Yoshimura Junzō (1908–1997), with whom he established a lifelong co-operation and friendship, as documented further in this book (p. 127). Maekawa soon left Raymond and worked independently. Paradoxically, however, it was precisely their three-year period of co-operation (1932–1935) that led to the definition of Raymond as a distinguished artist, who is even viewed by some historians as the founder of modern Japanese architecture.[16] The last fundamental change in Raymond's studio in the 1930s was the ever more intense engagement of Noémi Raymond, who after the birth of her son Claude returned to Japan, which inspired her deeply and where, according to the account presented in her memoirs, she felt thoroughly at home.

Noémi Raymond's work is immediately characterised by a number of striking elements. In her early production there is evidently a deep influence of the progressive Teachers College art school. Noémi Raymond was fundamentally influenced by the distinguished educator and also educational reformer, the Japonist Arthur Wesley Dow (1857–1922), about whom she states the following in her unfinished autobiography: "For some time he studied in Japan, and brought us all to his art. He was not an exceptionally talented painter, but like all who are not blessed with genius, he was an excellent teacher."[17] After graduating she worked as a successful graphic artist and illustrator. At the beginning of her long marriage to Antonín Raymond, especially during the period of his professional crisis, when he was seriously considering switching his focus to exclusively free artistic production, Noémi financed the family budget.[18] Another significant input at the outset of the career of both Raymonds was made by Noémi's friends and by her mother Marie Karcher Brooks. These long-term friendships had a positive influence not only in terms of work, but also on a spiritual level. Within the context of the "networking" of the time, such a function was performed for example Noémi's friend from the Paris art scene concentrated around l'École de la Grande Chaumiere, the painter St. Clair Breckons, whose friend Maude Miriam Noël (1869–1930) was also the companion and later second wife of Frank Lloyd Wright, which opened doors for Raymond to Wright's Taliesin studio in Wisconsin, and prepared the way for his journey to Japan.[19]

It was not only a study of spiritual life and her lifelong spiritual work on the ennoblement of her own existence, but also her concern for the spiritual welfare of those closest to her that attracted Noémi to the New York Theosophical Society (of which she was a member from 1919), whose international connections and affiliated groups in Japan and India she utilised for many years. Although her membership of the Theosophical Society was limited in terms of time, her correspondence with friends, in particular the Frenchman Philippe St. Hilaire (1894–1969), known as Pavitra, docu-

16 This epithet first appeared in the obituary "The death of the father of modern architecture, Antonín Raymond" in the journal *Mainichi*, 28 October 1976, and also under the title "Mr. Antonín Raymond" in the *Times* (London), 22 November 1976. See note on original study no. 47, Helfrich and Whitaker (eds.), *Crafting a Modern World* (2006), p. 29.

17 Excerpt from fragment of autobiography of Noémi Raymond np. (AA UPENN).

18 Helfrich and Whitaker (eds.), *Crafting a Modern World* (2006), p. 16.

19 Ibid., p. 21.

友人であった外交官・劇作家のポール・クローデル（1868〜1955年）の影響のもとで、キリスト教の神学と霊性にも関心を示していた[22]。ノエミはレーモンドが手がけた建物にも、チャペルや教会の繊細で親密な雰囲気の調度品デザインや、「正統な」キリスト教的瞑想の道具設計という形で関わり、こうした精神的な面を表現した。東京都目黒区にある聖アンセルモ聖堂（1952〜1956年）の独特なレリーフ「十字架の道行き」はその一例である（本書138ページ参照)。ノエミが事務所でより重要な役割を果たすようになった1930年代における、レーモンドのスタイルの非常に際立った特徴は、自然のディテールの具体化を重視したことである。ノエミの場合、それは現実の自然を取り入れつつ芸術的な力によって昇華された、特徴的な色彩として表れていた。東京にある赤星邸（1933〜1935年）のインテリアや、エロイーズ・カニンガム邸（1953〜1954年）がそのよい例である。

建物の設計のほか、独自色のある部屋や、その利用法とレイアウトなどにも携わったノエミのデザインには、日本の伝統的な美学と芸術への深い関心が反映されている。関係者の証言によると、ノエミは早いうちに日本語を流暢に操るようになり、日本人の友人も多くできたという。そのおかげでノエミは自然と、一風変わったグラフィックデザイナー・浮世絵師であり思想家の三田平凡寺（1876〜1960年）と知り合うことになった。三田はノエミをアントニンと共に、自らが主宰する珍品の収集家や好事家のクラブ「我楽他宗」（1919〜1940年）に招いた。このグループは定期的に集まり、パーティや小旅行を企画した。三田はまた（特に外国人の）希望者向けに、書道の講座や浮世絵を紹介する講演のようなことも行っていた。我楽他宗は現在の視点から見るといかにもレトロなクラブだったが、当時は驚くほどに先進的だった。たしかに変わったグループではあったが、（主な会員は日本人の著名な科学者や文学者やジャーナリストであったにもかかわらず）外国人に向けて開かれており、また女性に向けても開かれていた。さらに、見事な活字を盛り込んだ豪華雑誌『趣味と平凡』を定期的に発行し、会員の原稿を掲載していた。この我楽他宗で、レーモンド夫妻は先述のパヴィトラや、ポーランド人音楽家・神秘家のジナ・ウビエンスキーとシュテファン・ウビエンスキー (1893〜1976年) 夫妻[23]、さらにインド人陶芸家のグルチャラン・シン (1893〜1976年) と出会った。ノエミにとって、シンは精神世界の探求に向けたさらなる支えとなった。また、知識人や芸術家のコミュニティ、すなわち民芸運動とノエミとを引き会わせた人物でもあった。柳宗悦 (1889〜1961年) が率いた民芸運動は独特の美学思想を形成し、伝統的な民芸品の美こそ、現代日本、さらにはアジアのデザインと建築の生得的な部分であると主張した。レーモンド夫妻と民芸運動のつながりは戦後まで続いたが、残念ながら我楽多宗とのつながりは途切れてしまった。戦後にはすでに我楽他宗自体が存在していなかったからだ。民芸運動や、濱田庄司 (1894〜1978年) をはじめとする陶芸家たちとの交流に触発されたことで、レーモンド夫妻が数多くの陶芸制作を行ったことは疑いの余地がない。さらにノエミは茶道にも熱心に取り組んだ。しかしレーモンド夫妻の芸術的な創作活動が、何年にもわたって個別に発展してきたものであることは強調しておかなければならない。ノエミは自らの芸術の才能によって、権威あるティーチャーズ・

22 資料によると、ポール・クローデルはノエミをカトリックに改宗させようとしており、公教要理を学ぶために2人で会っている。またクローデルは息子クロードの教父でもあった。アントニンからノエミへの1926年4月30日の手紙、Helfrich and Whitaker (eds.), Crafting a Modern World (2006), p. 326に掲載。

23 友人の回想録からわかる限りでは、歌手、ダンサー、オカルティストであったジナ・ウビエンスキーの運命は波乱に富んだもので、また本人と同じように謎めいている。誕生日を秘密にしており、実際よりもかなり若いかのように振る舞っていた。どうやらポーランドのロシア貴族の私生児として生まれたらしいという状況から、血筋や生まれた場所も複雑である。死去した日も不明である。しかし誰もが、第二次世界大戦中にインドネシアの日本人捕虜収容所で死去したことを示唆している。この情報については、シュテファン・ウビエンスキーのご息女であるアドラ・マクウィリアム氏に感謝を申し上げる。ジナ・ウビエンスキーに関する言及は、シュテファン・ウビエンスキーの下記の自伝に見ることができる。Štefan Łubienski, Vor Der Schwelle, Lebenserzählung eines polnischen Künstlers und Suchers (敷居の前で——あるポーランド人詩人、そして探求者の物語) (Driebergen, Holland,1974, 個人出版)。

ments that questions concerning the spiritual nature of human existence and humanity represented a lifelong theme for her.[20] Pavitra, with whom Noémi became close in circles based around the Tokyo spiritual lodges, relocated to Puducherry in India and became the secretary of the ashram of Sri Aurobindo, as well as a close collaborator of his guiding spirit, "The Mother", namely the French occultist and painter Mirra Alfassa (1878–1973).[21] Noémi's interest in mysticism and the realm of the spirit was nevertheless not limited to texts of occult doctrines. For example, under the influence of her friend, the diplomat and dramatist Paul Claudel (1868–1955), she also focused on Christian theology and spirituality.[22] This spiritual level was reflected in the work of the Raymonds in the sensitive, intimate conception of the design of the furnishings of several churches and chapels, as well as in the rendering of the "canonical" environments of Christian meditation, for example in the individual Stations of the Cross in the Church of St. Anselm (1952–1956) in the Meguro district of Tokyo (see p. 143). An absolutely fundamental element of the Raymond style from the 1930s, thus at the time when Noémi was most active in the architecture office, was an emphasis on stylised natural detail, and in Noémi's case a characteristic colour scheme, which though it was based on real nature was augmented by a substantial artistic expression. A good example is provided by the interiors of the Akaboshi villa (1933–1935) in Tokyo and the small villa of Miss Eloise Cunningham (1953–1954). Noémi Raymond, who also participated in the architectural design of buildings, in the composition or layout of individual rooms and their utilisation, projected her deep interest in traditional Japanese aesthetics and art into her design work. Witness testimonies tell us that Noémi quickly learned fluent Japanese, which gained her several Japanese friends, including the extravagant graphic artist and intellectual Mita Heibonji (1876–1960), who invited her and her husband to the Garakutashū club of collectors and lovers of obscure knowledge (1919–1940). The club held regular meetings, and arranged parties and excursions. For a few interested individuals, primarily those from abroad, Mita conducted courses in calligraphy and a kind of introduction to the art of wood carving. From a contemporary perspective Garakutashū was a modern club, which was indeed surprisingly progressive in its time. Although it was marginal it was open to foreigners (even if its members were primarily distinguished Japanese scientists, literati and journalists), and in addition it was open to women and regularly published the luxurious, superbly typographically conceived magazine *Shumi to Heibon* (Hobbies and Ordinary Stuff), featuring contributions from its members. In the Garakutashū club the Raymonds met together with the aforementioned Pavitra, the Polish musicians and mystics Stefan (1893–1976) and Zina Łubienski,[23] and the Indian ceramic artist Gurcharan Singh (1896–1995). It was Singh who represented a further source of support for Noémi on her spiritual journey. He also acted as a mediator between Noémi and a group of intellectuals and artists – the famed Mingei movement, which under the leadership of Yanagi Sōetsu (1889–1961) formed a distinctive aesthetic stance, promoting the beauty of traditional folk crafts as a natural component of modern Japanese or Asian design and architecture. The Raymonds maintained con-

20 The correspondence stored at AA UPENN contains not only letters with Pavitra, but also with other members of the TS, e.g. with the Sikh Gurcharan Singh, Henry Bedinger Mitchell and the Breckons couple. Correspondence "conversations" continued up to the 1970s, indicating Noémi's enduring interest in spiritual values.

21 See Helena Čapková, Theosofie jako síť: Metodologické zamyšlení v kontextu meziválečného Japonska, in: Rostislav Švácha – Sabina Soušková – Anna Šubrtová (eds.), *Věda a umění; Sborník z 5. sjezdu historiků umění* (Artefactum, Praha 2017, pp. 216–224).

22 From the documents it ensues that Paul Claudel attempted to convert Noémi Raymond to Catholicism, that they met together at lessons in catechism and that he was the godfather of their son Claude. In: Letter from Antonín to Noémi dated 30 April 1926, reproduced in Helfrich and Whitaker (eds.), *Crafting a Modern World* (2006), p. 326.

23 The fate of the singer, dancer and occult enthusiast Zina Łubienska was as turbulent and mysterious as the artist herself, at least as we know it from the recollections of friends. She concealed her true date of birth and presented herself as considerably younger than she actually was. Her origin, and therefore also her place of birth, was complicated by the circumstance that she was probably the illegitimate child of Russian aristocrats living in Poland. The date of her death is also unknown. However, all sources attest to the fact that she died in a Japanese internment camp in Indonesia during the Second World War. For this information the author thanks the daughter of Stefan Łubienski, Adola McWilliam. We can find mentions of Zina Łubienska in the autobiography of Stefan Łubienski, *Vor Der Schwelle, Lebenserzählung eines polnischen Künstlers und Suchers* (Before the Threshold, the life story of one Polish artist and "seeker") (Driebergen, Holland: self-published, 1974).

カレッジに入り、ニューヨークのグラフィックデザイナーの激しい競争環境にn•i•pのイニシャルで参加して、新聞をはじめとするメディアに携わることができたのだ。この頃のノエミの自主制作作品も残されている(本書174〜177ページ参照)。またノエミは衣服制作を含む日本の伝統芸術に関心を持っており、着物を縫うことこそなかったものの、ヨーロッパ様式の衣服を制作したこともわかっている(本書38ページ参照)。しかし彼女が自主制作を行うことは徐々に少なくなっていった。対照的にアントニンは機会を見つけては絵画を制作し、1930年代からは陶芸にも打ち込んだ。彼の作品も本書に掲載している(168〜173ページ)。夫妻は共に日本の芸術作品を収集しており、そのコレクションは貴重な古代の埴輪といった古いものから、岡本太郎(1911〜1996年)や先述の濱田庄司など同時代の作品にまで及ぶ。

書簡でも触れられているこのコレクションは、アトリエの最も暗い時代である第二次世界大戦を乗り越えた。レーモンド夫妻はアメリカに移ることを長い間考えていたが、外交界からのシグナルがこの決断を速めた[24]。移動にあたっては、1930年代の前半を通じてずっと携わっていたプロジェクトを利用した。そのプロジェクトの始まりについては、ノエミとパヴィトラの書簡から伺い知ることができる。これらの手紙には、友情や、同じヨーロッパ系という出自——ノエミは「マザー」ミラ・アルファッサやパヴィトラと同じフランス生まれだった——そして霊的な共振や専門家としての名声から、パヴィトラ側にレーモンドのアトリエへ新しい宿舎の設計を委嘱する準備があることが記されている。集団生活の設備を備えた瞑想のための施設で、元フランス領インド、ポンディシェリにあるシュリー・オーロビンド・アーシュラムの本拠地に位置する「ゴルコンデ」だ。最初の話では、45人のサーダク(求道者)、つまりシュリー・オーロビンドとその教えに従う人々のための3階建て宿舎の建設計画が伝えられている[25]。それぞれの階には集団で使用するための設備があり、洗濯場など家事作業のための部屋は最小限に抑えて1階に配置する。階段1か所と長い回廊を設置し、建物内の動きやすさと方向感覚を確保する。同じ手紙の中でパヴィトラは、ボンベイから来た技術者をはじめ名前の明記されていないアシュラムのメンバーと「マザー」が建設の監督を務めることを伝え、レーモンドに提案書と設計図を送るよう求めている。

このプロジェクトではノエミだけではなく、建築家のジョージ・ナカシマ(1905〜1990年)とフランチシェク・サマー(1907〜1973年)も重要な役割を果たした。2人ともレーモンドの人生に深く関わった人物である。ナカシマは日系アメリカ人で、1934年にレーモンドの東京のアトリエに加わったが、まさにこのゴルコンデのプロジェクトが、創作面でも人生においても彼の転機となった。アシュラムの哲学と精神性に深い感銘を受けたナカシマはこのコミュニティに足を踏み入れ、スンダラナンダという名を受け、その後生涯にわたって貢献した。しかし戦争が間近に迫ったことで、スンダラナンダはインドを去ることを余儀なくされ、1939年に東京に戻った。その後、やはり日系アメリカ人の妻マリオンと共にアメリカに渡った。到着後は2人とも強制収容所に送られたが、アントニン・レーモンドの仲介で解放され、しばらく後にはペンシルバニア州ニューホープのレーモンドの会社で暮らした。戦後、ナカシマは木製家

24 ノエミの義理の姉妹であるジャネットが日本に暮らしており、その夫は東京のアメリカ大使ジョン・ムーア・アリソンだった。
25 パヴィトラからノエミへの1935年6月7日の手紙(シュリー・オーロビンド・アーカイブ)。

tact with members of Mingei also after the war, which unfortunately could not apply in the case of the Garakutashū club, since this no longer existed. Contact with Mingei and ceramic artists such as Hamada Shōji (1894–1978) undoubtedly inspired the Raymonds to experiment with their own ceramic art. In addition to this, Noémi studied the art of the tea ceremony. However, we must emphasise that the artistic production of the Raymonds had an individual development over the course of the years. Noémi's artistic talent brought her to the established Teachers College, and enabled her, working under the pseudonym "n*i*p", to assert herself within the competitive environment of New York graphic designers working for newspapers and other media. Her free artistic work has been preserved from this period (see pp. 174–177). We know that she focused on traditional Japanese art, including the production of fabrics, though she did not have these made into kimonos but rather dresses cut in European style (see p. 37). However, she gradually gave up working on her free art. By contrast, Antonín Raymond painted at every opportunity, and continued to focus on ceramics production (pp. 168–173). Both spouses collected Japanese artworks, from the oldest, such as rare primitive *haniwa* figures, to the production of their contemporaries such as Okamoto Tarō (1911–1996) or the aforementioned Hamada Shōji.

1 – A.レーモンドのアトリエ。ゴールコンダ宿舎、シュリー・オーロビンド・アーシュラム(ポンディシェリ、インド、1948年撮影)。

Antonín Raymond's studio, Golconde Dormitory, Ashram of Sri Aurobindo (Puducherry, India, photo from 1948)

This collection also was the subject of the correspondence that has been preserved from the darkest period of the studio, namely that of the Second World War. The Raymonds had already been considering relocating to America for a longer period of time, but signals from diplomatic circles hastened their decision.[24] For the purposes of relocating they made use of a project which accompanied them throughout the entire first half of the 1930s, about whose beginnings we are informed primarily by the correspondence of Noémi with Pavitra. It ensues from the letters that based on their friendship, their European origin (Noémi, like both the Mother Mirra Alfassa and Pavitra, was French by birth), their spiritual orientation and their impressive professional reputation, Pavitra was able to offer the Raymond studio an order for a new "dormitory", or more precisely a building designated for the purpose of meditation, which also housed collective accommodation: the Golconde at the seat of the ashram of Sri Aurobindo in Puducherry in French India. In the first specific mention, Pavitra informed Raymond that they intended to build a three-storey building for 45 sadhaks, followers of Sri Aurobindo and his teaching.[25] On each floor there were to be communal facilities, while other necessities such as a laundry etc. would be on a lower ground floor. A single staircase and a long corridor would ensure easy passage and orientation within the building. In the same letter Pavitra requested that Raymond provide a design for the building, stating that the supervision of the construction would be carried out by Mother together with an unnamed member of the ashram, an engineer from Bombay.

A significant contribution to the project was made not only by Noémi, but also by the architects George Nakashima (1905–1990) and František Sammer (1907–1973), who made a deep impression on Raymond's life. Nakashima was an American of Japanese origin, who began working at Raymond's Tokyo studio in 1934, and it was precisely the Golconde that became a milestone in his creative and personal life. The

24 Noémi's stepsister Jeannette lived in Japan together with her husband John Moore.
25 Pavitra to Noémi, 7 June 1935 (Sri Aurobindo Archives).

具のデザイナーとして知られるようになった[26]。ゴルコンデプロジェクトの第二の重要な協力者はチェコスロヴァキア人のフランチシェク・サムメルで、モスクワとパリでル・コルビュジエのアトリエに関わった後にレーモンドのもとにやって来た。1936年に東京のアトリエに参加して間もなくインドに向かい、関係者の中でもっとも長期間にわたってこの宿舎の建築を監督し、また自らも作家として参加して、質の高い建築とデザインを実現した。戦争によってサマーもポンディシェリを去らねばならなくなり、長い思案の末、1942年にビルマでイギリス軍に加わった[27]。戦後、戦闘で負った傷が癒えるとチェコスロヴァキアに戻り、共産党政権下での専門家による監督機関で積極的に活躍し、故郷プルゼンをはじめとする比較的大きな都市の開発や、大規模団地とインフラストラクチャーの建設に携わった。

1938年に日本を出た後も、レーモンド夫妻はアトリエの協力者たちと連絡を取り続けた。彼らは事務所の運営を維持し、レーモンドの財産を日本からアメリカへ送る手配をした。しかし戦況は短い間に急激に悪化し、会社の運営は完全に止まった。レーモンドともっとも親しく仕事をしていた吉村は、まさに運営が止まる頃、いくつかの依頼を手がけていたアメリカから戻ってきた[28]。

戦後になるとレーモンド夫妻は日本に戻ってきた。戦争の傷跡だけではなく、現地の住民とアメリカ人の間の敵意もまだ残っていた。こうした対立は日本の占領期が過ぎ去った後、1950年代まで続いていた。統治のための建物や航空基地の建設、さらに破壊された技術施設やインフラストラクチャーの再建でアメリカ占領軍を支援しようと、アントニン・レーモンドは個人的な計画から1948年に日本に戻った。東京の焼け跡でレーモンドは再び会社を設立した。この事務所は現在も東京にある。共に働いていた人々はレーモンドに忠実で、戦後のさらなる展開に向けて準備を整えようと、事務所の設備やプロジェクトの資料を大切に守り抜いていた。

ヘレナ・チャプコヴァー

26 George Nakashima, The Soul of a Tree. A Woodworker's Reflections (New York 2011)。

27 Shraddhavan (ed.), Golconde: A Look behind, Part 5. The Builders (2), Mother India, May, 1989, pp. 319〜322。

28 アントニン・レーモンドは、第二次世界大戦への協力を秘密にはしなかった。彼は建築家として日本の街の模型を設計し、アメリカ軍の爆撃訓練用の標的として使われた。日本の伝統文化の発祥の地である京都を護ったことも述べている。東京や他の都市は、しかし灰燼と化した。Antonín Raymond, An Autobiography (Rutland, Vt.: Charles Tuttle, 1973) pp. 188〜189. および、John W. Dower, Cultures of War: Pearl Harbor / Hiroshima / 9–11 / Iraq (New York, N.Y.: W. W. Norton, The New Press, 2010) p. 176。

philosophy and spirituality of the ashram held such a strong appeal for him that he became a member of the community, for whom he worked under the name Sundarananda until the end of his life. However, the approaching war forced him to leave India, and in 1939 he returned to Tokyo. He later left for the United States together with his wife Marion, also an American with Japanese roots. After their arrival in the United States both were interned in a concentration camp, from where they were released only following the intercession of Antonín Raymond, after which they lived for a period of time on Raymond's farm in New Hope in Pennsylvania. (After the war Nakashima found fame as a designer of wooden furniture.)[26] The second important collaborator on the Golconde project was the Czechoslovak František Sammer, who came to Raymond following his engagement at Le Corbusier's studio in Paris and Moscow. Almost immediately after commencing work at Raymond's studio in Tokyo in 1936 he left for India, where for the longest time of all those involved he supervised the construction of the "dormitory", guaranteeing its quality realisation and the high standard of its design, to which he himself contributed as an author. Sammer was also forced to leave Puducherry during the war. Following protracted negotiations he entered the British army in Burma in 1942.[27] After the war and his convalescence following an injury he returned to Czechoslovakia, where he worked as an active member of professional governing bodies subordinate to the communist regime. In this capacity he contributed to the urban planning of cities, above all his native Plzeň, and to the realisation of housing estate complexes and infrastructure.

After leaving Japan in 1938, the Raymonds remained in contact with their co-workers, who maintained the running of the office and organised the transport of Raymond's property from Japan to the USA. However, the wartime situation soon deteriorated to such an extent that the firm ceased to function entirely. Yoshimura, one of Raymond's closest collaborators, returned from America, where he had contributed to a number of orders, literally on the last ship.[28]

After the war the Raymonds returned to a Japan which was marked not only by the war itself but also by an enduring hatred between Americans and the local populace, which persisted throughout the entire period of peacetime occupation of Japan, up to the 1950s. Antonín Raymond returned to Japan on his own initiative in 1948 in order to assist the occupying American forces in constructing administrative buildings, air force bases, and in the reconstruction of destroyed technical buildings and infrastructure. In the charred ruins of Tokyo he reopened his company, which remains active in the city to this day. Raymond's co-workers were loyal to him, carefully maintaining the office furnishings and taking care of the project documentation so as to be prepared for the following post-war phase.

Helena Čapková

26 George Nakashima, *The Soul of a Tree*. A Woodworker's Reflections, New York 2011.

27 Shraddhavan (ed.), Golconde: *A Look behind*, Part 5. The Builders (2), Mother India, May, 1989, pp. 319–322.

28 Antonín Raymond did not conceal his engagements during the Second World War. As an architect he designed simulations of Japanese cities which served as training targets for American bombers. He states that he protected the cradle of traditional Japanese culture – Kyoto. However, Tokyo and other cities were reduced to ashes. In Antonín Raymond, *An Autobiography* (Rutland, Vt.: Charles Tuttle, 1973) pp. 188–189. Also in John W. Dower. *Cultures of War: Pearl Harbor, Hiroshima, 9–11, Iraq* (New York, N.Y.: W. W. Norton / The New Press, 2010) p. 176.

2 – 群馬音楽センターの現場にてア・レーモンド、五代氏、高崎、１９６０年頃。

Godai Yoshiko and Antonín Raymond on the construction of the Gunma Music Centre (Takasaki, approx. 1960)

五代美子

五代美子氏は第二次世界大戦後にアントニン·レーモンドが再来日し、事務所を再開して間もなく、1949年に入社した。1966年までレーモンドの秘書として、合計17年事務所で働いた。現在までレーモンドの家族との友情を保っている。

Godai Yoshiko

Mrs. Godai Yoshiko joined Raymond's firm shortly after its re-opening in 1949. She worked as Raymond's secretary until 1966, thus for seventeen years. She was friends with the Raymonds throughout her life, and maintains close contact with their family to this day.

3 – ノエミ・レーモンドと五代美子。八幡安川電機株式会社の上棟式出席のため、八幡安川へ向かい瀬戸内海を渡る船上にて。1955年。

Noémi Raymond and Godai Yoshiko on the deck of a boat on the inland sea, on a voyage to the Yahata Yaskawa electric corporation for the occasion of the jōtōshiki ceremony, commencing the construction of the roof (1955)

チャプコヴァー: 五代美子さんは第二次世界大戦後にアントニン・レーモンドが再来日し、事務所を再開して間もなく1949年に入社しました。1966年までレーモンドさん秘書として、合計17年事務所で働いていました。現在までにレーモンドのご家族との友情を保っています。

今日は、五代美子さんをお招きしています。彼女は、かつてアントニン・レーモンドの元で、秘書、速記者として活躍しておられました。また、レーモンドの会社および家族と生涯とても親密にお付き合いされました。家族ぐるみのものと言ってもいいでしょう。レーモンドは、第二次世界大戦の終わり、米政府に協力をします。まずは、彼がどのような形で米政府と関わりを持ったか、お尋ねするところから始めたいと思います。五代様、第二次世界大戦の終わった頃、東京はどのような様子でしたか。

五代: 私はそのとき、東京から離れていました。母の実家の新潟県新発田市におりましたので、話に聞くような大焼野原は実際に見ておりません。その後、東京へ戻ったのは1948年。でも1945年の、あの3月10日の大空襲で私の家が焼けた後、うちの近所が焼野原になった様子はよく見ています。青山墓地に避難して夜があけてから、自分の家の焼け跡に行くまでに、黒焦げになった人間の死体を何十体も目にいたしました。私たちも一瞬遅れれば、そういう目に遭っていた。そう思うと恐ろしくて。不安に押しつぶされそうになりながら親子5人で手を引いて青山墓地に避難した怖さは忘れられません。

チャプコヴァー: どのようなきっかけでアントニン・レーモンドのオフィスに入ったのですか？

五代: 戦後GHQの要請で、レーモンドが只見川にダムを造ることになりました。その際(1949)、アメリカからハイドロ・エレクトリック・エンジニアを連れてくることになり、ミスター・フロアーという、優秀な技術者を招聘したのです。戦前にレーモンド事務所で働いていた方たちは、昔の図面等を全部疎開保管して

HČ: For many years Mrs. Godai Yoshiko was the personal assistant to the architect Antonín Raymond, and a stenographer at his company. Their working relationship grew into a long-term friendship, and it could even be said with a degree of hyperbole that Mrs. Godai remains a member of the Raymond family to this day. Antonín Raymond returned to Japan shortly after the Second World War, specifically in 1948, as a co-worker of the American occupying forces. How did Raymond's return take place, and how specifically was it linked with the American forces? We shall focus on these themes in the introduction to our interview, but first of all I'd like to ask Mrs. Godai the following: "What was Tokyo like at the end of the Second World War?"

GY: Towards the end of the war we were no longer in Tokyo. We were staying with our mother's relatives in Shibata in the Niigata prefecture. I never actually saw the so-called "Great Bombsite" that I'd heard about with my own eyes. We didn't return until 1948. Our house had been burned down in the Great Tokyo Air Raid of 10 March 1945. I remember very clearly the bombed out ruins that still remained of it and the neighbouring houses for three years after the raid. The view of dozens of charred human bodies that I saw on the way home in the evening, when we were returning from our evacuation in the Aoyama cemetery, also made an indelible imprint on my memory. That would also have been our fate, if we'd delayed for just a moment. It's a terrible recollection. I still feel a sense of anxiety when I recall that fear that gripped me, my parents and my two sisters, when we held hands and fled to hide in the Aoyama cemetery.

HČ: Under what kind of circumstances did you start working for Raymond's studio?

GY: Upon the request of the General Headquarters of the American occupying forces, Raymond was commissioned with the construction of the dam on the river Tadami. In the same year (1949) the outstanding American expert in hydroelectric power stations Erik Floor was invited to Japan. It's necessary to point out that the employees from Raymond's pre-war studio had carefully stored all the diagrams and other property, including documents which remained in Japan, and awaited Raymond's return

4 – 笄町の事務所にて、デスクにつく五代さん。西麻布、1952年。

Mrs.Godai at her desk in Kogaichō, Nishi Azabu (1952)

HČ: Helena Čapková
GY: Godai Yoshiko
PH: Petr Holý

レーモンドの再来日を待っておりました。すぐにでも事務所を開きたい気持ちだったと思いますけれど、その頃は建物をすぐ建てたりする事も難しかったのです。そんな折、MITを卒業なさった鷲塚誠一さんという建築家が、レーモンドにパートナーシップを組まないかという話を持ち掛けてきました。その方は、建築家であると同時に多角的にいろいろビジネスをしていらっしゃいましたので、その頃はまだ日比谷にあったNHKの裏の地所にモルタル塗りの二階建てを二棟持っていらして、レーモンドがパートナーシップを組んだらその一棟に入って良いという条件だったようです。彼は新橋駅のガードの下の、列車が通るたびに物凄い音のする、狭い場所で英文タイプの学校を経営していました。私はその学校に入って、そこのコースを卒業したのですが、その際に「アントニン・レーモンドの事務所に行かないかと誘っていただきました。アントニン・レーモンドという名前も、生まれて初めて聞いた名前ですし、建築というものがどういうものかも全然わかりませんでしたけど、とにかく、仕事をして、収入を得ないと生活できないという状態でしたので、喜んで試験を受けに行きました。インタビューを受けたら、鷲塚事務所に受け入れてくださることになり、ほっとして次の日から、その頃住んでいました千葉県市川市行徳から総武線に乗って、新橋まで通い始めました。けれど、一か月ほど経った頃、レーモンドと鷲塚は、建築上の意見が合わなくて喧嘩別れ。私はせっかく仕事に就けたのに一か月でもうクビか、とがっかりしました。でも、幸いなことに、レーモンド事務所の方で「オフィスガールが要るからそちらで手伝えという嬉しいオファーをいただいて、働き始めました。それが私のレーモンド夫妻との幸運な出逢いとなりました。

5 – 宇野家の写真。右端に立つのが美子さん(長女)。東京、1930年代。

The Uno family, the oldest daughter Yoshiko on the right (Tokyo, 1930s)

チャプコヴァー: 戦後、レーモンド事務所が手がけた最初のプロジェクトはどのようなものでしたか。

五代: リーダースダイジェスト東京支社のビルディングを建てるのが戦後、最初の仕事でした。1948年には日比谷におりましたが、その現場が始まる1949年に、竹橋のリーダースダイジェストの現場に移りました。

チャプコヴァー: リーダースダイジェストの、思い出をお聞かせください。

五代: 普通は現場事務所ってあまり大きいものじゃないんですけれど、鷲塚と別れて行くところが無かったので、丸太小屋で、ずいぶん細長い建物を事務所としました。入ると、オフィスが右側の方で、ドラフティング・ルームは左側にありまして、その奥に、レーモンド自身のスタジオがありました。それから六本木の今井町へ移りました。六本木から溜池の方に降りる坂の左手の高台に戦前使われていた三井家の地所がありました。そこにアメリカ大使館館員のための宿舎を設計したんです。ペリーとハリスという２つのアパート。

ホリー: リーダースダイジェストの前に、イサム・ノグチの、「九輪」というと

6 – 福島山の歴史ある旅館の前に集まる只見ダム建設プロジェクト参加者たち。前列中央に座るのがエリック・フロアー、その左がアントニン・レーモンド、cca. 1949。

Participants in the project for the construction of the Tadami dam in front of a traditional ryokan hotel in Fukushimayama. In the middle of the first row sits Erik Floor, on his left is Antonín Raymond (approx. 1949)

after the war. Although they evidently wanted to open the studio immediately, the recovery of the construction industry progressed slowly. A solution to this situation came from the architect Washizuka Seiichi (Samuel), a graduate from MIT, who in addition to architecture was engaged in other commercial activities, and had two two-storey walled buildings in the Hibiya district in the centre of Tokyo, on a plot of land just behind the former buildings of the NHK television station. He offered the use of one to Raymond on the condition that he accepted the partnership. During that time, Washizuka was also running a school for stenographers in English, in cramped premises beneath the viaduct in Shinbashi. I enrolled at the school, and after I graduated Mr. Washizuka asked me if I'd like to start work at Raymond's office. I'd never heard his name before, and I knew nothing about architecture, but I needed work and an income, and so I gladly went to compete for the job. The interview went well, and I started in Washizuka's secretarial services. A weight fell off my shoulders. The next day I again took the Sōbu line to Shinbashi from my house in Ichikawa in the Chiba prefecture (in the neighbourhood of Tokyo). About a month later, Raymond and Washizuka had a disagreement on certain architectural matters, they fell out and their partnership broke up. I was sad because I'd lost my job after less than a month. However, fortunately they needed an administrator at Raymond's office, and so I started work for them. And that's how my lucky and fateful meeting with the Raymond couple began.

HČ: What was the first project you contributed to at Raymond's office?

GY: The company's first big post-war project was the building of the Tokyo branch of Reader's Digest magazine. In 1948 the firm was still located in Hibiya, one year later we moved directly to the Reader's Digest construction site in Takebashi.

7 – 五代さん、笄町の事務所にて。後方の写真はフランシス・ハール（1908〜1997）の作品。西麻布、1951年。

Mrs. Godai in the office in Kōgaichō. The author of the photographs on the wall is Francis Haar (1908–1997). Nishi Azabu (1951)

ても有名な、彫刻作品があったと思います。レーモンドとイサム・ノグチは何か関係があったのですか？

五代: とても仲良しでした。イサム・ノグチは、レーモンドと、父親ぐらい年が離れていたんじゃないでしょうか、よく遊びに来ていましたね。リーダーズダイジェストの建物には、彼のつくった彫刻が沢山ありました[1]。

チャプコヴァー: 笄町での日々についてお聞かせください。このオフィスでの毎日はどのようなものだったのですか。

五代: 外の門から入ると玄関があるんです。そこから向かって左手に、事務所。右手には、電気、下水道配管等のメカニカルに関する部門があって、さらに奥に行くとドラフティング・ルームがあります。いちばん奥は青図を印刷するところ。隣にはデザイン・ルーム。ここではレーモンドが何か建築のアイディアがでたとき、小さい紙切れに走り書きをして、それを建築家たちに見せて、図面を引かせるんです。デザイン・ルームに続いて下の方のところは、ミセス・レーモンドの部屋がありました。ミセス・レーモンドのところにもいつも女性の秘書の方がいらっしゃいました。ミスター・レーモンドのスチュディオはその左に。私は上の方の廊下のところにデスクがあって、境のふすまの陰におりました。私の窓からは中庭が見えましたね。レーモンドさんたちは、外気浴が好きなので、真冬のよほど寒いとき以外は外のテラスでいつも食事をしておりました。その前にはプールがあります。左の方には、バスルームがあって、それからキッチンがあって、サーバント・クオーターがありました。

ホリー: サーバントとして仕えた方は何人ぐらいいらしたんでしょうか？

五代: 日本人の女性のメイドと運転手、それから通いのシェフがそれぞれ一人ずついました。その方の料理をレーモンドがとても気に入っていまして。レーモンドはとにかくお肉が好きなんですよ。子供頃には時代的に肉類は食べることができなかったらしくて、ジャガイモとパンとバターを食べて過ごされていたらしいのです。ただ、ミセス・レーモンドは動物愛護の方なので、動物のお肉は一切召し上がらないんですよ。今でいう、ヴィーガンというか、ベジタリアンというか。ミスター・レーモンドがコックにいろいろ頼んだりしてるところに、ミセス・レーモンドが口を出されると、怒るんですね。'You don't know anything about cooking!'て言って。私、「そういうひどいことを言われて、どうして我慢していられるんですか？ってお聞きしたことあるんですけど、'Oh, he'll make it up other time.'っておっしゃるんです。いくらひどいことを言われても彼には優しいところがあって、埋め合わせはある。彼女はそれを理解している。そういういことですね。とても良いご夫婦でした。

ホリー: 見倣いたいですね（笑）。

8 – 事務所は一時的にリーダースダイジェスト社屋から西麻布の笄町に移設される。東京、1951年3月31日。

The temporary office moves to Kōgaichō (Nishi Azabu) from the construction of the Reader's Digest building (Tokyo, 31 March 1951)

9 – 五代さん、ノエミ・レーモンド、吉田美佐子（鷲塚氏の学生）。アメリカ大使館員宿舎にて。東京、1951年。

Mrs. Godai, Noémi Raymond and Yoshida Misako (teacher in Mr. Washizuka's school) on the construction of apartments for employees of the American embassy (Tokyo, 1951)

01 有名な彫刻家・デザイナーであったイサム・ノグチは、日本人の詩人であり英文学者の野口米次郎とアメリカ人で作家のレオニー・ギルモ

HČ: Could you share any of your recollections of that project with us?

GY: We had the temporary building of Raymond's studio on the construction site of that project. In a normal situation only a small office would be on the building site, but because Raymond had just parted ways with Washizuka, he built a long, narrow building on the site – a kind of hut made of rough-hewn boards, from material from the construction. To the right of the entrance was the secretariat, to the left the drafting office and behind it was Raymond's study. Then we relocated to Imaichō in the district of Roppongi. When you go from Roppongi in the direction of Tameike, you go downhill, and on a raised surface on your left you seen a plot of land that used to belong to the noble Mitsui family before the war. It was for this plot of land that we designed accommodation for employees of the American embassy, these were two houses for Mr. Perry and Mr. Harris.

PH: The sculptural work, for example Kurin, serving as a fountain, and the complex network of canals and reservoirs in front of the Reader's Digest building, were designed by the sculptor and designer Isamu Noguchi (1904–1988). Does this mean he was friends with Raymond?

GY: They were fond of each other. Raymond was a kind of father figure to Noguchi, and he often came to visit us. Several of his sculptures stood in front of the Reader's Digest building.[1]

HČ: Could you please tell us something about the daily routine in the office, I mean the permanent one in Kōgaichō? What was a normal day like there?

GY: Upon entering the building you found yourself in a corridor, what's known as a genkan. To the left was the office, to the right was a room with the technical facilities – an electricity meter, the sewerage piping and so on – behind that was the drafting office. Right at the end was the room where blueprints were printed, and next to it the studio. When Raymond had an idea, he quickly sketched it out on a piece of paper in the studio and handed it to the architects to elaborate on it in further detail. Further on was Mrs. Raymond's study, where she was always accompanied by an assistant. Mr. Raymond had his study on the left. My desk was there, I was separated from Mr. Raymond's study by a sliding partition. From the window I had a view of the building's inner garden. The Raymonds liked to be out in the fresh air, the only time they didn't eat out on the terrace was when it was really cold. There was a swimming pool in front of the terrace. The building also had its own bathroom, kitchen and sleeping quarters for the servants.

HČ: How many servants were employed there?

GY: A Japanese chauffeur, a housekeeper and a chef, the latter of whom commuted to the Raymonds. Mr. Raymond was very fond of his cooking, he liked meat a great deal. Apparently he was thin as a boy. He grew up eating potatoes and bread and butter. Mrs. Raymond was an active animal conservationist, and so they never ate meat together. Today she'd be called a vegan or vegetarian. He ordered what he liked from the chef, and whenever Mrs. Raymond commented on it he'd get annoyed: "You don't know anything about cooking!" Once I asked Mrs. Raymond how she could stand for

10 – 青山の自邸前の宇野美子氏、東京、1954。

Uno Yoshiko (later Godai) in front of the entrance to her house in Aoyama (Tokyo, 1954)

01 Ioguchi Isamu (1904–1988), Japanese-American sculptor and designer, descendant of distinguished Japanese writer, poet and essayist Noguchi Yonejirō and American journalist Léonie Gilmour. During the Second World War, because of his Japanese origin he voluntarily entered an internment camp in Arizona. He worked in both the USA and Japan, and sought ways to achieve a synthesis of Japanese and Euro-American aesthetics. For Reader's Digest he designed the critically acclaimed modern garden, inspired by the traditional design of Japanese gardens and historical technological approaches. The Reader's Digest project as a whole, i.e. as a fusion of Raymond and Noguchi's work, is considered a highly accomplished work, and in 1952 won an award from the American Institute of Architects (AIA). The building was demolished in 1963, but Noguchi's sculptures have been preserved. Kurin or the Nine Circles, one of the components of the tip of Buddhist pagodas, Noguchi's sculpture from 1951, stands on the campus of Macalester College in the inner garden of the Janet Wallace Fine Arts Center (St Paul, Michigan, USA).

11 – 軽井沢への旅行中　ノエミレーモンド氏とそのアシスタント、五代氏と戦前からの友達、元メイドさんおまささん、1950年代。

Trip to Karuizawa: Noémi Raymond, her assistant, Mrs. Godai and family friend of the Raymonds, former housekeeper Mrs. Omasa (1950s)

五代: ひとり息子のクロードの家族が戦後、日本に来たときは、1年ほどそのサーバント・クオーターに住んでいました。親子4人で一緒に。先ほども言ったように、サーバントとしては女性のメイドさんがいらっしゃいました。ある夏に、軽井沢の別荘で過ごしているときに使ったメイドさんをレーモンドが気に入って、東京まで連れてきて、そこの部屋に住み込ませていました。彼女はエンジニアの一人と結婚しましたね。

ホリー: レーモンドさんはお酒も飲まれたんですか？

五代: はい。レーモンドは夕食の時間の前になると一人でキッチンへ行って、戸棚からスコッチウイスキーを出してグラスを持って来るんです。ある日、シェフがボソッと「僕はちっともアルコールが飲めないから、レーモンドはずいぶん得してる」って（笑）。普通は、こういう台所のお酒はシェフがこっそり飲むものなんだって言ってました (笑)。

チャプコヴァー: 所員の方も一緒にご飯を食べられたんですか？

五代: 西麻布の建物に移ったとき、その建物が傾斜地に立っていたんです。低い方の部分に、私たちがカフェテリアと呼ぶ食堂がありました。そこに、女性の調理師がいて、お昼ご飯を提供してくれました。確か一食50円だけ自分が負担して、後は会社が援助してくれて。毎日、日替わりでランチタイムをそこで過ごしたのを覚えています。ランチと言えば、高崎の井上房一郎さんという方

アの間にロサンゼルスで生まれた。第二次世界大戦中アメリカの日系人の強制収容にいた。戦後世界的に活躍し、レーモンドと共にリーダーズ・ダイジェスト東京支社のお庭を設計した。その彫刻とデザインが和洋折衷として考えられる。1952年にリーダーズ・ダイジェスト東京支社の設計が日本建築学会賞を取れた。1963年に取り壊されたが、ノグチの彫刻、例に九輪が移転され、ミシガン州セントポールのマカレスターカレッジのジャネットウォレスファインアーツセンターの屋内庭園にある。

12 – レーモンドと井上房一郎氏、高崎現場、1958。

Antonín Raymond and Mr. Inoue on the construction site in Takasaki (1958)

such insults, but she just said: "Oh, he'll make it up another time." She could also see his good side – they were a good couple.

PH: I wouldn't mind something similar myself. *(Laughs)*

GY: When their son Claude and his family came to Japan, they lived in the servants' quarters for about a year. All four of them. That summer the Raymonds took a liking to a housekeeper who worked in their summer residence in Karuizawa. They invited her to their place in Tokyo, and there she married an engineer.

PH: Did Raymond like alcohol?

GY: Yes, every day before dinner he went to the kitchen and brought back a bottle of Scotch and some glasses. Once the chef whispered to us with a smile: "I hardly drink alcohol, so Mr. Raymond will drink almost all of that himself." Of course, it's reportedly commonplace for chefs to drink secretly in the kitchen.

HČ: And did the employees eat together?

GY: The building we moved to in Azabu was on a slope. At the foot of it was a canteen, which we called the Cafeteria. A local cook prepared lunches. We paid 50 yen for the food, the remainder was paid for by the company. I remember well that we went there every day, and my memories of those lunches are linked to a recollection of Mr. Inoue Fusaichirō from Takasaki (1898–1993), who was a close friend of the Raymonds.[2] Whenever he came to Tokyo, he would stop by and come to lunch with us. Mr. Inoue was the initiator of the project for the Music Centre in the Gunma prefecture, and he'd lived in France for a long time. In France he stayed with a butler and studied painting, but he didn't learn much French. He spoke English with

02 Inoue Fusaichirō, owner of the construction firm Inoue Kōgyō, made a significant contribution to cultural life in the city of Takasaki in Gunma prefecture. He studied art in Paris and endeavoured to revive folk art in Gunma (he sold products in Tokyo). His interest in crafts brought him together with Antonín Raymond. His firm also produced furniture from a whole range of modern designers (e.g. Bruno Taut, who during the time when Inoue was designing lived close to the company headquarters, in the Senshintei pavilion by the Darumaji Shōrinzan temple in Takasaki). A number of Raymond's projects in Gunma, above all the Music Centre, originated on Inoue's initiative.

がレーモンド夫妻の親しい友人で、彼が東京へいらしたときには必ずレーモンド邸を訪ねて、昼食を一緒にしました。井上房一郎さん(1898～1993)は群馬音楽センターを出て、フランスに長くいらした方なんです。執事を連れてパリに留学され経験をお持ちで[2]。ただ、絵画の勉強のための留学だったので、フランス語は習得されなかったみたいなんです。だからレーモンド夫妻と話すときは英語でした。大方は私が通訳していましたけれども。井上さんもレーモンドのシェフが作る料理を美味しいと褒めていました。よっぽど腕の良いシェフだったんだと思います。ある日、そのシェフが休んでいた際に井上さんがいらしたことがあって、事務所の近くにあるフレンチレストランに行きました[3]。そのお店ではムール貝が出たんですけれど、井上さんは「ムール貝は労働者が食べる貝だ」と言って、ご機嫌が悪くなってしまって。

チャプコヴァー: 五代さんは、岡本太郎の家のすぐ隣に住んでいたとお聞きしています。岡本太郎との関わりについてお話できますか？

五代: これは私たちが住んでた家です。戦後、私たちは市川から東京へやってきました。レーモンドが、私たちがあまりにひどいところに住んでるものだから、白石建設と言うレーモンドの住宅を最もたくさん手がけた会社に交渉してくださったんです。「美子のために家を建ててやってくれ、そしてその支払いは毎月彼女の月給から差っ引いて返すことにしてやってくれ」と話してくださって。それが今、高樹町3番地の30坪の土地に建っている、2階建ての家です。2階は1部屋で私たち娘3人が住み、下にはみんなで食事のできるダイニング・ルームと両親のための8畳の間があって。もちろん、お風呂場もキッチンも付いていました。そして、その路地の反対側に、岡本太郎が住んでいらっしゃいました。写真に写っているこのブロック塀は岡本太郎の家のブロック塀です (31ページを参照)。2階の窓から、人の話し声が聞こえたり、人の出入りが手に取るようにわかってしまうんですね。しょっちゅう見てたわけではないですけれど、「とても面白い方だなと思っていました。

ホリー: お美しい。

五代: 岡本さんのブロック塀のところに立って写真を撮りました。これ、撮ったときのカメラはレーモンドさんに拝借した、ライカ。カメラなんか買う余裕は私にはありませんでしたけど、時々お借りして写真を撮っていましたわ。

チャプコヴァー: レーモンドさんと岡本太郎は、どうやってお知り合いになりったのでしょうか？

五代: 岡本太郎さんの家を設計して建てた、坂倉準三さん (1901～1969)を通じて知り合ったんだと思います。レーモンドが西麻布に住んでいて、「太郎さんって面白い。ちょっとクレイジーだけど変わった画家だと。」時折、レ

13 – 青山の自邸前の五代氏、東京、1954。

Godai Yoshiko in front of her house in Aoyama (Tokyo, 1954)

02 群馬県高崎の井上工業社長井上 房一郎は高崎市の文化的な活動の一人として有名な人である。1923年にフランスのパリに留学。1930年に帰国し井上工業に入社。高崎の民芸品を売り込むのために、東京の西銀座のお店を始まった。そこでレーモンドとあって、友達になって、一緒に高崎の群馬音楽センターなどを仕始める。井上工業は前衛的デザイナー何人とコラボをして、そのグループの中に1933から来日したブルーノ・タウト（1880～1938）もいた。タウトは仕事だけではなくて、2年間高崎の達磨寺少林山の洗心亭にすんでいた。

03 現在は表参道にある “Figaro”。

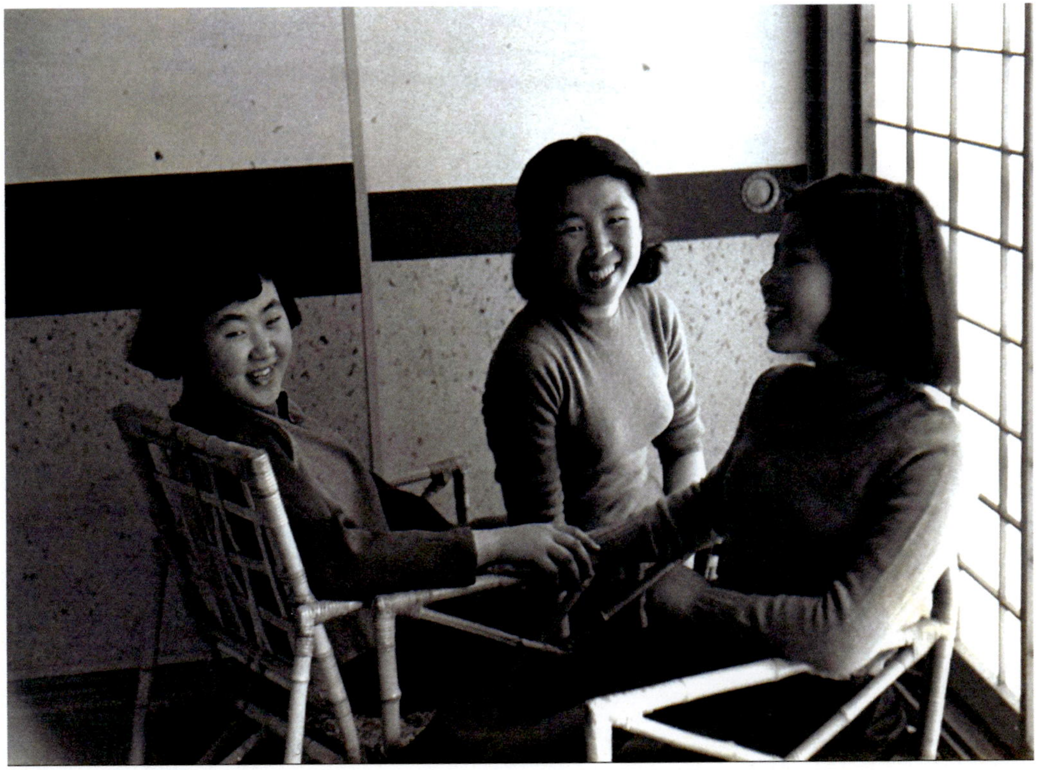

Raymond, but mostly I interpreted for him. Every time Mr. Inoue complimented the chef on his dishes, so they probably truly were exceptionally good. Once the chef had the day off, and so we went to a nearby French restaurant.[3] That day they were serving fresh mussels, but this spoiled Mr. Inoue's mood, and he declared: "Mussels are a type of shellfish that are eaten by no-one but labourers."

HČ: I heard that you lived right next door to the painter Okamoto Tarō (1911–1996).[4] Could you tell us something about Okamoto and his relationship towards Raymond

GY: Yes, our house is in the photograph (fig. 13). After the war we moved from Ichikawa to Tokyo. Mr. Raymond didn't like us living so far away and not in a particularly nice place, and so he approached the construction firm Shirashi Kensetsu, with which he collaborated for many years. He told them: "Build a house for Yoshiko, she'll pay it in monthly instalments from her wage." So they built me a two-storey house on a land plot of 30 tsubo (99 m2) in Takagimachi number 3. On the first floor there was one large room, where I lived together with my two sisters. On the ground floor there was a dining room and my parents' bedroom, on a surface of about eight tatamis (approximately 13 m2). There was also a kitchen and bathroom. Okamoto Tarō lived opposite us, across the street. In the photograph you can see the low wall which belonged to Okamoto's house (fig. 15). From the window on the first floor we heard what the Okamotos were saying, we heard people coming and going, it was literally within touching distance. Although I didn't follow him with any kind of concentration, it was clear to me that he was a very interesting person.

14 – 高樹町３番地のリビングルーム 次妹 美子 末妹, 東京、1954。

In the living room of Godai Yoshiko's house in Takagimachi no. 3. From left: middle sister, Mrs. Godai and youngest sister (Tokyo, 1954)

15 – 美子 岡本太郎と北側隣家の境界ブロック塀, 東京, 1960年代。

Mrs. Yoshiko by the wall separating from the neighbouring land plot on the northern side of the house of Okamoto Tarō (Tokyo, early 1960s)

03 Today the restaurant is named Figaro and is located on Omotesandō street in the Tokyo district of Minato.

04 Okamoto Tarō (1911–1996) is among the most distinguished Japanese artists, especially of the post-war period. In the inter-war period he studied in Paris, focusing on philosophy, and in 1933 he became the youngest member of the group Abstraction-Création. After the Second World War he systematically focused on painting, photography, sculpture and also large projects, of which the most significant is Tower of the Sun – the symbol of EXPO in Osaka (1970).

ーモンドは太郎さんの所を訪ねては、彼の作品を見ていました。「座るのを拒否する椅子」(1963)とか、それから「梵鐘ー歓喜が出て」(1965)っていうのを叩いてみたり。それから後に万博の、あの有名な「太陽の塔」なんかを見て。

ホリー: 現在、レーモンド設計事務所のメモリアル・ルームは代々木にあると思います。その後、西麻布から引っ越されたんですか?

五代: 西麻布の土地を売って、代々木に土地を買いました。オリンピックの青少年センターの、はす向かいのところです。5階には西麻布のレーモンドのスチュディオを移して、レーモンド・メモリアルルームとして現存しております。そこでホリーさんとお会いしたんですよね。

ホリー: そうです、初めてお会いしました。そのときに、テラスへお邪魔させていただいたんですが、岡本太郎の椅子があって。こんな野ざらしでいいのかなぁって(笑)。

五代: 雨に会おうが、風に吹かれようが変わりませんから。でも座ると本当に痛いですよね(笑)。

チャプコヴァー: ホリーさんは旦那様の五代信作さんとも事務所でお会いになりましたか?

ホリー: いえ。会っていません。

五代: 彼は、残念ながらアルツハイマーでしたので、千葉の施設に入ってました。ただ、その施設には病気のために入ったのでは無いんです。彼は「もう都会に住むのが嫌になったから僕は田舎に住みたいと言って。北海道から九州まで体験入居して歩いたんですよ。それで千葉の君津の施設が気に入ったみたいで。私にも「一緒に来ないか」って言ったんですけど、田舎に行くとちょっと、虫に刺されたりなんかいろいろあるので、嫌だと言って行きませんでした(笑)。主人があの病気になってからは娘と私と交代でいつも見舞いに行っていました。一日がかりで。木更津から久留里の方まで単線に乗って行くんですよ。そりゃあ、もう、大変なんです。

ホリー: だから私はお目にかかれていないんですね。

五代: レーモンド事務所に関しては、西麻布が彼の最後の職場となりました。代々木には全然行っておりません。と言うのは、ちょうどレーモンドが、帯状疱疹になって、ひどい痛みのために。ペンシルヴァニアの農場に移ったんです。1973年のことです。それで結局、そのまま引退。

16 – 左 五代信作 群馬音楽センター 高崎 1960。

Godai Shinsaku (left), Gunma prefecture Music Centre (Takasaki, approx. 1960)

PH: Superb!
GY: Those photographs were take with Raymond's Leica camera. At the time I couldn't have afforded a camera like that, but I occasionally borrowed it.
HČ: How did Raymond meet Okamoto?
GY: I think they met through a mutual acquaintance, the architect Sakakura Junzō (1901–1969) who designed Okamoto's house.[5] When Raymond lived in Nishiazabu, he often used to say: "That Mr. Tarō's a strange one. An interesting, but slightly cranky painter." They visited one another and Okomoto showed Raymond his works. He also tested out the Chair for not Sitting on (Chaise pour ne pas s'asseoir, 1963) and another sculpture: Joy – Temple Bell (La joie – Cloche du temple, 1965).[6] He also saw the famous Tower of the Sun that Okamoto designed for the occasion of Expo in Osaka.
PH: I think that they (Okamoto's chairs) are now in the memorial hall in Raymond's architecture firm in Yoyogi. – Under what circumstances did the office move from Nishiazabu?
GY: They sold the land plot in Nishiazabu and bought the one in Yoyogi. Right opposite is the National Olympic Centre for Youth. On the fifth floor is part of the original studio, the so-called memorial hall. I think that's where we met together with Mr. Holý.
PH: Yes, that's where we met for the first time. They even let us onto the terrace where Okamoto's aforementioned chairs were. They're a bit uncomfortable. *(Laughs)*
GY: The rain just runs off them, the wind can't blow them away, they're actually indestructible, but sitting on them is genuinely painful. *(Laughs)*
HČ: Mr. Holý, when you were at the office did you meet Mrs. Yoshiko's husband, Mr. Godai Shinsaku?
PH: Unfortunately not.
GY: My husband was beginning to show signs of Alzheimer's disease, and so he moved to the sanatorium in Chiba prefecture. But he didn't choose Chiba only because he was ill, he wanted to move out to the country. He'd travelled throughout Japan from Hokkaido to Kyūshū, and he liked it in Chiba. He wanted me to move with him, but the country's not for me. You're constantly being bitten by insects and all kinds of things, so I stayed where I was. *(Laughs)* When he got ill, I went to visit him with our daughter. It was arduous, the travelling took us all day – on one line from Kisarazu in the direction of Kururi.
PH: So that's why I didn't meet him…
GY: His last job was with Raymond in Nishiazabu, he no longer commuted to Yoyogi. At that time Raymond took very ill, he had shingles and was in a lot of pain. In 1973 he moved to the farm in Pennsylvania. So in fact he left the firm and retired.
HČ: I heard that your wedding reception was held in the company premises in Kōgai-chō…
GY: Yes, that's right. At that time Raymond had started working together with the American architect of Slovak origin L. L. Rado.[7] Rado had a firm in New York, and wanted me to work there in the secretariat. He vouched for me at the American em-

17 – 旅行中の五代さん。
Mr. Godai Shinsaku on his travels

05 Japanese architect, one of those who studied under Le Corbusier in France in the 1930s. Sakakura bore the responsibility for Le Corbusier's only Japanese realisation – the Museum of Western Art in Tokyo (1959). His other prestigious realisations include the Japanese pavilion at EXPO in Paris (1937) and West Plaza at the Shinjuku station in Tokyo (1967).
06 Thanks are due to Mrs. Sugitao Shinju, art historian and specialist in Okamoto's work, for the identification of the French names of the work which A. Raymond saw at Okamoto's house.
07 Ladislav Leland Rado (1909–1993), American architect of Slovak origin, graduate from the Czech Technical University in Prague (1932), Brno colleague of Bohuslav Fuchs (1932–1939). After 1939 he lived in exile in the USA, studying at Harvard University under Walter Gropius (graduated 1940). In the period of 1946–1982 he was the co-owner of the company Raymond & Rado. Professor of architecture at Yale University (New Haven, USA).

18 – 会社週末旅行（串本） 写真後列左より森径子（青図機）、五代美子、森悦子（カフェテリア、森径子と姉妹）、吉田美佐子（事務）、大久保（電気）、名前なし、土屋重隆（会計）、五十嵐謙司（会計）、西嶋泰親、松岡保夫、萩野栄子、五代信作
前列左より 豊泉、大村六郎、小坂寿男、後藤、田辺博司、斉藤（見積）、三沢浩、1957の秋。

Employees of Raymond's office on a weekend trip to Kushimoto.
Back row from left: Mori Michiko (worked in blueprint office), Godai Yoshiko, Mori Etsuko (worked in cafeteria, sister of Michiko), Yoshida Misako (administrator), Mr. Ōkubo (electro), unidentified, Tsuchiya Shigetaka (accountant), Nishijima Yasuchika, Matsuoka Yasuo, Hagino Eiko, Godai Shinsaku. Front row from left: Toyoizumi, Ōmura Rokurō, Kosaka Kazuo, Gotō, Tanabe Hiroshi, Saitō (surveyor), Misawa Hiroshi (autumn 1957)

チャプコヴァー: ウエディング・レセプションを笄町で開かれたとお聞きしています。

五代: はい。あのときは、ミスター・レーモンドが、L. L. Radoというチェコスロヴァキア出身の建築家と、パートナーシップを組んでいたんです[4]。彼はニューヨークに事務所を持っていたので、私がラドの事務所でセクレタリーとして働けるように連れて行くと、言って下さったんです。それでアメリカ大使館に行って、彼らは聖書の上に手を置いて、この女性の保証人になると言う宣誓をしてくれて・それから渡航の手続きを始めました。けれども、私の母が「そんな地の果てのような遠いアメリカのニューヨークへなんか行くなと言って、反対して脳溢血を起こして倒れてしまったんです。それが原因で渡航は取り止め。レーモンドも「そういう状態の母親を置いてニューヨークに行くのは、お前も気がかりでできないことだろう」って。それで、彼は「会社のドラフトマンの中から誰かを選んで、結婚させるって言い出したんです。

ホリー: それが旦那様に？

五代: 五代と言うドラフトマンがいるけど彼はどう？って。レーモンドのゴルフ友達の甥だったんです。彼は鷲塚のリーダースダイジェストの頃に、入社したんです。私よりは遅かったんでしょうか。彼と結婚する前、10年間ほどでしょうか、会社の若い人たちのグループで、いろいろ遊んではい

19 – 結婚式の準備中。笄町、東京。

Preparations for the Godai wedding ceremony

04 ラディスラフ・レラント・ラド(1909〜〜1993) スロヴァキア出身、アメリカの建築家。プラハのチェコ工科大学卒業 (1932年)、ブルノでボフスラフ・フックスとともに働く(1932〜1939年)。1939年にアメリカに亡命し、ヴァルター・グロピウスのもと、ハーヴァード大学で学ぶ(1940年卒業)。1946年から1982年にかけてレーモンド&ラドの共同オーナーとなる。イェール大学建築学教授（ニュー・ヘイヴン)。

bassy, swearing on the Bible, and we began preparing documents for the journey. But my mother was against it, and pleaded with me not to go so far, to a foreign culture; eventually it gave her a brain haemorrhage and she collapsed. As a result I decided to stay. Even Raymond acknowledged that under such circumstances I couldn't abandon my mother. And then he said: "I'll find you someone from the drafting office and you'll get married!"

PH: And so he chose your husband for you?

GY: "There's a designer here, Godai, who might appeal to you," he said. He was the nephew of one of Raymond's golfing associates and he'd come to the firm at the time of the partnership with Washizuka, during the Reader's Digest project, but later than me. About ten years before our wedding I used to see him, and we went on trips together with the others. But it never occurred to me at all that we might marry.

PH: So you met your husband at work.

GY: Yes, it was just at the time when we were finishing the designs for the Gunma Music Centre. The Raymonds came in the summer, they rented a cottage from the Mitsui family in Karuizawa, which is nearby, and that's where we worked. At the time my husband had finished the designs and came for Raymond's signature. Then we started talking and we fell in love. The Godai family were Shintoists, and so we approached a Shinto cleric to request a wedding ceremony. The ceremony was held in the residential premises in Kōgaichō, which we rented. We built an altar by the outer wall of the studio, prepared everything and arranged the chairs and stools for seating.

PH: Every time I see it I say to myself what a simple and attractive design it is (of the chairs and stools).

GY: They used those three-legged stools on the farm in Pennsylvania. Originally they had even shorter legs and were used during milking. At that time Raymond approached the furniture company Kobayashi Kaguten to produce about a hundred of them for him.

PH: I'd also have liked to buy them. They're not sold any more.

GY: The people who'd purchased them brought them to the wedding, they each brought about two or three. Even though they looked unstable, they're in fact very stable, you don't need to worry that the stool will topple over when you stand up.

PH: When did the ceremony take place?

GY: The Raymonds used to spend the hottest summer months in Karuizawa, and returned to Tokyo in the autumn. We had our wedding on Saturday 4 October (1958). It was a beautiful autumn day and everyone from the company was in attendance. The Shinto clerics played gagaku on shō mouth organs and on a hichiriki flute.[8] I remember how we took our wedding vow and drank sake from a cup. Then we moved the tables outside, where the garden reception was held. I couldn't afford to have a wedding kimono made, and so I borrowed it from my friend's sister from the girls' school. I wore a wig on my head. Mrs. Raymond's dress was made of kasuri type Japanese silk.[9]

PH: I heard that kasuri was very popular at one time.

20 – レーモンドと井上房一郎氏。高崎の建設現場にて。1958年。

Antonín Raymond and Mr. Inoue on the construction site in Takasaki (1958)

08 Gagaku is the ceremonial music of the Japanese imperial court, which is also a part of Shinto ceremonies. The instruments used include the flute, sometimes also the oboe, also the hichiriki and shō – a small organ played with the mouth.

09 Kasuri is a method of dyeing fabrics of the ikat type (during dyeing part of the thread is intentionally not dyed, the effect and technique is reminiscent of batik). The pattern of materials decorated by this technique forms uncoloured or only pale covered surfaces on a dark background; it has several variations and is very popular. The kasuri technique enables the creation of an inconspicuous, cut-up, elegant design of fabrics.

21, 22 – 五代氏の結婚式　笄町、東京、1958年10月4日。

At the wedding ceremony of the Godais in Kōgaichō (4 October 1958)

ました。けれど、まさかお互いに結婚する相手になるとは思っていませんでした。

ホリー: 仕事上の付き合いというか。

五代: ええ。ちょうどその年に、群馬音楽センターの図面の最後の仕上げが、あったのですね。レーモンド夫妻が日本にいらした夏でしたので、軽井沢の三井さんの別荘をお借りして、そこで仕事をしてました。夫は、群馬音楽センターの図面が仕上がると、軽井沢のミスター・レーモンドのところに、サインをもらいに来るんですよ。それで、仕事が済むと、二人で話して会ったりなんかして。そこから恋愛が始まりました。五代の家は神道なんです。だから、神主さんを呼んで、リビング・クォーターを全部借りて、式を挙げました。ミセス・レーモンドと、ミスター・レーモンドの、ステュディオの境の壁のところを神殿にしていろいろお供えして。椅子やスツールなんかも並べて。

ホリー: いつも思うんですけれど、シンプルで素敵なデザインですね。

五代: この三角スツールは、ペンシルベニアの農場で使われていたもので。本物はもっと足の低いもので、持ち歩いて、牛のそばに持って行って座って、乳を絞るんですね。それを、その頃レーモンドの家具を専門の様に作っていた小林家具店に100脚ぐらい頼んだんですよ。

23 – 五代氏の結婚式　笄町、東京、1958年10月4日。

At the wedding ceremony of the Godais in Kōgaichō (4 October 1958)

24 – 左から レーモンド夫妻 清家清氏 由良滋氏 五代氏の結婚式　笄町、東京、1958年10月4日。

From left: the Raymonds, Seike Kiyoshi and Yura Shigeru (both renowned architects) at the Godai wedding ceremony in Kōgaichō (4 October 1958)

GY: Silk was used for formal dresses, for summer dresses cotton kasuri or chequered ichimatsu was used. Well woven cotton fabric clings nicely to the body and doesn't cause any skin complaints. – In the photograph (fig. 24) you can see the Raymonds and the architect Seike Kiyoshi.[10] Standing next to him is Mr. Yura Shigeru, a graduate from the faculty of architecture at the Academy of Fine Arts. Yura, together with the architects Hashimoto and Suzuki made up the three musketeers of Washizuka's office. Mr. Suzuki's father was the head of the Tokyo branch of Reader's Digest, his name was Suzuki Bunshirō and unfortunately he died of cancer.

HČ: The prestigious post-war projects include the Gunma Music Centre. Let's focus on this if we may.

GY: The film "Spring" from 1955 presents a good account of the history and development of the Symphonic Orchestra of the Gunma prefecture. I don't know if you know, but it was in Gunma that amateur musicians began to associate. And as the ensemble grew in size, they sought a larger and larger rehearsal room and concert hall. At that time Mr. Inoue offered a project to Raymond. The costs for the construction were collected from donations from the population of the city (Takasaki). When we went to Karuizawa by train, we went through Takasaki – it was the city with the largest number of television aerials. Takasaki was the city that was known as the cultural centre of the prefecture, unlike the capital of the prefecture, Maebashi. That's why the music centre was to be based there. First of all it was supposed to be a theatre with a circular ground plan, but that kind of concept was too modern for the time.

10 Seike Kiyoshi (1918–2005) was a renowned Japanese architect of the post-war period, a professor of architecture at the Tokyo Institute of Technology. His most prestigious works include the house for Dr. Mori (1951), his own house (1954) and the campus buildings of the Tokyo Institute of Technology (1960s).

ホリー: 買いたいな、とずっと思うんですけど、今買えないんです。

五代: 当時、2、3脚ずつ買った方は持ってらっしゃると思います。三角はとても不安定のような感じがしますけど、非常に安定してるんですよ。立ち上がっても怖くないくらい。

ホリー: 結婚式はいつ頃？

五代: レーモンド夫妻は夏は軽井沢に避暑に行くんです。それで、戻ってきた秋の、(1958年) 10月4日の土曜日に結婚式をここでやらせていただくことになりました。幸いなことに、とても綺麗な秋晴れで、会社の皆様にも出席していただくことにして。神主さんが笙、篳篥で、雅楽を演奏してくださって。結婚の誓いをしました。固めの盃をしたのを覚えています。それから、庭の方のテーブルに移って、ガーデン・パーティーを開きました。私には着物を作ったりするほどの余裕がありませんでしたから、女学校時代のクラスメートの姉上のものを借りて着ました。頭はかつらです。ミセス・レーモンドのお召しになっているドレスは、日本の絣の生地、絹の和服地です。

25 – ノエミレーモンド、五代さんの結婚式、1958年10月4日。

Noémi Raymond at the Godai wedding reception (4 October 1958)

ホリー: 絣はよく身にまとわれたというお話を以前、聞いたことがあります。

五代: ドレス用には絹をお使いになるし、夏のワンピースは、木綿の絣とか市松でしたね。しっかりした木綿地のものは、肌に直接つけても、悪い影響はありませんし。ミセス・レーモンド、ミスター・レーモンド。それから清家清さんですね。その隣は由良滋さん。芸大を出て、由良さんと橋本さんと鈴木さんという三羽ガラスが、鷺塚事務所にいました。鈴木さんのお父様は、リーダースダイジェストの東京支社の社長でした。鈴木文史朗っていう方でしたけど、癌で亡くなりました。

チャプコヴァー: レーモンドの戦後の主なプロジェクトは、高崎にある群馬音楽センターでした。その話をもっとお聞かせいただけませんか？

五代: 『ここに泉あり』(Here Is a Fountain, 1955)という映画があって、あれを観ると群馬交響楽団の成長の仕方がよくわかります。昔の方はご存知かしら。群馬県のアマチュアの音楽家が最初集まって、音楽をしていたらしいんですね。それがだんだん大きくなって、自分たちの練習場などを作りたいという希望が出てきて。そこで、井上さんからレーモンドにそういうものを設計して欲しいという依頼がありました。建築費、費用は、ほとんど市民から集めたお金だそうです。軽井沢に行ったりするとき、汽車で高崎を通りますと、他の市や町よりもテレビのアンテナが多いんですね。高崎は、群馬県の県庁所在地の前橋より、文化的で、昔から名が売れていると聞いております。それで、そこに音楽センターを建てるという話になって。設計が始まっ

26 – 群馬音楽センター、高崎、1961年。

Completed construction of the Gunma Music Centre, Takasaki (1961)

PH: And now it looks like a frog…

GY: A frog? *(Laughs)* Yes, sure, like a toad! *(Continues laughing)* When the plans were finished, a lot of large construction firms sent offers – Taisei Kensetsu, Shimizu Kensetsu, Takenaka Kōmuten and others. But still, we wanted the order to be given to Mr. Inoue and his firm Inoue Kōgyō.

PH: And was Mr. Inoue Fusaichirō the director at that time?

GY: Yes, that man from the district of Taitōku. In comparison with Taisei or Shimizu it was a small firm, but since it was an order financed by money collected from people from Takasaki in Gunma and it was a building for them, we wanted the it to be given to the firm Inoue Kōgyō.

PH: Of course, after all Raymond also built a house for Inoue.

GY: That was a bit different. Mr. Inoue wanted the same house that Mr. Raymond had in Kōgaichō, and he also brought a daikusan (carpenter) to survey the house. And then he constructed the same house, but with the difference that it was a mirror image.

PH: And is it still standing in Takasaki?

GY: Yes, it was converted into a study.[11] It's a wooden structure more than fifty years old, and so the wood darkened, it looked dirty. – But it seems that they recently renovated it. – Mr. Inoue was among the local dignitaries, and in the town he looked after the development of youth. He was responsible for the tradition of practical skills such as dyeing fabrics, he purchased domestic silk moths and supported silk production, the spinning of silk thread and eventually also weaving. He also employed people in furniture production.

27 – 群馬音楽センター後方。高崎、1961年。

From the construction of the Gunma Music Centre, Takasaki (1961)

11 The former residence of Inoue Fusaichirō is now managed by the publicly accessible foundation Philosophy Study in Takasaki.

て最初は円形の劇場という話だったのですけれど、円形はちょっとその頃ではモダンすぎて。

ホリー: それで蛙みたいな？

五代: 蛙ですか (笑)？確かにガマガエルみたいね (笑)。それで設計が仕上がって、いろんな建設会社から入札があったんです。大成建設、清水建設、竹中工務店。でも、どうしても井上工業が、この仕事はやらせてほしいと。

ホリー: 井上工業っていうのは井上房一郎さんが社長をされていた頃ですね？

五代: そうです。台東区の方にある、大成とか清水組とかに比べたら規模は小さい会社ですよね。でも、群馬県の高崎市民から集めたお金を使って作る、市民のための建物だから、何とか井上工業にやらせてくれないかって。

ホリー: 確か、レーモンドさんは井上房一郎さんのために家を造りましたよね。

五代: いや、それは違うんです。レーモンドの住宅と同じものを建ててよいかと井上房一郎さんが大工さんを連れて見に来たんです。それで、レーモンドの住宅と左右反対のものを造られて。

ホリー: 現存してますよね、高崎で。

28–30 – 高崎の現場、1950年代。

Project in Takasaki, construction supervised by the Raymonds, Mr. Godai, Mr. Inoue and other members of the team (late 1950s)

31 – 高崎でのプロジェクト、コンサートホール内観。50年代末。

Project in Takasaki, construction of interior of concert hall (late 1950s)

PH: He also sponsored Bruno Taut.
GY: Bruno Taut came to Japan during the war and hid in the Shōrinji temple for several years.[12]
PH: In his time Mr. Inoue ranked among the distinguished patrons. You don't see that these days.
GY: Although he had the same house built as Antonín Raymond, I think his was slightly bigger. He also built a stage for rehearsing nō theatre and so on.
PH: So he studied it at Hōshōryū school?[13]
GY: Probably, if he was involved with *nō*. His wife devoted herself to the tea ceremony, flower arranging and similar things. Their son unfortunately died of leukaemia at a young age. He was married and had two sons. When they grew up they took over the management of the Inoue Kōgyō company.

12 See note 02, p. 29.
13 One of five historically established nō theatre schools, famed for its conservative approach and introspective style of acting. Inoue was also interested in another significant tradition of Japanese theatre, the form of kabuki (see p. 213).

32 – 高崎でのプロジェクト。五代氏と語るレーモンド夫妻。

Project in Takasaki, the Raymonds in the interior discussing with Mr. Godai

五代: はい、哲学堂になっています。木造で50年以上経っておりますから、もう見た目は黒くて汚らしい。でも、今、直されて綺麗になったらしいですけれど。井上房一郎さんは、高崎の素封家なんですよね。若い人たちのために、染色とか、例えば蚕を買って絹を作ってその糸を作って、織物を作るための方法とかを教えていらっしゃった。家具も作らせてらっしゃいましたよね。

ホリー: ブルーノ・タウト(28ページを参照)とかを支えたりしたとか。

五代: ブルーノ・タウトが、戦争中、追われて日本に来たときは、少林寺というお寺に何年か匿ってあげたんですよね。

ホリー: 井上さんが行っていた当時のメセナ活動って素晴らしいんです。今は、もう、そういうことをする人がいなくなってしまいましたから。

五代: 井上さんはご自宅にレーモンドと同じものを建てたとき、もう少し大きくなさったと思います。なんでも、ご自分が能の練習をなさる舞台もお建てになったとか。

ホリー: では、宝生流ですよね。

五代: そうでしょうね。能をやってらっしゃいましたから。奥様はもちろん、お

33 – 群馬音楽センター、基礎部分。

Construction of the Gunma Music Centre, technical buildings

34 – 群馬音楽センターオープニング 左から五代夫妻、高崎市役所の方、三沢浩、高崎、1961年。

Ceremonial opening of the Gunma Music Centre. From left: the Godais, employee of Takasaki Municipal Authority and architect, member of Raymond's studio Misawa Hiroshi, Takasaki (1961)

PH: In this shot we can see that Mrs. Godai is standing on a model of the building (fig. 34). What are you doing there?
GY: It's a stress test of the model of the Gunma Music Centre. At that time I weighed less than fifty kilograms.
PH: That's truly excellent architecture!
GY: In the photograph (fig. 35) I have a pleated skirt which I received from the Raymonds when they returned from America after about six months. At that time pleated fabrics or clothes were completely unavailable in Japan.
HČ: It's evident from the photographs that the Raymonds enjoyed spending time outdoors. Let's talk about their summer houses, specifically the villa in Hayama.
GY: The summer villa in Hayama was in Horinouchi. When they built it, there were not other summer chalets there, just a small gazebo with a surface for two tatamis in the corner of the garden. They used logs here also. On the ground floor, which was constructed on a concrete base, Mr. Raymond practised pottery, and he also had a pile of canvases and frames there, he painted there. On the first floor there were three bedrooms and a kitchen. The housekeeper and cook didn't have their own rooms here, they stayed close by, with the caretaker of the land, who was a fisherman, or with a friend.
PH: Did Mr. Raymond donate a boat to this fisherman?
GY: Their own boat was really very old, and they couldn't use it after the war. "Your life would be more cheerful with a boat," said Raymond, "but unfortunately I don't have the savings for it now." But at least he gave him another gift. Raymond was on

茶やお花とかいろいろなさってらっしゃったようですし。残念なことに一人の息子さんが、白血病で早く亡くなってしまわれたんです。ご結婚はされていて、二人のお孫さんを残されました。その二人が後に、井上工業の社長と専務になりました。

ホリー: 五代様が模型の上に立ってらっしゃる、この写真はなんでしょうか？

五代: これは、群馬音楽センターの模型を何分の一かの強度で作って、その強度テストだったんです。この頃、私50キロ近くあったと思うんですけど。

ホリー: でも、びくともしない、その建築の素晴らしさ！

五代: このとき履いている、このプリーツのスカートは、レーモンド夫妻がアメリカにお帰りになって、また半年ぐらい向こうで過ごして日本へ戻って来られるときのお土産に持ってきてくださったものです (45ページを参照)。その頃にはまだ日本にはプリーツなんてもの、なかったんです。

チャプコヴァー: レーモンド夫妻は自然の中で時間を過ごすこと大好きだったようですね。今からちょっと夏の別荘の話をしたいと思います。こちらは、葉山の別荘ですね。

五代: 葉山の堀之内にあった別荘。これを建てるときには、畳2畳の東屋が庭の隅にあっただけで、彼らの別荘の建物は無かったですね。これもやはり、丸太を使って造ったものです。1階の部分は全部コンクリート打ちっ放しのフロアーになっていて、そこで彼は、陶芸などをされた。それからイーゼルなどを置き、絵を描いたりしていました。階段を上って2階に、ベッドルームが3つあって、キッチンがあるんですね。当時は、メイドさんやシェフはここには泊まれないので、近くの、この土地の管理をしていた、路地の向こうの葉山の漁師さんの家に泊まらせてもらったか、もしくは、そこからのお世話で近所に泊まったりしてました。

ホリー: レーモンドさんは、その漁師さんに船を贈ったそうですね。

五代: 戦後、彼らの持っていた船はもう使い古して、使えなかったんです。「船があれば生活が楽になるんだけど、今はちょっとそれだけつくるほどの余裕が無い」と仰っていて、それでレーモンドがプレゼントしたんです。レーモンドさんと漁師さんは仲が良くて、ずっと土地の管理をしてもらってたんですね。そういう関係性もあったので、お金を出して、船を贈呈しました。そのときは、おじいさんと息子とその子供、みんなとっても喜んでました。私の夫なんかは、一艘漕ぎの扱い方を知っていたので、私たちが行ったときにはお借りしたりしました。いつも漁に出ている訳ではないですからね。定置網はだいたい朝早く戻ってくるのです。

35 – 五代美子が立つ群馬音楽センターの模型 西麻布前庭にて 1950年代。

Godai Yoshiko on model of the Gunma Music Centre (garden in Nishiazabu, late 1950s)

good terms with the fisherman, who took care of his land. Then he bought him a boat and this made the family very happy. My husband could steer a boat, and so we occasionally borrowed it. Though not for fishing – fishing with nets is done too early in the morning.

HČ: What was the fate of the villa in Hayama?

GY: When Mr. Raymond left the firm and moved to his farm in America, he sold it with a condition: the new owner could change the layout of the rooms, but the exterior form of the villa had to be retained. Unfortunately the buyer didn't keep this promise. When I went to Hayama some time later, I found just a block of concrete there.

PH: Surely not! They demolished it?

GY: Yes, because of the concrete box. The summer villa in Karuizawa was bought by a former employee, and so it's standing there to this day (see p. 147).

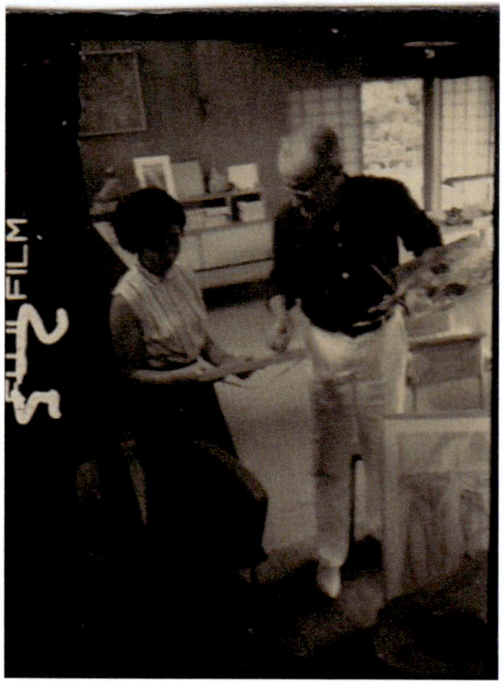

チャプコヴァー: 葉山の別荘はその後どうなったんですか？

五代: レーモンドがペンシルバニアの農場にリタイヤするときに、内部は変更してもいいけど外装はこのまま残すっていう条件で売ったんです。けれど、買った方が、その約束を守って下さらなくて。しばらく経って私が葉山にどうなってるか見に行ったら、コンクリートの箱が、デンッとありました。

ホリー: え？　潰したんですか？

五代: 潰されちゃってました。ただのコンクリートの箱に。私も自分の目を疑いましたよ。軽井沢の方は元所員の方が買ってくださったので、未だに軽井沢にありますけどね (147ページを参照)。

ホリー: 葉山の別荘は、すごく綺麗な写真で紹介されていました。『新建築』や『建築文化』などの週刊誌か何かに。それだけに勿体ない。

五代: あそこ、夏は若者が多くて、海岸がうるさいんですよね。レーモンド夫妻は、秋から冬にかけていらして一階をスタディオとして使っていました。ベッドルームを2階にあげたんですね。その方が暖房が効きやすかったのかしら。

チャプコヴァー: レーモンドさんとの最後の出会いはいつ頃でしたのか。

五代: 1974年の春にレーモンドさんが病気になって、横浜の山手病院 (The Bluff

36–38 – 絵画のモデルとして五代美子、軽井沢にて、1950年代。

Mrs. Godai modelling for Antonín Raymond (Karuizawa, 1950s)

PH: Some of the beautiful photographs of the villa in Hayama have been published. Perhaps in the weekly journals Shin-kenchiku (New Architecture) and Kenchiku Bunka (Architectural Culture), which documents how outrageous it is that it's been destroyed.
GY: In the summer a lot of young people are on the coast and there's a lot of noise. The Raymonds came from autumn to winter and used the ground floor as a studio. They slept on the first floor, probably because of the heat.
HČ: When did you last see the Raymonds?
GY: In the summer of 1974 Mr. Raymond fell ill with painful shingles, he was hospitalised in the Yamato district of Yokohama, but his condition didn't improve and so he hastily flew to America. By doing so he also resigned from his position in the Japanese firm. In the summer I went to the United States with my daughter, and we also visited the farm in New Hope, Pennsylvania. That was the last time I saw him. After that I only went to the funeral. Mrs. Raymond was now showing symptoms of her illness, and she was only dimly aware that Mr. Raymond had died. The same year the Church of St. Anselm was completed in Meguro in Tokyo, where they held a requiem mass for Mr. Raymond. It was attended by his son Claude (Jean-Francois), with his son Claude, but Mrs. Raymond's dementia had advanced to such a degree that she did not come back to Japan again.

39 – 隠居した漁師さんと五代美子、はやまにて、1950年代。

Mrs. Yoshiko with a fisherman and the caretaker of the villa in Hayama (1950s)

40 – ノエミレーモンドと五代氏、葉山、1959年2月。

Noémi Raymond and Godai Yoshiko in Hayama (February 1959)

41 – 葉山の防風バルコニーに腰掛ける五代さん。50年代。

Mrs. Godai on the railings of the balcony of the villa in Hayama (1950s)

Hospital) に入院した。帯状疱疹になって、アメリカへ早めに帰った同時に会社退院した。娘と同年の夏にペンシルヴァニアの農場 New Hope へ最後の訪問をした。1976年のレーモンドさんのお葬式も参加し、ミセス・レーモンドはもう病気で誰が亡くなったとよく分からなかった。その時東京の目黒の聖アンセルモ教会が完成され、追悼ミサをそこに行って、クロードさんとその息子のクロードも参加した。ミセス・レーモンドは病気で来日できなくなっていた。

42 – 前列左から斉藤大工、レーモンド夫妻、隠居した漁師夫妻、葉山、1950年代。

Front row from left: builder Saitō, Noémi and Antonín Raymond with a fisherman (Hayama, late 1950s)

松坂屋百貨店での展示
住宅と別荘

Exhibition in the Matsuzakaya department store, residences and the summer villas

44 – 祝儀の後。この時のアントニン・レーモンドの装いは、著名な「旭日章」第三グループによるもの。左から黄田多喜夫氏外務事務次官、レーモンド夫妻、建築家吉村順三。1964年4月21日。

After the ceremony, during which Antonín Raymond was decorated with the honour of the third degree of the Order of the Rising Sun. From left: diplomat Kida Takio, the Raymonds and architect Yoshimura Junzō (21 April 1964)

43 – 笄町の自宅にて、ソファーに座るレーモンド夫妻。1962年。

The Raymonds in their house in Kōgaichō (Azabu, approx. 1962)

45 – 仕事机に向かうアントニン・レーモンド。麻布にて、1970年。

Antonín Raymond at his desk (Azabu, 1970)

46 – アントニン・レーモンド、笄町の従業員たちと。麻布、1970年。

Antonín Raymond with his employees in Kōgaichō (Azabu, 1970)

47–48 – アントニン・レーモンド展 “Antonin Raymond and His Work”、松坂屋百貨店のギャラリーにて。左手よりA.レーモンド、F.井上氏、レーモンド設計事務所元社長石川氏、高松宮、N.レーモンド。銀座、東京、1970年。

From the exhibition Antonin Raymond and His Work in the gallery of the Matsuzayaka shopping centre/ department store. From left: A. Raymond, F. Inoue, director of Raymond's firm Mr. Ishikawa, Prince Takamatsu and Noémi Raymond (Ginza, Tokyo, 1970)

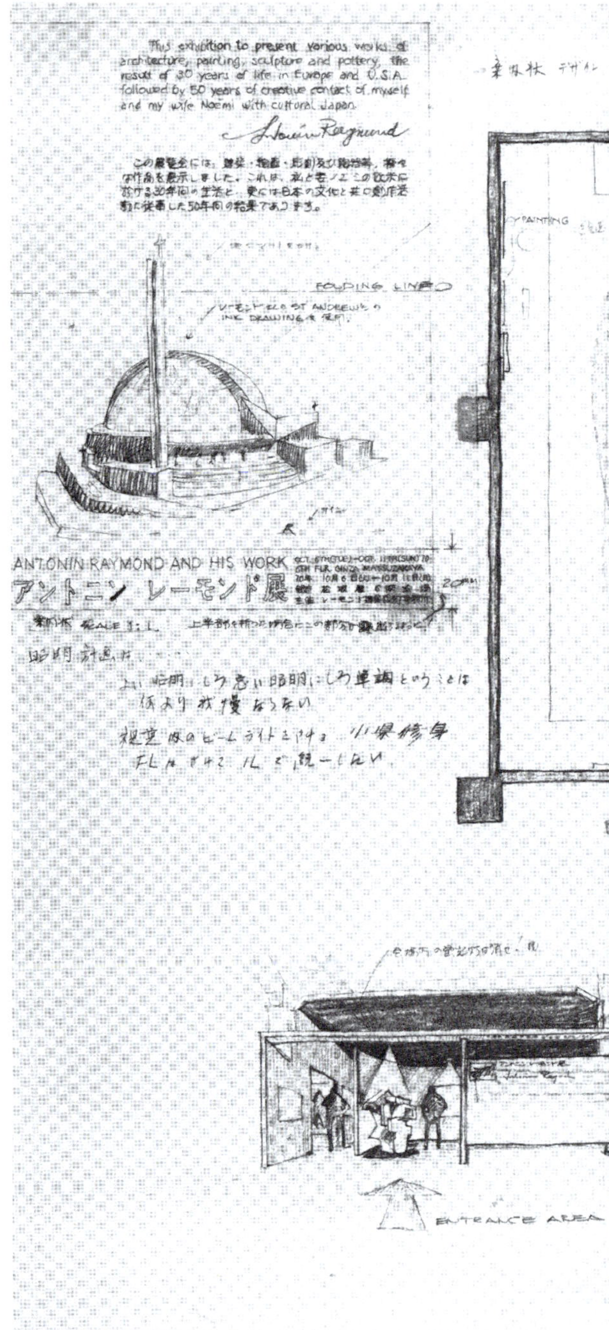

49 – 北澤興一、アントニン・レーモンド展の図案。展示場の建築はA.レーモンド案。

Kitazawa Kōichi, design of installation of the exhibition Antonin Raymond and His Work in the Matzukaya gallery, thus in the building constructed according to the design of Antonín Raymond (1970)

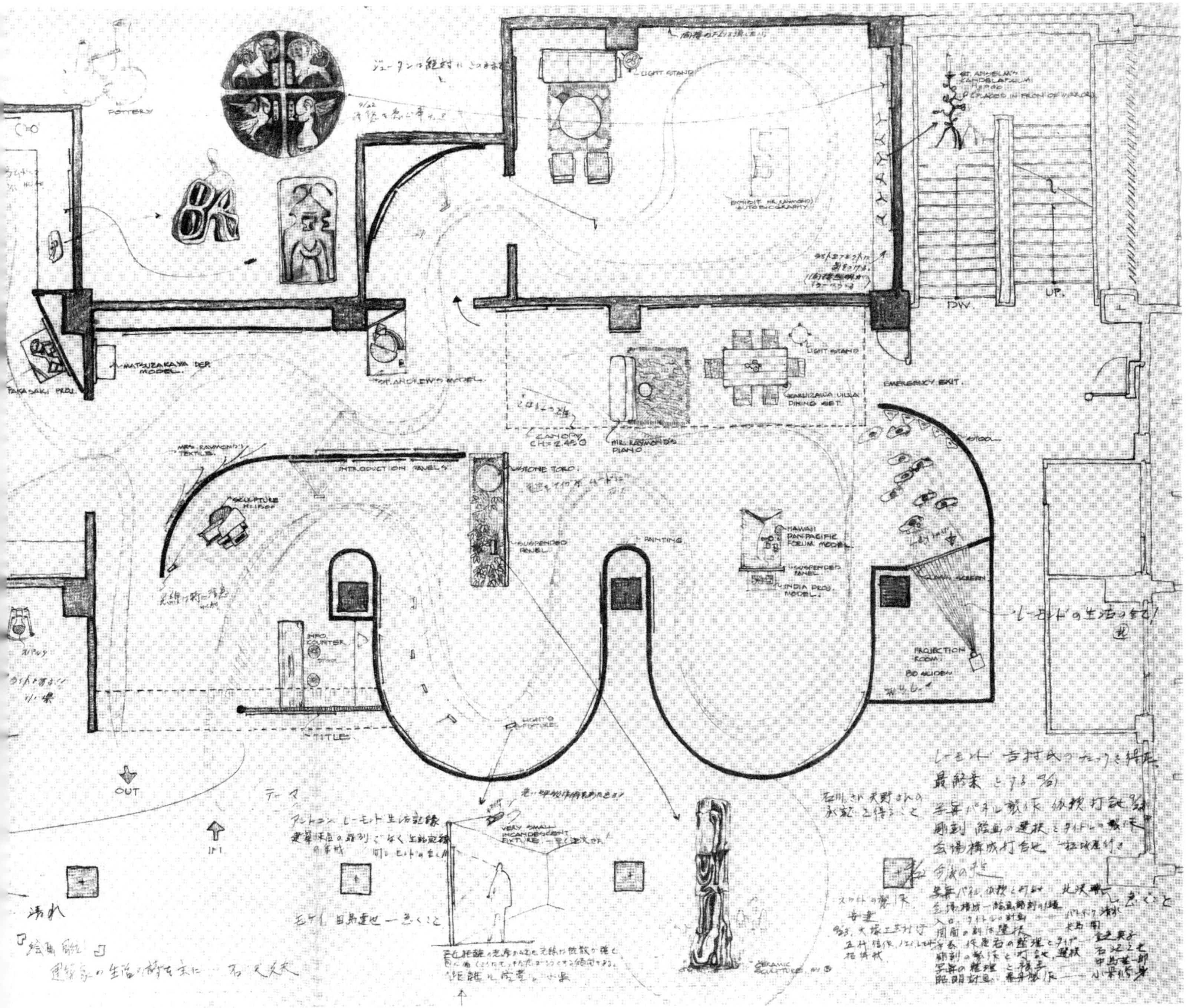
POTTERY
LIGHT STAND
EXHIBIT MR. RAYMOND'S AUTOBIOGRAPHY
MATSUZAKAYA DEP. MODEL
TAKASAKI PROJ.
ST. ANDREW'S MODEL
LIGHT STAND
KARUIZAWA VILLA DINING SET
EMERGENCY EXIT
CANOPY CH=2,450
MR. RAYMOND'S PIANO
MRS. RAYMOND'S TEXTILES
INTRODUCTION PANELS
SCULPTURE
SUSPENDED PANEL
PAINTING
HAWAII PAN PACIFIC FORUM MODEL
SUSPENDED PANEL
INDIA PROJ. MODEL
PROJECTION ROOM
INFO. COUNTER
TITLE
LIGHTING FIXTURE
OUT
IN
DW.
UP.
VERY SMALL INCANDESCENT FIXTURE
CERAMIC SCULPTURE
レーモンドの生活の全て!
テーマ
アントニン レーモンド生活記録
流れ

50 – 霊南坂のレーモンド宅。東京、１９２４〜１９２６年。

Raymond's Tokyo residence Reinanzaka (1924-1926)

51 – 霊南坂のレーモンド宅。東京、１９２４〜１９２６年。

Raymond's Tokyo residence Reinanzaka (1924–1926)

52 – 霊南坂のレーモンド宅のリビング。東京、１９２４〜１９２６年。

Living room in Reinanzaka house. (Tokyo, 1924–1926)

53 – 笄町邸宅にて。中庭からプール眺め。麻布、1951年。

Villa in Kōgaichō, view of swimming pool from patio (Azabu, 1951)

54 – 笄町邸宅内観。麻布、1951年。

Interior of villa in Kōgaichō (Azabu, 1951)

55 – 笄町邸宅にて。麻布、1951年。

Villa in Kōgaichō (Azabu, 1951)

56–58 – 葉山海岸の別宅。1958年。のちに建て壊し。

House on the coast in Hayama (Kanagawa, 1958, later demolished)

59–61 – 軽井沢の新スタジオ。長野、1962年。

New studio in Karuizawa (Nagano, 1962)

62–64 – 軽井沢の別荘。長野県、1932年。のちに移転、現在はフランスの画家レイモン・ペイネの常設展として使用されている（ペイネ美術館）。

Summer house in Karuizawa (Nagano, 1932, later relocated, now serves for the permanent exhibition of the works of the French painter Raymond Peynet (Musée Peynet)

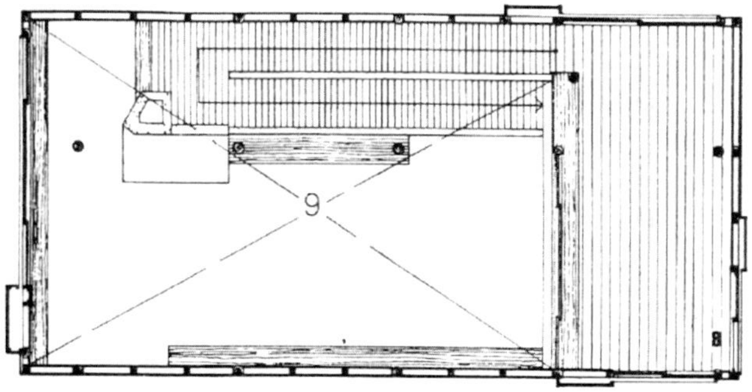

Second floor; scale: 1/150

1 LIVING ROOM (EXHIBITION ROOM-1)
2 STORAGE
3 PANTRY (RECEPTION)
4 KITCHEN (OFFICE)
5 BEDROOM (EXHIBITION ROOM-3)
6 BATHROOM (STORAGE)
7 HOUSE MAID'S ROOM (demolished)
8 ATELIER (EXHIBITION ROOM-2)
9 VOID
10 POOL

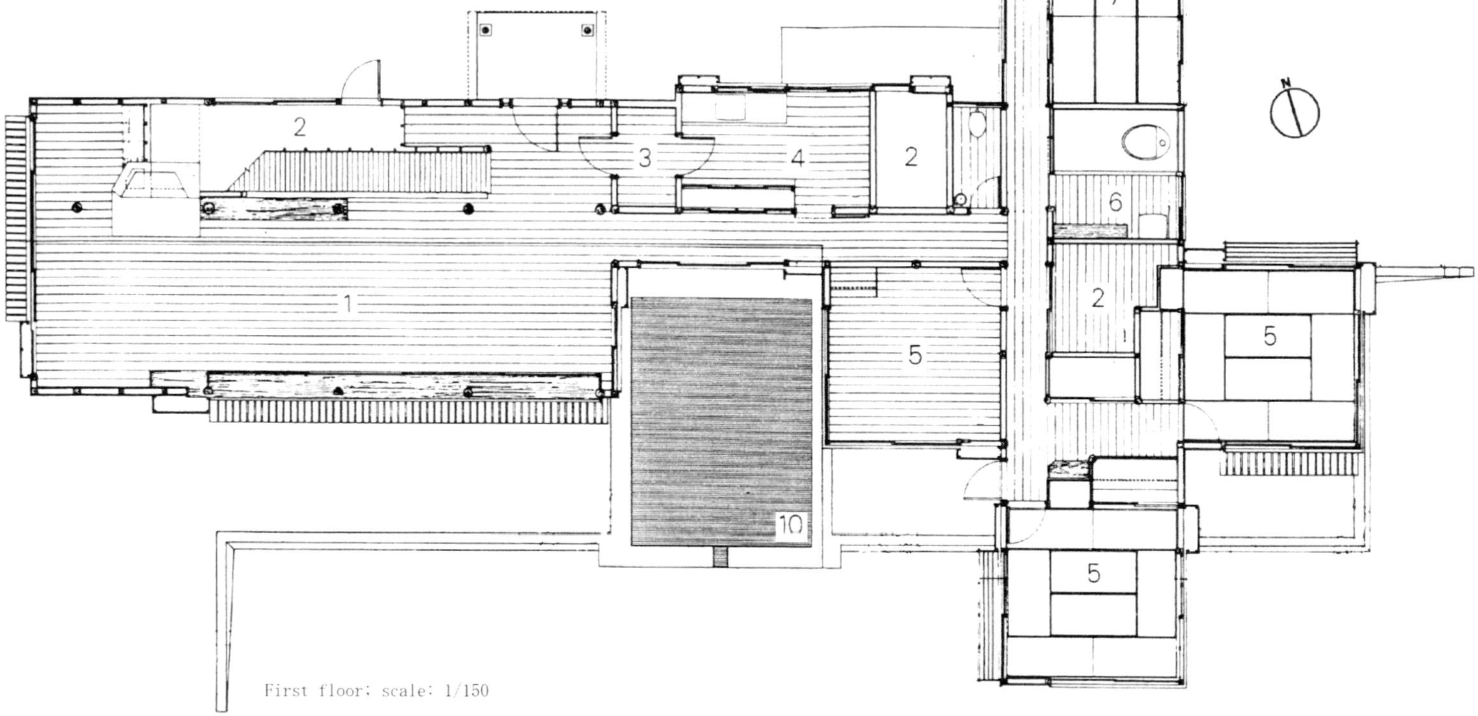

First floor; scale: 1/150

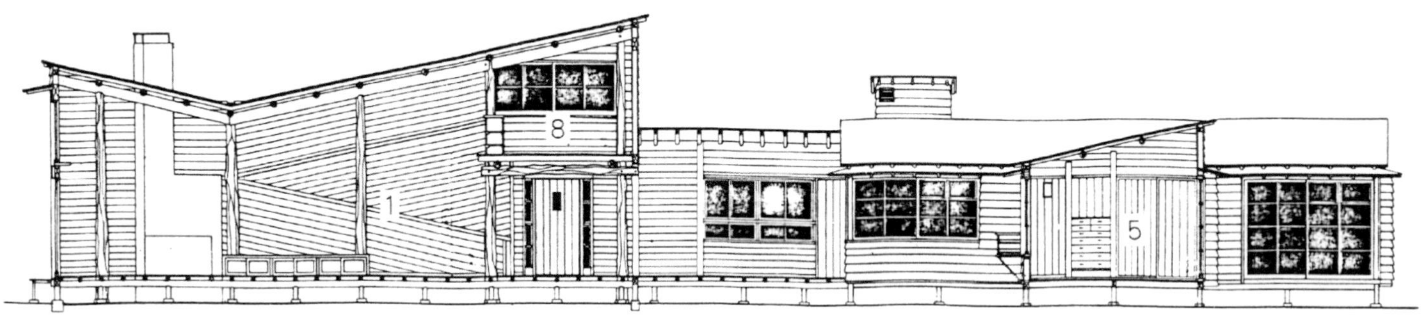

Section; scale: 1/150

1932 軽井沢 夏の家(旧アトリエ)

65 – 軽井沢別荘の図面。1932年。
Plans of summer house in Karuizawa (1932)

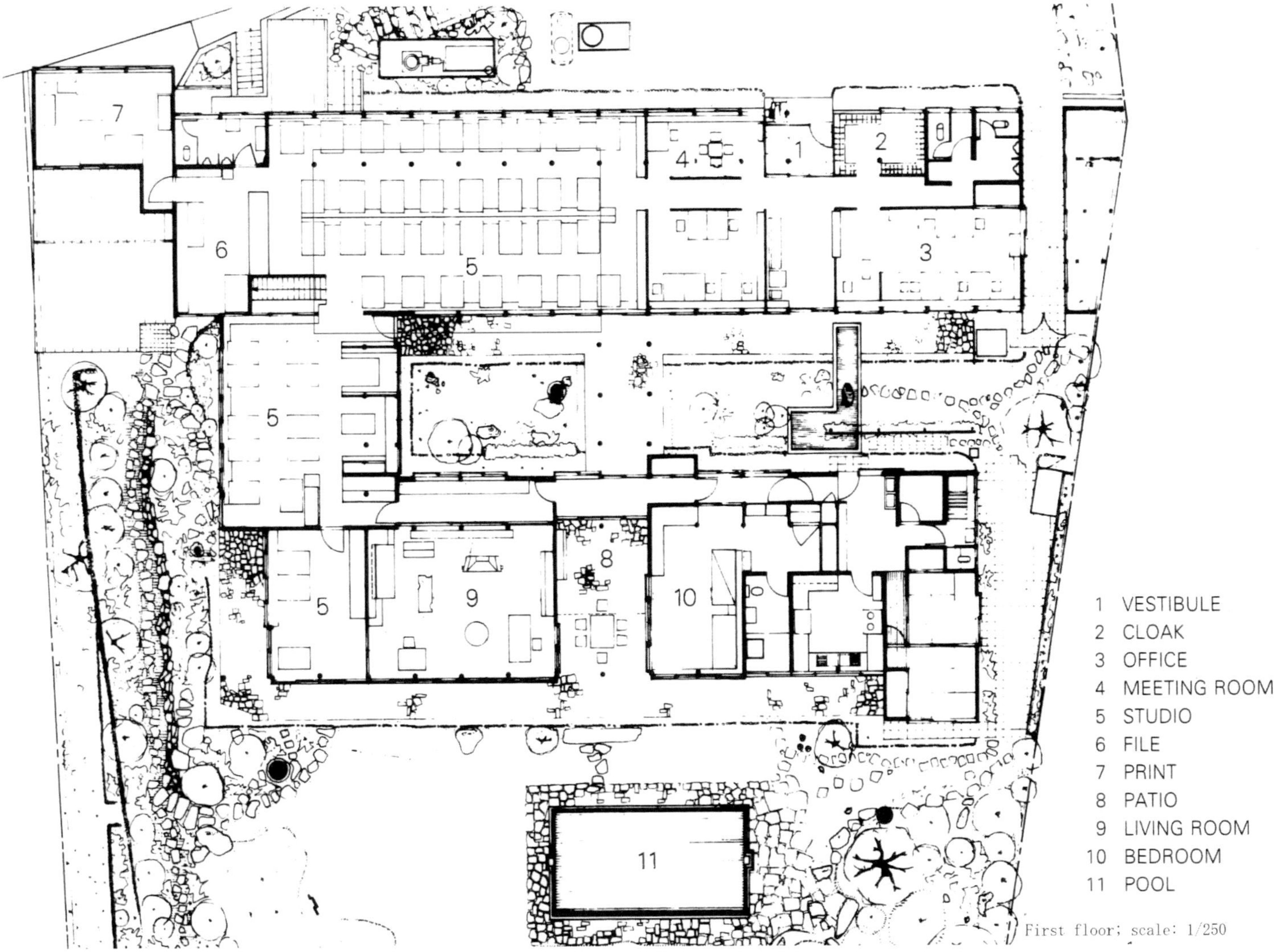

First floor; scale: 1/250

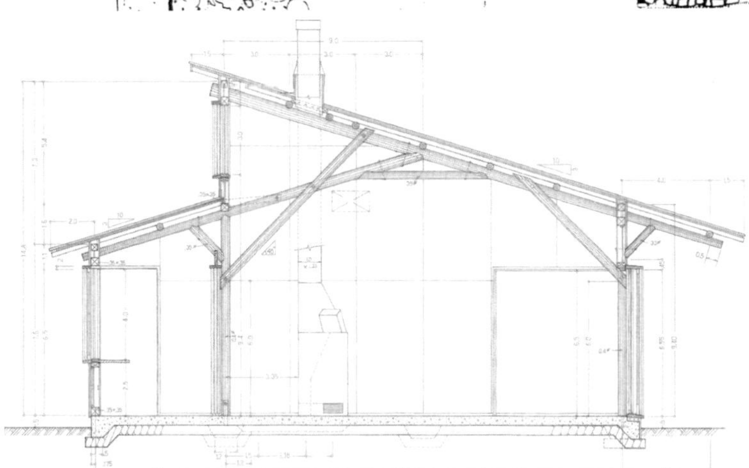

Section; scale: 1/100. module: shaku (1shaku=303mm)

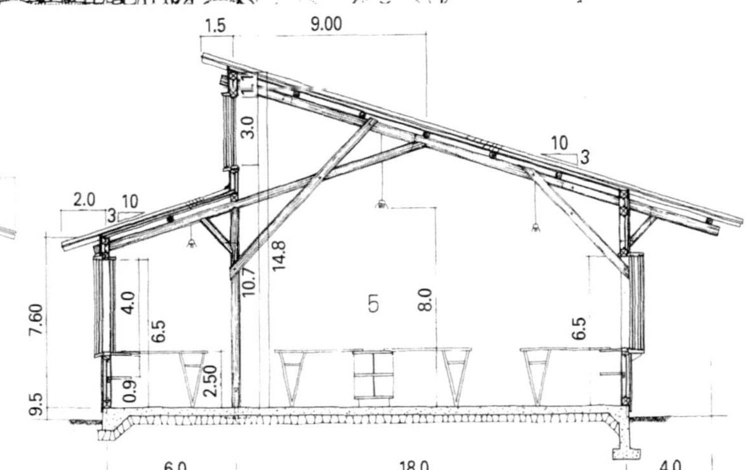

24 1951 レーモンド設計事務所兼自邸

66 – 笄町邸宅図面。1951年。
Plans of building in Kōgaichō (1951)

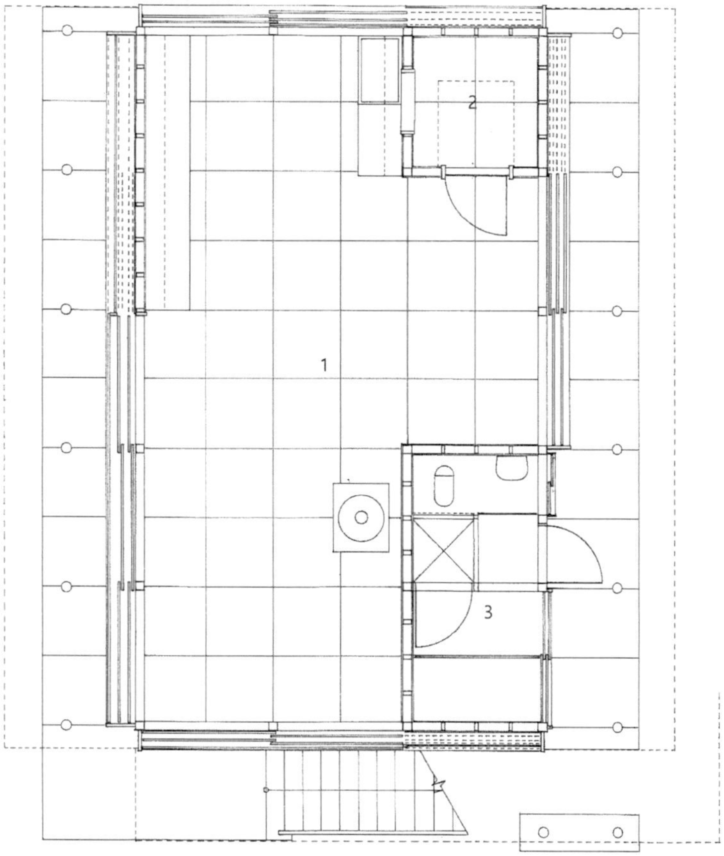

First floor; scale: 1/100

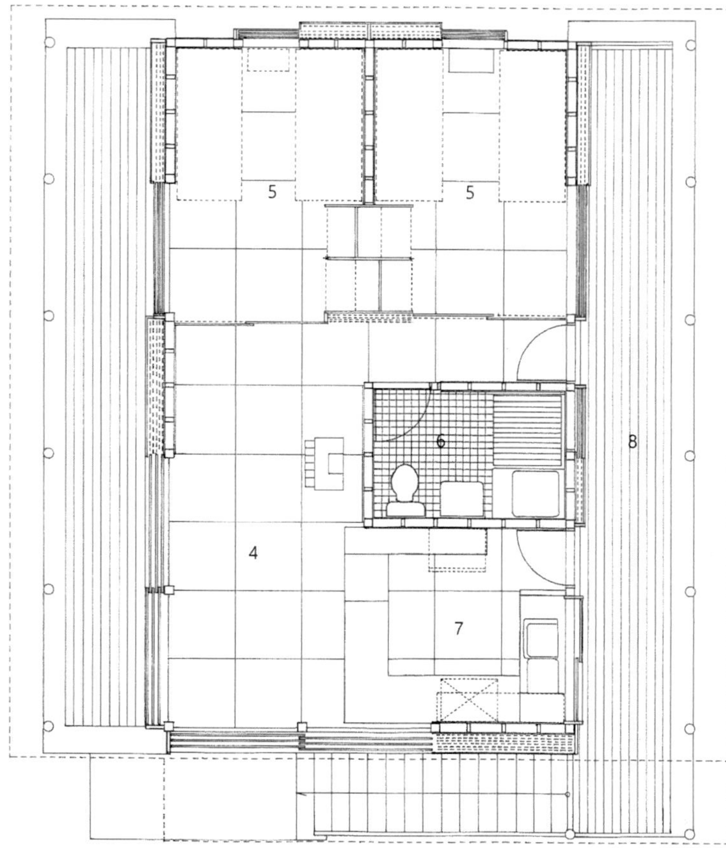

Second floor; scale: 1/100

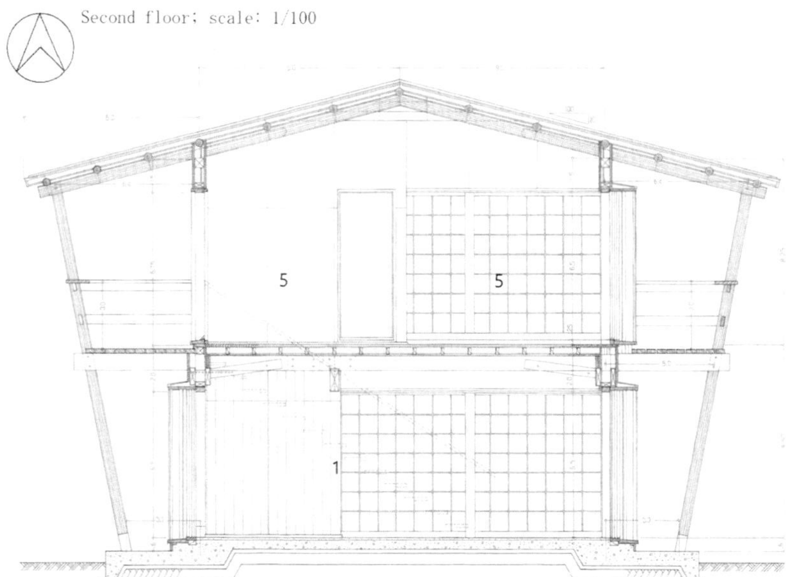

Section; scale: 1/100

1 STUDIO
2 STORAGE
3 MAIND'S ROOM
4 LIVING AND DINING ROOM
5 BED ROOM
6 BATH ROOM
7 KITCHEN
8 BALCONY

1958　葉山　海の家

67 – 葉山海岸の別宅図面。1958年。
Plans of house on the coast in Hayama (1958)

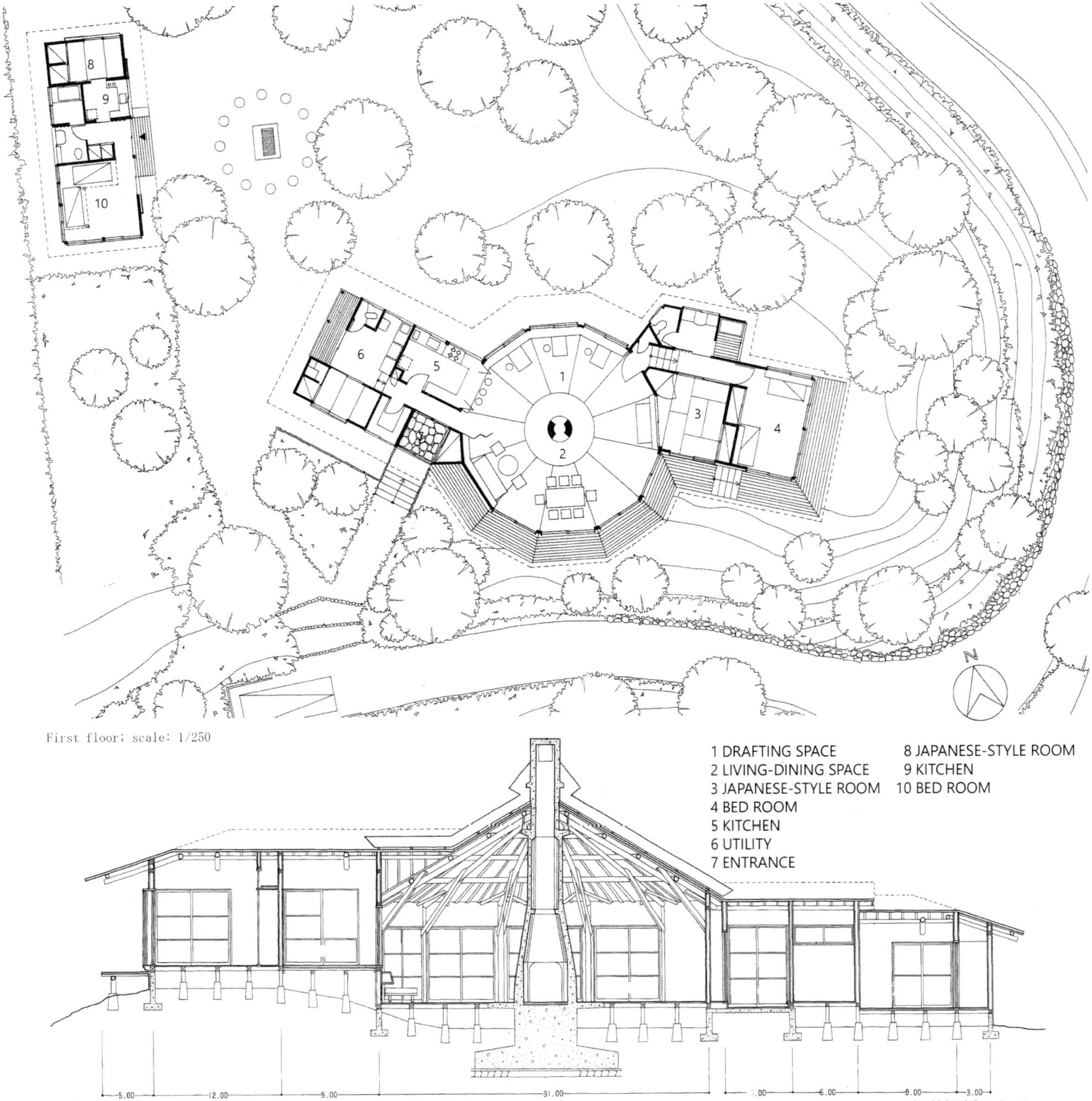

68 – 軽井沢新スタジオの図面。1962年。
Plans of New Studio in Karuizawa (1962)

69 – 群馬音楽センターの階段、高崎、1961年。

Staircase of the Gunma prefecture Music Centre (Takasaki, 1961)

内藤恒方

建築家・ランドスケープアーキテクト内藤恒方氏は東京芸術大学建築学科に卒業後、５年間、レーモンド設計事務所勤務。カリフォルニア大学大学院修了後、ササキ・ドーソン・ディメイ・アソシエイツに勤務、ニューヨーク州立大学助教授を経て帰国。1972年にＡＬＰ設計室を主宰。レーモンドの建築を熱心に世に広めた。

Naitō Tsunekata

Mr. Naitō Tsunekata joined Raymond's firm in 1958, immediately after completing his studies of architecture at the Tokyo University of the Arts. Five years later he left for the USA, where he studied Landscape Architecture. In 1972 he returned to Japan, opening his own office here. He actively promotes the work of Antonín Raymond to this day.

チャプコヴァー: さて、今日は内藤恒方さんをお招きしました。1934年生まれの内藤さんは、1954年に東京芸術大学美術学部建築科に入学され、1958年に卒業、その年の4月よりレーモンド設計事務所の所員として5年間、事務所で働かれました。その後、1963年9月より、アメリカ、カリフォルニア大学バークレー校、環境デザイン学部大学院に入学され、1966年、同学部のランドスケープ・アーキテクチュア学科より、MLAの学位を受けられました。その後、マサチューセッツ州、ボストンにあるササキ・ドーソン・ディメイ・アソシエーツに入社し、アソシエートとして3年間、1969年まで働かれます。そして、1969年より1972年まで、ニューヨーク州立大学環境科学学部ランドスケープ・アーキテクチュア学科で助教授として教鞭を取られ、1972年8月に、日本へ帰国されました。同年9月より大阪芸術大学、その他、数々の大学を教えながら、ALP設計室を設立。主宰として、建築設計、ランドスケープ・デザイン、広域計画や設計を、日本での一級建築士、アメリカ・マサチューセッツ州の登録ランドスケープ・アーキテクトとして遂行し、今日に至っておられます。東京芸術大学美術学部建築科を卒業し、レーモンド設計事務所に入社される時に、大学の先生である吉村順三教授より、[1] お薦めがあったと伺いました。その経緯をお聞きして良いでしょうか？ また、東京芸術大学の授業は、どの様なものだったのでしょうか？

内藤: 私が東京芸術大学に入学した時は、美術学部建築科の新入生は15人でした。それまでは、毎年10人ほどしか入学できず、明治40年に初めての卒業生が出て以来、数えると300人くらいしか卒業生がいない計算になるんですよね。その年は15人取るのに400人以上の応募の人達がいたと聞いてて、後で考えると、よく入れたと思います。建築科では、岡田捷五郎先生が学科長で教授でした。その他、吉田五十八先生と二人が教授で、吉村順三先生と山本学治先生が助教授だったかと思います。その他非常勤の先生達、建築史の蔵田周忠、都市計画の石川栄耀、高山英華、バウハウスで勉強をされて来られた水谷武彦先生など、[2]今振り返ると大変偉い先生達がいたんだなと。

70 – アントニン・レーモンド、内藤氏、同僚。南山大学の模型を前に。笄町、60年代初頭。

Antonín Raymond and Mr. Naitō with a colleague by the campus of Nanzan University, Nagoya (Kōgaičō, early 1960s)

01 吉村順三は著名な日本の建築家であり、1928年からレーモンド設計事務所にインターンとして入社した。レーモンドのもとで長く働き、友情関係を築いた。東京美術学校（現 東京芸術大学）で建築を学び、1931年に卒業後、アントニン・レーモンドに師事。1941年、吉村順三設計事務所を開設。1962年、東京藝術大学教授に就任。代表作は国際文化会館 (前川國男、坂倉準三と共同設計、1955)、皇居新宮殿基本設計 (1968) など。

02 水谷 武彦は 日本の美術教育者。建築教育者。日本で最初にバウハウスへ留学した人物。帰国後、様々な活動を通じて、日本にバウハウスを

71 – アントニン・レーモンドと内藤恒方。50年代末。

Antonín Raymond and Tsunekata Naitō (late 1950s)

HČ: Helena Čapková
NT: Naitō Tsunekata
PH: Petr Holý

HČ: My guest today is Mr. Naitō Tsunekata. Mr. Naitō was born in 1934. In 1954 he began studying architecture at the Faculty of Arts at the Tokyo University of the Arts (Tokyo Geidai), and completed his studies in 1958. In April the same year he started work at the Raymond Architectural Design Office, where he worked for a further five years. In September 1963 he commenced his Master's degree at the College of Environmental Design at the University of California in Berkeley, where he was awarded the title of MLA in the discipline of Landscape Architecture in 1966. He then entered the company Sasaki, Dawson & DeMay in Boston, Massachusetts, where he worked as a partner for three years, until 1969. From 1969 to 1972 he taught landscape architecture at the Faculty of Environmental Design at the State University of New York. In August 1972 he returned to Japan, and from September that year he began teaching at the Osaka University of Arts (Osaka Geidai) and a number of other Japanese universities. At the same time he founded the architecture studio ALP (Architecture Landscape Planning). As president of ALP, and as an authorised first category architect in Japan, as well as a registered landscape architect of the state of Massachusetts, to this day he focuses on architectural projects, territorial planning and landscape architecture.
I heard that when you completed your study of architecture at Tokyo Geidai, you obtained a recommendation for a position at the Raymond Architectural Design Office from professor Yoshimura Junzō (1908–1997).[1] Could you tell us something more about this? I would also be interested in the form that teaching took at the Tokyo Geidai.
NT: At the time when I was accepted onto the course at the Faculty of Arts at the Tokyo Geidai, there were fifteen new students of architecture. Until that time they had taken on approximately ten students per year. If we counted up all of the graduates, starting from 1907, when the first generation of students completed their studies, then up to 1954 there were less than three hundred graduates. I later heard that the condition for them to take on fifteen first year students in 1954 was that more than four hundred candidates had to apply. When I thought about that later, I was amazed

01 Yoshimura Junzō was a distinguished architect, friend and from 1928 a colleague of Antonín Raymond. After graduating from the department of architecture (Faculty of Art, Tokyo University of the Arts) he realised several prestigious projects: The Shōfūsō teahouse in the garden of MOMA in New York (1953, in 1957 relocated to Philadelphia) the International House in Roppongi (1955, together with K. Maekawa and J. Sakaura) and the buildings for the Imperial Palace in Tokyo (1968). In 1941 he opened his own office and after 1962 he was appointed professor at his alma mater, the Tokyo Geidai.

チャプコヴァー： 吉村先生や吉田先生から直々に教えを受けたんですね。どのようなことを当時は学ばれたんですか？

内藤: 吉村先生は、ニューヨークで日本の書院造りの木造建築を作っておられる時で、さらにMotel on the Mountainと、ニューヨークでのお仕事を沢山かかえておられました。「建築概論」の講義があり、ご自分の経験に基づいたお話を伺うことができましたね。吉田五十八先生も、丸の内に事務所を持っていましたが、講義は持っていなくて、学生達のエスキースを見て、ご自分の経験に基づいた貴重なお話をされていました。私たちは、よく真剣に聞いたものです。住宅設計の課題で、一年先輩のTさんのエスキースを見て、玄関の入り方が良くないと、吉田先生が30分以上滔々と指導されていたことを覚えております。多分、先生と云うよりは、親が子供に教える様に、懇切丁寧に話す感じだったんでしょうね。でも、大学に入学したばかりの我々にとっては、あまり長いお話しだったので、T君は、皆の前でトレペに書かれたエスキースを取って、幾つかのピースに引き裂き、「先生、よく分かりました」と言って帰っちゃったんですよ（笑）。当時の芸大建築科は、この位、家庭的な雰囲気を持った、素晴らしい学校でした。

ホリー: 学校はどんな様式の建築だったんでしょうか？

内藤: 教室のある建物は、レンガ造りの2階建の建物で、窓は上下に上げ下げする窓が付いていました。学生の人数が少ないので、上級生、下級生のエスキースの時間には、だれでも聞く事ができました。この当時、建築科の建物は、古いレンガ造の建物で、職員室以外には、講義室と各学年の製図室には電気がなく、暗くなったら、家に帰らなければなりませんでした。また暖冷房も、全くなく、冬や暑い夏は、ここで仕事をするのは、大変でした。

チャプコヴァー： レーモンド事務所に入社する経緯はどのようなものでしたか？

内藤: 1958年1月になって、卒業の目処が立ち、吉村順三先生に就職の相談に伺ったんです。そうしたらその時に吉村先生から直接、「大学にレーモンド事務所から募集が来ているので、行って見たらいい。僕も多くの事を学ぶ事ができたよ」と言われ、応募する事にしました。

チャプコヴァー： レーモンド事務所に入社するのはそんなに簡単なことではないでしょう。

内藤: レーモンド事務所では入社試験がありました。約40名が応募し、建設設計2人と構造設計1人が、入社する事ができました。今、考えて見ますと、芸大の入学、レーモンド事務所への入社と共に、本来は狭き門なのに、私は大変ラッキーにもパスできたんです。

紹介し、その教育を実践した。東京美術学校建築科に復職後、「構成原理」の講義を受け持つ。戦後も東京都立大学で図学講師など、講師歴多数。

that they had accepted me as a student there. – The department of architecture was headed by professor Okada Shōgorō. Another professor was Yoshida Isoya (1894–1974), and Yoshimura Junzō and Yamamoto Gakuji also taught there. External lecturers included the historian of architecture Kurata Chikatada (1895–1966), the town planners Ishikawa Hideaki and Takayama Eika, and also Mizutani Takehiko (1907–1969), who studied at the Bauhaus.[2] It's now that I realise that at the time they were among the most successful teachers.

HČ: So you studied directly under professors Yoshida and Yoshimura. What did you study specifically?

NT: Mr. Yoshimura had a large number of projects in progress in New York. He was working there on a project of a wooden building in the traditional Japanese style of shoin-zukuri,[3] and also on the building Motel on the Mountain. During his lectures in the course Introduction to Architecture he primarily related his own experiences. Professor Yoshida Isoya had his architecture study in the Tokyo district of Marunouchi. Instead of lecturing, he inspected our designs and commented on them, based on his wealth of experience. We always listened to him attentively. I recall that he surveyed a diagram of a family house drafted by T, a fellow student of mine a year older than me, and then explained to him for a full thirty minutes that he had put the door in the wrong place. I would say that rather than a teacher he appeared to us more like a parent who tried to explain things patiently to his children. But for us fresh university students his explanations were too long, and so T. took the diagram and tore it into pieces in front of everyone, declaring: "Professor, I understood you!", and walked out of the class. *(Laughs)* At that time there was such a homely atmosphere in the department of architecture at the Geidai. It was a wonderful school.

PH: What style was the university building constructed in?

NT: The classrooms were located in a two-storey brick building with sliding windows. There were only a few students, and so anyone could come and attend classes of drafting and sketching in the higher and lower years. At that time the building of the department of architecture was an old brick structure, and with the exception of the offices of the employees, the lecture theatres and studios of all years were without electricity. When it got dark, we had to go home. In addition there was no heating or air conditioning in the building, and so it was fairly difficult to work there in the winter or during a hot summer.

HČ: How did you come to work at the Raymond Architectural Design Office?

NT: In January 1958 it seemed that I was on course to conclude my studies successfully, and so I went to professor Yoshimura Junzō for a consultation on my future employment. Professor Yoshimura told me straight out: "We've just received an advertisement from the Raymond Architectural Design Office. You ought to take a look at the place. I learned a great deal of things there." And so I decided to reply to the advertisement.

HČ: But it can't have been easy to start work at the firm.

NT: I had to take entrance examinations. I managed to secure a position in the firm despite the fact that out of forty candidates they took on only two architects and one

02 The architect Mizutani Takehiko was evidently the best known and first regular Japanese student at the Bauhuas in Dessau, where he spent two years (1927–1929). After returning to his homeland he worked as a lecturer, in particular as an assistant at the Tokyo Geidai.

03 Shoin-zukuri is a traditional Japanese style of architecture based on the central space of the building, and the simple design of the study of the literary aristocrat. A "shoin" is a highly aestheticised sanctuary of the scholar, containing a tokonoma alcove in which artistic objects are traditionally placed. In the alcove is a chigaidana shelf; like the tokonoma it is built into the wall, and represents a fundamental element of the building's architecture. "Asymmetrical" shelves enhance the sense of asymmetry of this style, which was developed in the Middle Ages in Japan. With the gradual decline of the importance of the aristocracy and thus also their property, the popularity of shoin-zukuri increased, which was compact, aesthetically refined and accentuated asymmetry and irregularity.

ホリー: レーモンド事務所に入社した後の生活についてお聞かせください。

内藤: その当時、レーモンドさんは70才で、まだまだ精力的にお仕事をしておられました。レーモンドさんは、朝、遅刻するのが非常に嫌な方で。規律には厳しかったですね。生活のリズムを作ることが建築家にとっては大事なんだっていうことを私は教わりました。1958年4月1日、初めてレーモンド事務所に出社し、大きい製図室の中庭に面した中央位の窓側に席を与えられました。製図板の上に、白い紙を貼った瞬間、扉を開けて、レーモンドさんが入ってきて、紹介をされ、私の建築家としての生活は始まりました。レーモンドさんは私の椅子に座られて、"Architect should put chaos into order"と書かれ、辞書で引いてよく考える様にと言って立って行かれました。この事は、トランスビュー社の『アントニン・レーモンド：チャーチ&チャペル』に書いています。

チャプコヴァー： レーモンド事務所ではどのような仕事から始めたのですか？

内藤：私が初めて加入したチームの仕事は、T先輩のチームで、四国の広見町と云う町役場の設計中の図面作りの仕事でした。T先輩は、レーモンドさんの言うことを聞かないんですよ。レーモンドさんが仕事のチェックをしに、彼のテーブルに行かれる時は、日に日に、大争いの連続となり、事務所中に聞こえる様な大声で、レーモンドさんは怒っておられました。この仕事は、レーモンドさんの建築が好きな広美町の町長さんが依頼したものだったんですね。レーモンドさんの建築に対する哲学に基づいて、設計しなければならない事、これは最も大切な事であると、事務所に入所した一番初めの仕事を通じて、教えられました。また、一方、建築家という仕事は、Tさんがとったような誤った行動には、身を張って対処しなければならない職業でもある事を、目前で、知らされました

チャプコヴァー： 軽井沢のレーモンドさんの別荘には行かれましたか？

内藤：はい、その夏、私は7月から9月まで、その年一緒に入社したM君と共に、軽井沢に、3ヶ月連れて行かれ、合宿訓練を受けました。レーモンド夫婦と我々2人での生活の中で私達は、建築家としての仕事に対する心がまえや、生活とは本来どうあるべきかを多く学びました。東京にレーモンドさんが一人で出張される時は一等車で行かれ、ノミエ夫人は、必ず3等車で行かれるんです。軽井沢の別荘は、戦前、大きな建築物でして、今はこれが南軽井沢に残されております。また、新しい別荘は、私が事務所を退社する頃はまだ工事中で、私は、ここのファイヤー・プレスを設計いたしました。

チャプコヴァー： 軽井沢のレーモンド邸での生活はどのような雰囲気だったのでしょうか。

72 – 船上のアントニン・レーモンド、瀬戸内海、1955年。

Antonín Raymond on the deck of a boat on the Inland Sea (1955)

73 – レーモンド設計事務所の従業員、五代さんの結婚式にて。笄町、1958年。

Employees of Raymond's firm at the celebration of the wedding of Mrs. Godai (Kōgaichō, 1958)

civil engineer. When I look back on it, I have to say that luck played a big part in my acceptance at both the Geidai and the Raymond Architectural Design Office.

PH: What was your everyday life like when you started work at the Raymond Architectural Design Office?

NT: At that time Mr. Raymond was seventy years old and he was still working actively. He didn't like anybody to come to work late in the morning; he strictly demanded that we all follow the rules. I learned how important it is for an architect to set an everyday rhythm. When I first came to the firm on 1 April 1958, they allocated me a place in the studio by the middle window, with a view of the courtyard. At the moment I attached the white paper to the drawing board, the door opened and in walked Mr. Raymond. They introduced us, and that's how my life as an architect began. Mr. Raymond sat down on my chair and wrote: "Architects should put chaos into order", and he then told me to look it up in a dictionary and contemplate it thoroughly. Then he got up and left. I write about that incident in the book published by the Transview publishing house, entitled Antonín Raymond: Churches and chapels (Tokyo 2013).

HČ: What was your first project in Raymond's office?

NT: They put me in my colleague T's team, and my first job was to draft diagrams for a design of the town hall in the city of Hiromi on Shikoku island. But you know my colleague T didn't follow Mr. Raymond's instructions, and they argued loudly every day. Every time Mr. Raymond went to his desk to inspect the progress of the project, within a short time his angry voice could be heard throughout the entire

内藤： まず、私達が、この1958年の夏、3ヶ月滞在した別荘はI氏の持っておられた物件です。旧軽井沢銀座まで歩いてすぐの広い土地に小さな建物が数件あった家を3棟借り、1棟がレーモンド夫妻、1棟がM君と私、ここでレーモンド夫妻、セクレタリーと5人で朝昼晩の食事を共にしましたね。その他、コックさん、運転手、女中さんの為の1棟があって、皆そこで寝泊まりしていました。私達のところでは、朝、早く起き、皆様が来られる前に、布団をたたみ、食事のテーブルを出しておかねばなりませんでした。日曜日は、コックさんのお休みの日で、皆、5人で外で夕食を取ります。レーモンドさんは、いつも、たわいのない事を云って、皆を笑わせて下さいました。でも、夕食には必ず、ワインが付き、土曜日には、スコッチの水割りも付きました。1958年の日本の夕食では、考えられませんリッチなものでした。

ホリー: レーモンドさんは葉山にも別荘をお持ちでしたよね

内藤： はい。でも、後年、壊されてしまいました。絶対に壊さないという約束で暖炉屋さんに売ったんですけども、あっという間に壊してしまって。それで、私がアメリカ留学した後に、帰国して、その暖炉屋さんに「暖炉を造りたい」と言ったら、「うちに余っているのがあるからそれをやる。新しい煙突だけこしらえれば良い」と。それが葉山の別荘の暖炉な訳です。だから、葉山の別荘の暖炉はひとつ、うちに残っています。

ホリー: 救世主だ。

内藤： うちの家宝ですから。

チャプコヴァー： ところで、内藤先生はそこで群馬音楽センターのお仕事をされたと伺っています

内藤： そうなんです。ここでの私の仕事は、高崎音楽堂の入口ロビーの周り階段の基本設計でした。この実施設計は、東京事務所の佐藤さんが担当されました。このことは「INAX REPORT 103号」に掲載された香山寿夫氏とのインタビューに細かく述べられております。

ホリー: 他に軽井沢での思い出って何かありますか？

内藤：軽井沢に滞在していた間に、戦前、レーモンドさんに会って感銘を受けたというアメリカ人で、カリフォルニア大学バークレー校の教授をしていたM.チャヤさんが、フルブライトの奨学金を取って、尋ねて来られたんです。一週間位、軽井沢に滞在され、私達と寝起きを共にしました。彼は、建築家の先生でしたが、アートや美術方面を教えておられ、フルブライトの奨学金のテーマは、日本の道祖神の研究で、地方の道端に立っているレリーフの付いた石柱のスタディーをしておられ、これに墨をつけた布で湿らせた紙に型取る事を沢山

company. That order had been commissioned by the mayor of Hiromi, a great fan of Mr. Raymond's architectural work. Thanks to that first project I learned that the most important thing is to design in accordance with Raymond's conception of architecture. I saw with my own eyes that among other factors the profession of architect also requires the ability to deal with the problematic behaviour of people such as Mr. T.

HČ: Did you ever visit Mr. Raymond's summer residence in Karuizawa?

NT: Yes, that summer when I started working in the firm I underwent an induction for three months in Karuizawa, from July to September, together with my friend M. M and I started work at the firm at the same time. During that time we spent with the Raymonds, we learned a great deal about their stance towards the vocation of the architect and about life in general. - If Mr. Raymond went to Tokyo on business he always travelled first class, whereas Mrs. Noémi would only ever travel third class. The villa in Karuizawa, which they built before the war, was an imposing structure, you can find it today on the south side of town. At the time when I left the company they were just building the new villa (Raymond sold the pre-war villa). I designed the fireplace for it.

HČ: What was life like in the Raymonds' summer residence? What kind of atmosphere was there?

NT: The house we lived in for three months in 1958 was the summer residence of Mr. I. The Raymonds rented three smaller houses on an expansive plot of land close to the district of Kyū Karuizawa Ginza. They lived in one of them, I lived in the second together with my friend M, and five of us – including the secretary – used to eat breakfast, lunch and dinner there. The cook, chauffeur and servant slept in the third house. In our house we had to get up early in the morning, clear away the futons and prepare the dining table before the others arrived. On Sunday the cook usually had the day off, and so the five of us ate in one of the local restaurants. Mr. Raymond always used to amuse us with an entertaining story. In the evening we drank wine and on Saturday we drank Scotch with water. They were genuinely luxurious dinners by the standards of Japan in 1958.

PH: Did Mr. Raymond also have a summer residence in Hayama?

NT: Yes, but that was later destroyed. It was sold to a stove fitter in exchange for a promise that the house would be preserved, but he almost immediately went back on his promise and had it demolished. Later, when I returned from my studies in America, I told that stove fitter that I wanted a stove fitting for myself. He answered that he had one spare at home, and if I had a new chimney made then I could use it. It was the one from the house in Hayama. And so now I have the stove from Mr. Raymond's villa in my home.

PH: You salvaged it!

NT: It's my treasure.

HČ: I heard that you also worked in the Gunma prefecture Music Centre.

NT: That's true. My task was to prepare the basic design for the staircase leading from the entrance to the lobby of the concert hall. Mr. Saitō from the Tokyo studio was in

行って帰国されました。一週間、共に生活した時に、私は、レーモンド事務所を退職した後、カリフォルニア大学での都市計画の勉強の可能性をたずねたところ、彼も賛成し、その時は、保証人になると言ってくれました。

チャプコヴァー： その後、東京の事務所に戻ってからはどのようなお仕事をされたんですか？

内藤：9月には東京の事務所に帰り、次の様な仕事を続ける事になりました。国際キリスト教大学の図書館の設計や、そこの教会。元々ヴォーリスの設計した建物の改修、木造建築による教員の為の宿舎。その他、武蔵カントリークラブ・クラブハウスも手がけました。そこでトイレのタイル割りを経験したんですが、この手の設計にはタイル割りが必要である事を初めて知ったんです。また、門司カントリークラブ・クラブハウスの暖炉の図面もやりましたね。煙突を2本にすることになったんですが、暖炉の床が広い為、人工的に煙を出す様にファンをつけるなど工夫しました。屋根が茅ぶきの白河高原カントリークラブ・クラブハウス、白河高原スキー場山小屋宿泊施設、東京カントリー・クラブ内のラウンジの中央暖炉なども手がけたのを覚えています。これは六角形をした暖炉で、その中央にこの地階にある男子浴室の湿気抜けの円形の60センチ直系のパイプが入っているんです。他に覚えているところでいうと、木造2階建住宅の渋谷にあるラザーソン邸、新しいレーモンド軽井沢別荘暖炉といったところですか。新しいレーモンドさんの別荘は茅ぶき屋根のため、煙が外部に出る前に、煙突の下に水溜めの上を少し走らせる必要があったんです。こうした仕事の他、南山大学のマスター・プラン作りもやりました。

チャプコヴァー： こういったお仕事から学ばれた事はなんですか？

内藤： これらの仕事を通じて、設計の進め方、図面の作り方、特に木造の建物のディテールの作り方などを多く勉強する事ができました。さらには、レーモンドさんに図面を見てもらう時には、ディバイターが必要であり、良いプロポーションを作るのには、ディバイダーが不可欠だってことも知りました。レーモンドさんはディバイダーにはこだわっていましたね。それから、日本古来からの畳、建具の寸法、3尺×6尺（90センチ×1m80センチ）の測り方も学びました。これに基づいて、日本の本来の木造建築を作る素材は全て作られているんだって。

ホリー: レーモンド事務所は当時、どんな作りでしたか？

内藤： レーモンド事務所に入社した時、全ての壁面は90センチ×1m80センチの3mmのラワンベニアで出来ており、それが真鍮釘で1インチ（2.5mm）間隔に打ってあり、美しさが感じられました。その当時は建費は安く、ベニア板は高いものでした。今日では違います。日本の風土から生まれた材木、紙、タイル、色、ベンガラ色、コゲ茶色、色のくすんだ白、と言った具合に、どこかに

74 – 群馬音楽センターの建設現場。高崎、1961年。

On the construction of the Gunma prefecture Music Centre (Takasaki, 1961)

75 – 群馬音楽センター、メインホール。高崎、1961年。

View of the concert hall of the Gunma Music Centre (Takasaki, 1961)

charge of the project preparation. I focus on it in detail in the interview with Mr. Kōyama Hisao for the magazine INAX REPORT no. 103 (Tokyo 1992).

PH: What other recollections do you have of your days spent in Karuizawa?

NT: During the time I resided in Karuizawa we were visited by the American professor Michael E. Czaja from the University of California in Berkeley. Before the war he'd been

76–77 – レーモンド建築事務所（株）10周年記念パーティにて。笄町、1960年。右上には内藤恒方。

From the celebration of the jubilee of the Raymond Architectural Office. In the circular cross-section Cunekata Naitō Tsunekata stands at the top right (Kōgaichō, 1960)

日本古来の感じのする物を、取り入れることが、レーモンド夫妻は上手だったんです。そういった大学では教えてもらわっなかったこと、真の意味の建築設計をすることをレーモンド事務所では学ぶことができました。この様な実務的な事と同時に、私が学んだ最も大切なことは、建築家とは、社会に対して、何をしなければならないのか、建築家としての人間の生き方を知らされました。これは、今も私の生き方の中央に残されており、レーモンドの話をする時、一番に話します。

チャプコヴァー： それから内藤先生は渡米されますね。

内藤： ええ。1963年の正月になって、58年の入社時に軽井沢で会った、M.チャヤさんに手紙を書き、カリフォルニア大学バークレー校大学院に都市計画の勉強に行きたい旨を伝えたところ、早速、数々の書類が来て、入学が受理されたんです。8月10日には家内と結婚し、25日にサンフランシスコに渡米。家内は6ヶ月後に私とアメリカで生活できる様にして、出発する事ができました。レーモンド事務所は、7月に円満に退社する事ができました。

チャプコヴァー： アメリカではどのように生活が始まっていきましたか？

内藤： サンフランシスコの空港に、M.チャヤさんが迎えに来て下さり、ひとまず、彼の自宅、ウォールナット・クリークまで自動車で連れて行って下さりました。日本の様に、パブリック・トランスポーティションは、バスしか

very captivated by Mr. Raymond's work, and he came to Japan thanks to a Fulbright grant. He lived with us in the house in Karuizawa for about a week. Although he was a professor of architecture, he lectured more on the theory and history of art, the theme of his grant project was the phenomenon of dōsojin, Japanese deities of borders and paths. In ink on paper he sketched out a whole range of reliefs from stone pillars by village paths. Later he returned to the USA. When we spent time together in Karuizawa, I asked him if there would be any opportunity for me to study town planning at the University of California. He not only endorsed my plan, but said he'd act as a guarantor.

HČ: What project did you work on after returning to the Tokyo studio?

NT: I returned to the studio in Tokyo in September 1958. I continued working on other projects, I designed a library and church for the International Christian University. For the same university I also headed the project for the repairs, which were originally designed by William Merrell Vories (1905–1964). I designed wooden bungalows for the teachers. I also worked on the design of the Musashi Country Club, where I first attempted the tiling of the toilets, thanks to which I realised the importance of first of all preparing a laying plan. I also worked on a project for a fireplace for the Moji Country Club. The fireplace had two chimneys, and because the grate was spacious I had to think of a way to get the smoke out – for example, among other things I added a ventilator to it. I remember that I also worked on the design of a building with a thatched roof (kayabuki), the Shirakawa Kogen Country Club, and also the Shirakawakōgen ski resort and the central fireplace in the salon of the Tokyo Country Club. The fireplace in the Tokyo Country Club had a hexagonal shape, in its centre was a duct with a diameter of 60 cm for the exhaust of moisture from the men's showers in the basement. And I also recall a two-storey wooden structure in the district of Shibuya for Mr. Lazerson, and a fireplace in Mr. Raymond's new summer residence in Karuizawa. Mr. Raymond's new summer residence had a thatched roof, and so it was essential that before the smoke was discharged through the chimney it first of all had to be cooled in a water tank located underneath it. As well as those projects I also worked on the main design of Nanzan University.

HČ: What did you learn from working on those projects?

NT: Thanks to those projects I learned a great deal about the procedure in architectural design, about the creation of diagrams and mainly about the production of the details of wooden constructions. When Mr. Raymond checked the diagrams using a pair of compasses, I realised that this was absolutely essential for the creation of the proportions. Mr. Raymond was rigorously insistent on the use of compasses. I also learned how to use the traditional Japanese unit of 3x6 shaku (90x180 cm) for tatamis or furniture. All the components of original Japanese wooden architecture are produced on the basis of these dimensions.

PH: How was the studio of the Raymond Architectural Design Office built?

NT: At the time when I started working in the studio, all the walls were made of plywood, with dimensions of 90x180 cm and a thickness of 3 mm. The walls were nailed together with brass tacks an inch apart. I really liked the look of it. At that time labour

78 – 群馬音楽センターの階段、高崎、1961年。

Staircase of the Gunma Music Centre (Takasaki, 1961)

79 – 南山大学校舎の建設現場を眺める建築チーム。校長ゲルハルト・シュライバー神父、アントニン・レーモンド、五代さん。名古屋、60年代前半。

Construction team, including school headmaster Father Gerhard Schreiber, Antonín Raymond and Mr. Godai, inspecting the construction of Nanzan University (Nagoya, early 1960s)

なく、ショックを受けました。やがて、２～３日後、チャヤさんの友人でB.エリスさんというご婦人に会い、彼女がバークレーの大学に連れて行って下さったり、また、すぐ下宿捜しを手伝って下さいました。徒歩で大学から、10～15分の処で、ルーミング・ハウスが見つかり、１階は屋主のお祖母さんが住み、２階の３室の小部屋に、私の他に二人のアメリカ人 ——— １人はロサンゼルスの郊外のパセディナから来ている白人、もう１人は、サンフランシスコの東北、車で４～５時間かかる処から来ている中国系の人 ————が住んでおりました。１階の台所は使っても良いとの事でしたが、３人で、外に行き、マクドナルド等で、簡単に過す事が多かったです。懐かしいですね。マクドナルドは当時、もうアメリカでは有名なチェーン店でした。その時、バスに乗ってサンフランシスコまで行き、ハーマン・ミラーで買った勉強机に向かうためのイームズの座がグラスファイバーでできた椅子は、今日でも重宝して使っております。

チャプコヴァー： アメリカでは社交的な生活が求められますよね。

内藤： パセディナから来ている白人、レナックス・スウィニーの家に、クリスマスに呼ばれて行ったりしましたね。彼の家にはバークレー時代には、２～３度行きました。彼のお父さんは、ハリウッドの女優さんの美容師で1ドル/360円の時代に、時給が700ドルと聞き、驚きました。日本へも「八月十五夜の茶屋」

was cheap, but plywood was expensive. Today that's not so much the case. The Raymonds were proficient in the use of Japanese materials: wood, paper, tiles and also paints: ochre, brown and off-white. Thanks to this their works were reminiscent of the old, traditional Japanese style. I wasn't able to learn such things at university, and it was in Raymond's studio that I learned them. In addition to practical skills, that was the place where I also learned what was most important for me: the responsibility I have to society as an architect, the way an architect ought to live. To this day this is the core of my philosophy of life. When I talk about Mr. Raymond I never forget to mention it.

80 – 南山大学。名古屋、1964。
Nanzan University (Nagoya, 1964)

81 – 南山大学。名古屋、1964。
Nanzan University (Nagoya, 1964)

で来られたとか。私は、R.ノイトラ(1892〜1970)の自宅に連れて行かれ、彼の自伝の本にサインをしてもらったのを、今でも大切に、持っております。日本の私共の家にもご夫婦で数度、来られました。長いお付き合いでした。

ホリー: 内藤先生の英語はどうやって勉強されたんですか？

内藤： 大学が始まり、英語の聞き取りのコースを、外国人留学生は、みんな取らされました。ケネディのキューバの核武装に対する演説を、毎日、聞かされましたね。

ホリー: そっか、ケネディ政権の時代か。

内藤： その時、ケネディが、テキサス・ダラスで銃弾によって殺害されたニュースは、大変、ショックでした。B.エリスさんと大学のカフェテリアで朝のコーヒーを飲むのを日課としておりました私は、アメリカという国の、別な側面

82 – 南山大学。名古屋、1964。
Nanzan University (Nagoya, 1964)

HČ: Later you travelled to the USA.

NT: Yes. At New Year in 1963 I wrote a letter to Michael Czaja, with whom I became acquainted at the time when I was starting at the firm in Karuizawa in 1958. I told him that I wanted to study urban planning at the University of California in Berkeley. I soon received a number of documents. I was accepted onto the course. On 10 August I got married, and only fifteen days later I left for the USA. Within six months I managed to arrange for my wife to live with me in America. But before that, in July, I smoothly ended my contract of employment at the Raymond Architectural Design Office.

HČ: How did your life in America begin?

NT: I was picked up at San Francisco airport by Michael Czaja, and he drove me to his home in Walnut Creek. I was surprised that apart from buses there was no other kind of municipal public transport, just like in Japan. After about two or three days I met Mrs. B. Ellis, Michael Czaja's friend, who took me to the university in Berkeley and helped me find accommodation. I moved into a tenement house about 10 or 15 minutes' walk from the university. The grandmother of the owner lived on the first

を知らされました。バークレーの郊外の私立の大学教会で大きなミサがあり、エリスさんが連れていって下さりました。

チャプコヴァー： アメリカ生活は順調だったんですね。

内藤：1964年の2月になって、妻の嬰子がバークレーに来ることができました。エリスさんが、私ども二人と、レネックス・スウィーニー、ジェフ・リーの4人の為に家を一軒買って下さいました。彼女のご主人は、お医者様で、アメリカでは医者だと、ダウンペイメントは5ドルで、後は、銀行がローン組んでくれ、私達4人は、このローンだけを支払うことにより、今までよりも安く住む処を得る事ができ、皆、ハッピーに住み代える事となりました。エリスさんには、全てにおいて、大変、お世話になり、私と妻のバークレー時代の大恩人でした。1965年に、私達の間に、男の子が生まれました。アメリカでは名前が決まらないと、病院から退院ができず、大急ぎで「久方」という名にしました。私の名前は、恒方であり、「恒」という字は、父が就職した時に世話になった、おじ、小林恒四郎の恒を貰い、「方」は、父の実家、石橋の先祖にいた、石橋政方から、「方」取って、私の名前としたんですね。そこで私は、祖母、久良さんの「久」を取り、私達の子供の名前としました。

チャプコヴァー： アメリカの大学ではどのようなことを学ばれたんですか？

内藤： カルフォルニア大学バークレー校では、この年から環境デザイン学部が新設され、今まで別々の学部であったり、他の学部の中にあった学科が、1963年の秋から、4つの学科、つまるところ、都市計画学科、建築学科、ランドスケープ・アーキテクチュア学科、それに、インテリア・デザイン学科が集まって新しい学部になりました。建物も、一つの新しい建物が新設され、ウールスター・ホールと云う名の基に、新しい時代を迎えようとした年でありました。ハーバード大学の大学院も、この様な変化が起こりました。私は、カリフォルニア大学へは、都市計画を学ぶために来たので、都市計画学科に席を置きました。授業の選択は、どこの学科の授業も受講できますので、M.チャヤ先生と相談して、どの先生の授業を取るのか、定めました。都市計画学科の中では、M.スコット先生のヨーロッパ都市計画史、建築学科の授業ではC.ムーア先生とJ.エシュリック先生の建築概論。インテリア・デザイン学科のウェリントン先生の実習も受けましたね。このウェリントン先生の実習は、「二人の大学生の寮の部屋のデザイン」という全米の学生の懸賞設計があり、私の案は、全米の学生の中で最優良案に選ばれました。戸棚の収納がフレキシブルに棚を変えられる案で、選ばれたんです。

ホリー: すごいですね。しかし、素晴らしい環境にいらっしゃったのですね。

内藤： おかげさまで環境だけはいつも素晴らしかったですね。この頃、サンフランシスコに事務所を持つランドスケープ・アーキテクト、L.ハルプリ

floor, and there were three flats on the second floor. Besides me there were two Americans living there, one white guy from Pasadena, the suburb of Los Angeles, and an ethnically Chinese guy who came from the north-eastern part of San Francisco, about 4 or 5 hours' drive away. Although we were able to use the kitchen on the first floor, we often went out and ate in McDonald's or somewhere similar. They're nostalgic memories for me. McDonald's was already a well-known chain in the USA by that time. – At that time I took the bus to San Francisco, and I bought an Eames type fibreglass chair from the Herman Miller furniture shop to go with my desk. It's a fine chair, and I still use it to this day.

HČ: In the USA it's usually expected that people will be very sociable. Is that the case?

NT: Lennox Sweeney, the white guy from Pasadena, invited me to his home for Christmas a couple of times. When I was studying at Berkeley I went to his family home about twice or three times. His father was a hairdresser for Hollywood actors, and at the time when the dollar was worth 360 yen he was earning 700 dollars an hour. I was absolutely shocked by that. He even came to Japan when they were making the film The Teahouse of the August Moon (1956). He was a make-up artist and his name was Keester Sweeney (1910–1996). I also visited the house of the architect Richard Neutra (1892–1970), and to this day I cherish the biography he signed for me. I stayed in contact with him for a relatively long time. He also visited our home in Japan together with his wife.

PH: How did you learn English?

NT: When teaching began at the university, all the foreign students had to take a mandatory English course. Every day I had to listen to Kennedy's speeches about nuclear weapons in Cuba.

PH: Aha, it was actually at the time of the Cuban missile crisis.

NT: The news that Kennedy had been shot dead in Dallas was a terrible shock to me at the time. I was sitting in the canteen drinking coffee with B. Ellis like I did every day, and suddenly I realised that America also had its dark side. – Mrs. Ellis took me to a huge mass at the church of a private university in the suburbs of Berkeley.

HČ: But was life there otherwise in accordance with your expectations?

NT: In February 1964 my wife Eiko also managed to come to Berkeley. Mrs. Ellis bought a house for me, my wife, Lennox Sweeney and Jeff Lee. Mrs. Ellis's husband was a doctor, and in the USA it was enough for doctors to pay five dollars advance payment and take a loan for the rest. So the four of us took out a loan, and thanks to this we were able to live far more cheaply and freely than previously. Mrs. Ellis was a great help to us with everything. During the time when we were living in Berkeley, we were greatly indebted to her. In 1965 my son was born. In the USA the rule is that until you give your child a name they won't let you leave the maternity hospital, so in a hurry we named our son Hisakata. My name is Tsunekata, and the character that reads as "tsune" comes from the name of Kobayashi Tsuneshiro, an uncle of mine who helped my father greatly when he was looking for work. The character "kata" is from the family of my ancestors on my father's side, specifically from the name of Ishibashi

ン (1916〜2009) が４〜５年間かけて現地の自然条件を調査するという事業を始めました。既存の樹木の樹形を調べ、どの位直立し、どの位の角度で風によって曲るのかを調べ、建築物の形も、これにふさわしいものにするという提案付きのマスター・プランでした。当時は、サンフランシスコから100マイルほど北方に行った場所に、別荘群が姿を現し始めた頃だったのを覚えています。建築家は連棟型の形を提案したC.ムーア氏と、個建てを提案したJ.エシュリック氏でした。カリフォルニアって、温暖な気候とはいえ、海からの潮風は強く、植生に対して厳しい環境なんですね。だから、別荘群もこの自然とどう立ち向かうか問われたわけです。

ホリー: 先生がたはどのような先生でしたか？

内藤： J.エシュリック先生とC.ムーア先生とは対照的な先生でした。エシュリック先生は大変理論的な先生で、作品は優等生なんですけど、あまりおもしろ味がないんですよ。ムーア先生は説明が上手ではなく、汗をかきながらよくお話しされていましたけれど、作品は大変おもしろかった。空間を作る発想自身、多くのボキャブラリーをお持ちで、多くを学ぶことができました。二人とも、レーモンドさんとは違う、カリフォルニアならではの発想でした。

チャプコヴァー： カリフォルニア的な発想の中で多くを学ばれたんですね。

内藤： そうですね。M.スコット先生のランドスケープ・デザインの実習は、バークレー市の中心部の街並のスタディーをし、もし、変更した方が良い部分があれば、提案をすると云う実習でした。街並のスタディーに関しては、どの様な基準を設けるか、という事から考えなければならないんです。そこで私は、カミロ・ジッテの広場の基準、周りの建物の高さ、道路の幅とのプロポーションによって快適な空間かどうかを調べ、更に、そこにどの様な色があり、人々の眼を引くかなどを加え、良い街並かどうかを考えてみる方法を提案しました。J.スコット先生は、都市計画のM.スコット先生の奥様であり、プランティング・デザインの先生でもありました。あとで触れますが、D.カイリーという、バーモント州のランドスケープ・アーキテクトが、バークレー市の隣の、オーランド市の美術館のランドスケープ・デザインをする時に、彼女をコンサルタントに依頼した人です。また、J.スコット先生は、大の日本びいきで、日本通で、私はいろいろと教わりました。

チャプコヴァー： どのようなことを日本人であられる内藤先生が教わったのでしょうか？

内藤： 京都の圓通寺の借景のすばらしさも、この先生から教えられました。スコット先生ご夫妻は、毎年、個人として大学と契約を結ばれ、テニュアルな資

Masakata. For my son I decided to use a combination of the character "kata" and the character "hisa", which my grandmother Kura had in her name.
HČ: What did you learn at the American university?
NT: It was that very year that they established the Faculty of Environmental Design at the University of California in Berkeley. In the autumn of 1964, four departments: architecture, urban planning, landscape architecture and interior design, which had previously belonged to other faculties, were joined together in a new faculty. A building was also newly designed for the faculty – Wurster Hall. It was a year that heralded the dawn of a new age. At that time similar changes were also taking place at Harvard. I enrolled at the Department of Urban Planning, understandably, since I'd gone to the University of California to study urban planning. I was able to choose my subjects independently of the department, and so I enrolled for the lectures by the teachers recommended to me by professor Michael Czaja. At the Department of Urban Planning I chose professor M. Scott, who taught the history of European urban planning, and at the Department of Architecture I chose professors C. Moore and J. Esherick, who lectured on an introduction to architecture. I also attended classes held by professor Wellington from the Department of Interior Design. Professor Wellington headed the all-America student competition Design of a Student Room for Two, in which my design won. It was a design of a wardrobe with flexibly interchangeable shelves.
PH: You were in an inspiring environment.
NT: I've always been lucky to be in an excellent environment. At that time the landscape architect Lawrence Halprin (1916–2009), who had an office in California, was starting a project on the research of the local natural conditions, which lasted for four or five years. He examined the shape of trees, whether they grow straight or at the angle they're bent at by the wind. Part of the project was a plan for producing architecture that's suitably adapted to the natural conditions. I remember that at the time a settlement of cottages was built about a hundred miles north of San Francisco. The type of mutually interconnected cottages was promoted by C. Moore, while the type of detached cottages was designed by J. Esherick. Even though the weather's mild in California, the wind from the sea is strong, and that places a burden on the plants. It was therefore necessary to think of how to manage the natural conditions when building the settlement of cottages.
PH: What kind of teachers were the professors you mentioned?
NT: Professors J. Esherick and C. Moore were very different from one another. Professor Esherick was a great theoretician, and even if his work had a range of advantages, it was somewhat lacking in features of interest. Professor Moore wasn't good at explaining, he expounded at great length and sweated a lot during the process, but on the other hand his designs were very interesting, his work was rich in terms of expression. His conceptions of the formation of space were also very interesting. I learned a great deal from him. Both of them differed from Mr. Raymond, their way of thinking was typical of Californians.

格を取ることを拒否していたんです。常に新しいチャレンジの心がまえを持って物事に取り組むように、教えて下さりました。授業に出て来ない生徒には、下宿、自宅に電話を掛けて、出て来ない理由を問われる事もあると聞いておりました。私自身、ランドスケープ・アーキテクチュアの学問の教え以外に、教育者としてのすばらしさに、大変、感銘を受けました。日本に帰国して、今の私の家が出来上がってから、楽しみに立ち寄られ、お二人から、ご本を頂戴し、家宝として持っております。

ホリー: 素晴らしいアメリカ体験ですね。

内藤： ええ。この様ないろいろな事があり、一年が、なんとかして終了いたしました。この間に、日本人の学生の紹介で、中古の自動車、フランスのシトローエンを買いました。この自動車のおかげで、B.エリスさんの紹介で、バークレーから一山越えた町で設計事務所をやっておられた、カンフォーさんという方の事務所に赴く事ができました。アッという間に夏休みは終わり、９月から二年目が始まりました。

チャプコヴァー： アメリカ生活二年目のお話もぜひお聞きしたいです。

内藤： 今まで都市計画学科に在籍しておりましたのを、建築科に移籍しましたが、建築科は、コンピューター導入の時代でした。先生達も、今までの方々とあまり変わらなかったのですが、一方で、ランドスケープ・アーキテクチュア学科は、この年から、ローマ大賞の奨学金でイタリーからアメリカに帰国されたばかりの若い２人の先生、R.マーティン先生、I.ズービー先生が加わりました。私はこちらの実習を取り、新しい事を勉強できる事をめざしました。始めの課題は、環境デザイン学科のウールスター・ホールの周りのランドスケープ・デザインをするテーマだったかと思います。ウールスター・ホールというのは新しく建てられたばかりの建物で、建築は出来上がってたんですが、未だ、何の植栽も施されておりませんでした。課題を出し終えた後、丁度、その時、オークランド美術館の仕事で来ておられたD.カイリー(1912〜2004)が、私達の作品である、ウールスター・ホールの周りのランドスケープ・デザインの発表会に出席して、批評をしてくれる事になり、大変、楽しみでした。D.カイリー氏の作品は雑誌等でよく知っていましたが、実際には見た事はなく、オークランド市の美術館には、大変興味を持っていたんです。なので、実際にお目にかかって、お話をうかがう事ができるのを大変光栄な事と思っていました。

ホリー: 内藤先生の案はどのようなものでしたか？

内藤： 私の案は、日本的な樹木の配置、大きな樹木を７本、５本、３本と樹木をグループ化して、建物の周りに配置する案でした。長い時間をかけて図面を作りました。プレゼンテーション用の図面製作は、芸大、レーモンド事務所時代に鍛えた腕があり、見た目には美しい図面を作ることには自信があったんで

HČ: And it was precisely this "Californian way of thinking" that seems to have inspired you a lot.

NT: Yes, that's true. Our practice in professor Scott's landscape architecture lessons consisted of studying the urban scenery of the central part of Berkeley. It was our task to propose adjustments and improvements. When studying the civic development it was necessary to begin with the choice of a suitable criterion on which the survey would be based. I chose as my criterion the town square according to Camillo Sitte, and based on the proportions of the height of buildings and the width of the routes in the centre of town I examined whether the space was suitable. To this I added a further survey concerning the colours in the city centre, whether they attract people's attention, and proposed a method for determining whether the urban scenery is good or bad. Mrs. J. Scott, the wife of professor M. Scott, taught the use of plants in architecture, I'll return to this later. The landscape architect D. Kaylee from Vermont, who designed the garden for the art museum in neighbouring Orlando, hired her as a consultant. Professor J. Scott was also an enthusiastic admirer of Japanese culture, she had extensive knowledge of Japan. I learned a lot from her.

HČ: What could you, as a Japanese man, learn about Japan?

NT: For example, she explained to me what is remarkable about shakkei, the loaned scenery in the garden of the Kantsūji temple in Kyoto. – The Scotts concluded a contract with the university every year as private individuals, they didn't want to be employed for an indefinite period. They taught us how important it was to be open to new things and to have an appetite to always take on new challenges. I heard that they sometimes phoned students in the halls of residence or at home in order to find out why they hadn't attended the class, they wanted to know the reason for their absence. I was personally greatly impressed by their erudition in landscape architecture, as well as by what fantastic teachers they were. When I finished my own house after returning to Japan, I was greatly pleased to be able to welcome them as visitors, and they gave me their book, which I appreciate very highly.

PH: You have some valuable experiences from your stay in America.

NT: Well, all kinds of things happened, and the first year flew by. I bought myself a Citroën, and on Mrs. B. Ellis's advice I commuted to Mr. Canfore's architecture studio, which was in a town on the other side of the mountains. – Then the summer holidays suddenly finished and in September I went into the second year.

HČ: Please tell us about your second year in the USA.

NT: Until that time I'd been at the Department of Urban Planning, but then I switched to the Department of Architecture. This was just at the time when they were introducing computers at the department. My teachers didn't change much, but the Department of Landscape Architecture was joined by two young teachers, R. Martin and I. Zoubi, who had just come back from Italy, where they'd been on a grant from the Roman Prize at the American Academy in Rome. In an endeavour to learn something new, I enrolled for their lectures. I think that our first task was a design for the layout of the landscape within the surrounding area of the Environmental Faculty –

す。私の案には、先生がたのまあまあの良いコメントが集まり、時間が少し残ったので、私はD.カイリー氏に「なぜ、貴殿はいつも、美しく幾何学的に大きな樹木を配置されるのですか？」と尋ねました。すると、D.カイリー氏は、幾何学とは人間が作り出したものであり、私は、いつも、デザインのスタートは、それに頼りたいと思っています、とお答えになられました。私は、「7、5、3、という奇数を主とした配置、これは、長く日本に伝った考え方に基づいた樹木の配置であり、これにより、このプロジェクトが、人々の目に柔らかく映るのではないでしょうか」とお話ししました。これ以来、D.カイリー氏とは大変仲良くなり、彼は、IFLA（国際ランドスケープ・アーキテクト連合）、ASLA（アメリカ・ランドスケープ・アーキテクト連合）等に属する事は、大嫌いだったんですが、ILFAがボストンであった時も、そっと、朝食を一緒にしようと、ニューヨークから、彼の家のあるバーモントに帰る途中に寄ってくれたこともありました。また、2度程、日本に来た。

内藤： あと、R.ヴィニョーリ(*1944)が、旧都庁の跡地で行われた東京国際フォーラムの設計コンペで一等になられた時、広場の設計をD.カイリー氏に依頼して、一緒に仕事をしようとしていたんです。けれど、D.カイリーが体調をくずし、日本までは来られず、彼のスケッチに基づいて、私がこの仕事を担当した、なんてこともありました。

チャプコヴァー： アメリカでの残りの学生生活はどのようなものだったのでしょうか。確か、カリフォルニア大学バークレー校はその頃、G.エクボ (1910〜2000) が学科長を務めたかと思いますが。

内藤： そうですね。1965年になり、ランドスケープ・アーキテクチュア学科は、G.エクボ先生が学科長になって来られることになり、私のカリフォルニア大学への留学のおもたる目的であった、ラディカルな都市計画の勉強がやっと叶えられる事になったんです。そこで、所属を建築科からランドスケープ・アーキテクチュア学科に移し、マスター・コースを修了することにしました。卒論の委員会では、エクボ先生を主として、M.チャヤ先生、M.アルバギャスト先生の3人にしました。エクボ先生は、大阪府大の久保寛先生が大阪に一年呼ばれ、府大で講義をされこともあり、日本の事をよくご存じだったんです。また、M.アルバギャスト先生は、日系の方で、アメリカ人の方と結婚された、植物の先生なんですけど、バークレーの市内を植物を覚えさせるために、私を連れまわしてくださった先生でもありました。この頃は、既にT.チャーチ先生がカリフォルニア大学をリタイヤされてはおられましたが、キャンパス内を腰にハサミを入れて、散歩をしながらいらない枝を切って歩いていた姿をよく目にしましたね。このT.チャーチ先生の作られたカリフォルニアの住宅のお庭、フリーな形の曲線によるスイミング・プールは、近代ランドスケープ・デザインのスタートを感じさせるもので、私など若者はアメリカ、カリフォルニアならではの美しさにみんな感激いたしたものです。

Wurster Hall. Wurster Hall was a newly constructed building, and although it was completed in terms of architecture, no plants had yet been planted in its surroundings. When we completed the task, the presentation of our conception of the landscape adjustment of Wurster Hall was also attended by Daniel U. Kiley (1912–2004), who was nearby due to his work for the Art Museum in Oakland. I was greatly pleased by his enthusiastic reaction. I was familiar with the work of D. Kiley from magazines, but I'd never seen his buildings with my own eyes, and so I was very interested in the museum in Oakland. It was a great honour for me to meet and talk to this architect.

PH: How did you manage the task you're referring to?

NT: I proposed planting groups of three, five and seven trees in the area surrounding the building. I selected types which were evocative of Japan. I spent a long time preparing the diagrams. I felt fairly confident when I was creating the diagrams for the presentation of the design, because I'd been trained both at the Geidai and at the Raymond Architectural Design Office. The professors evaluated my design relatively positively, and since I had a little time left I asked D. Kiley why he always used beautiful, large, symmetrical and geometrically arranged trees. He answered that geometry is a science created by man, and that in his judgement every design must be based on geometry. I told him: "The essence of my design is odd numbers, three, five and seven, that's the traditional Japanese way of laying out trees. I think that as a result the whole conception will create a relaxed visual impression." From that moment D. Kiley and I became friends. Even if he couldn't stand the fact that he was a member of organisations such as IFLA (International Federation of Landscape Architects) or ASLA (American Association of Landscape Architects), at the time when IFLA had its representation in Boston, he stopped by at my place several times on the way from New York to Vermont, where he lived, and we went out for breakfast together. I recall that he also came to Japan twice. Later, when Rafael Viñoly (born 1944) won the architecture competition for the building of the Tokyo International Forum, it was D. Kiley that he asked for the plan of the town square. D. Kiley and I had been planning to work together, but he was no longer in good physical condition, he was unable to come to Japan, and so I took on the task myself, based on his sketches.

HČ: How was the end of your period of study in America? As far as I know, the head of the department at the University of California in Berkeley was Garrett Eckbo (1910–2000).

NT: Yes, you're right. In 1965 Garrett Eckbo became the head of the Department of Landscape Architecture. My main objective, the reason I came to study at the University of California, namely to study radical urban planning, was finally fulfilled. I transferred from the Department of Architecture to the Department of Landscape Architecture, and decided to complete my master's course there. I chose professors G. Eckbo, M. Arbegast and M. Czaja for the thesis defence commission. Professor Eckbo had previously spent a year in Japan, where he lectured at the Osaka Prefecture University upon the invitation of professor Kubo Akira, and he understood Japanese well. Professor M. Arbegast was of Japanese origin, she'd married an American and

チャプコヴァー： 失礼ですが、内藤先生の卒論のテーマを伺っても良いでしょうか？

内藤： 私の卒論のテーマは「日本での、パブリック・オープン・スペース」というテーマでした。バークレーに来て以来、大変お世話になったB.エリスさんが無償で、私のつたない英語を直し、タイプを打って下さり、全て、皆々様の善意の基に進められました。一方、その間に、ランドスケープ・アーキテクチュア学科の実習のコースを取り、前期は、「ナパ・ヴァレーで美味なワインを作る葡萄畠が、住宅地、主に別荘地に浸食されて来ている事に対して、どう対処するべきか？」という課題でしたかね。ナパ・ヴァレーにはバークレーに来て以来、いつも、大変、親切に面倒みて下さるB.エリスさんの別荘があり、そこに、何度も連れて行ってもらっており、ワイナリーも、良く知っているところが多かったんです。

チャプコヴァー： 自然と土地の関係についても熱心に学ばれたんですね。

内藤： というのも、当時、現在でも大変影響力の強い、ペンシルベニア大学のI.マクハーグ先生の地域計画の手法が流行ったんですよ。ちょうどこの頃出版されたDesign with Natureで、マクハーグ先生は自然の諸要素が土地利用にどの様に影響するかを説いていて、その本を通じて地域計画の基本を学ぶ事ができました。卒論に戻りますと、ある一人の同級生と一緒に作業をし、発表会に来られたG.エクボ先生、その他多くのサンフランシスコ湾内の設計事務所の諸先生がたに満足していただく発表ができました。後期は、サンフランシスコの南側でジャイアンツの野球場のそばで、ハンタース・ポイントという地区の住宅地の開発のプロジェクトを行いました。レーモンド事務所に在籍中は、個々の住宅を多く担当していたのでそれに関する見識はありましたが、住宅地全体の開発の計画を考えたのは、初めての事でした。

ホリー： プロジェクトは内藤先生お一人で？ それともチーム作業でしたか？

内藤： このプロジェクトの仕事は、私、一人でやる事にし、まず役所に行き、土地の価値を調べ、それに対して、上の建てられている建物の価値を調べました。アメリカの場合、建物の価値に対して、土地の価値は低いのですが、このプロジェクトの場所は逆で、建物の価値は低い。この事も、一番初めにプレゼンテーションに取り入れました。道路の配置と幅員等、今まで考えた事もなかった事柄などを考慮にいれなければなりませんでしたが、日本の一級建築士を持っている私としては、ただ四角い建物を提案するだけではなく、もう少し未来的な住居の形を取り入れたかったんです。

チャプコヴァー： 未来的な住居といいますと？

内藤： コンクリートのパネルを組み込み、取り外し可能なジョイントを施し、

taught botany. She was the professor who took me out into the field so that I could remember the individual plants in Berkeley. By that time professor T. Church had already left the university for a rest, but I often saw him walking through the university campus with a trimmer on his belt, here and there pruning excess branches. The garden of his family house in California and the gradual curves of the swimming pool that professor T. Church designed were considered the beginning of modern landscape architecture. I and the other young students were enchanted by this typically American, or more precisely Californian beauty.

HČ: May I ask about the theme of your master's thesis?

NT: The theme of my thesis was Open Public Space in Japan. Mrs. B. Ellis, who had helped me with everything right from the moment I came to Berkeley, corrected my poor English and typed out the text for me for no recompense. I completed the thesis only thanks to the co-operation and willingness of my friends. At the same time I enrolled on a practical course in the winter semester at the Department of Landscape Architecture, which consisted in an assignment entitled: In what way is it necessary to respond to the increasing number of residential buildings and cottages that are taking up space at the expense of vineyards in the Napa Valley? It was in the Napa Valley that my great supporter Mrs. Ellis had her cottage, and she often brought me there with her, in addition to which she was also very well acquainted with viniculture.

HČ: So you had an opportunity to learn a lot about the relationship of nature and built up areas.

NT: That was thanks to the method of territorial planning according to Ian McHarg from the University of Pennsylvania, which had a considerable influence, and remains popular to this day. The book Design with Nature had just been published, in which professor McHarg explained the influence that various natural elements have on the utilisation of the soil. Thanks to this book I learned the basics of territorial planning. I worked together with a fellow student, and successfully completed the project, which met with the satisfaction not only of G. Eckbo but also a series of other experts from a number of architecture firms from the San Francisco bay area. In my work for the Raymond Architectural Design Office I headed several projects for residential buildings, and so I had experience in that field, but this was the first time I'd been in charge of preparing a design for an entire residential district.

PH: Did you work on the project alone or as part of a team?

NT: I decided to take on the project by myself. First of all I went to City Hall, where I found out the prices of lands and the prices of the houses built on them. In the USA land plots are mostly cheaper than the houses that stand on them, but in the case of this project it was the other way round: the prices of the houses were lower. I included this fact in my presentation right at the beginning. I had to take into consideration things I'd never previously thought about whatsoever, for example the position of the road and its width. As an authorised first category architect in Japan, I wanted to design a futuristic dwelling, not just an ordinary boxy house.

HČ: What do you mean by "futuristic dwelling"?

これが基本的なコンクリートの構造体の枠組みの中に入っている様な建物を作り、その一例をもって完成とした提案を打ち出しました。午前10時からのプレゼンテーションだったのですが、それらの図面が出来上がったのが午前8時ごろ。それからサンフランシスコの地図を見ながら、サウサリートからバークレー、オークランドまでの全体的な地域の透視図と、部分的な透視図を作り、大学まで持って行き、プレゼンテーションを行いました。このプレゼンテーションは全ての先生達の大喝采を頂きました。先生がたは私がその学期で卒業と分かっておられたので、先生がたの事務所まで来てほしいとの声がかかりました。

チャプコヴァー： 大変優秀な学生でいらしたんですね。羨ましい限りです。

内藤： と、いいたいところなんですが、後日、このコースの成績をエクボ先生に伺った処、A−と言われたんです。どうしてマイナスが付くのですかと尋ねると、学校で仕事をしないで、ほかの学生の面倒を見なかったからだと言われました (笑)。自分のことしか考えなかった学生なんですね。エクボ先生は、多くのランドスケープ・アーキテクチュアに対する哲学の持ち主であり、1956年にはThe Art of Home Landscaping、1964年にはUrban Landscape Designを、それから1969年にThe Landscape we seeと、立て続けにランドスケープ・デザインのご自分のフィロソフィーをまとめた本を出版されており、いずれも日本語に訳されております。先出のD.カイリー氏、オーストラリアの首都であるキャンベラの都市計画をコンペで取られたJ.ローズ氏、それとG.エクボ氏は、1920年代に、ハーバード大学で同級であられたんですね。大学では、ヨーロッパのランドスケープ・デザインの講義ばかりで、アメリカの新しいムーブメント、例えば、先程のカリフォルニアのランドスケープ・アーキテクト、T.チャーチの話などが無い事に抵抗をし、授業をストライキした話は有名です。また、エクボ先生は、私が帰国してから仕事をした、M不動産の「湘南国際村」の開発事業で、中央に作られた公園のデザインにご参加いただきました。公園の浜をZEN・PARKにしようという事まで決まり、図面をいろいろと作って下さりったんです。彼は、三度、この仕事で、東京まで来られて、この時の報酬でホンダの小さな自動車が買えたらしく、ありがとうと言っていました。それからしばらくご無沙汰だったのですが、1993年のクリスマス・カードに、「83歳になったので、もう、日本には行けない」と書いておられて、少し寂しい思いをしました。

チャプコヴァー： まさにアメリカでの恩師ですね。そこから最終的に、ササキ・ドーソン・ディメイ・アソシエーツ入社するわけですね。

内藤： エクボ先生に、無事、卒論にサインをいただき、就職の相談に乗ってもらったんです。東海岸に行き、設計事務所に就職したいと申し出ると、ボストンのササキ・ヒデオ氏(1919〜2000)の事務所はどうかといわれ、私はためらいもなく「イエス」といいました。すると、その場で電話を掛けて下さって。そ

NT: I designed a building that created the impression that the basic concrete frame construction was composed of concrete panels, interconnected with variable joints. The presentation of the design began at ten o'clock, and I finished the diagrams at eight. Later, with a map of San Francisco in my hand, I produced a perspective diagram of the entire region from Sausalito and Berkeley to Oakland, and then diagrams of the individual areas. I brought the diagrams to the university and presented my design. The presentation won applause from the group of professors. The professors knew that it was my final semester, and so they invited me to visit them in their studies.
HČ: I see that you were an exceptional student. I have to admit I envy you a little.
NT: The only thing is, a few days later I went to ask professor Eckbo about my final grade, and found that I'd got an A-. When I asked why I'd got a minus he explained that I hadn't worked in the school or helped the other students. *(Laughs)* I'd only thought about myself. – Professor Eckbo had a distinctive conception of landscape architecture, and had published his ideas on this theme in a series of books. In 1958 his book The Art of Home Landscaping was published, followed in 1964 by Urban Landscape Design and in 1969 The Landscape We See. All of these books were also published in Japanese translation. The aforementioned J. Kaylee and J. Rose, who won the architecture competition for an urban planning design for the city of Canberra in Australia, studied together with G. Eckbo at Harvard in 1922. It's a well-known story that they protested against the fact that it was primarily European landscape architecture that was being taught at the university, while the new architectural current that was just in its inception in America didn't gain any opportunity. For example, T. Church, the representative of Californian landscape architecture, wasn't mentioned whatsoever in the lessons. At the time Kaylee and Rose organised a strike in the lesson. – After I returned to Japan, when I was working on the Shōnan Kokusaimura project for the real estate agency M, professor Eckbo collaborated with me on the design of the central park. He decided to turn the beach into a park in the style of Zen gardens and drew up several different diagrams. I had to fly to Tokyo three times because of that project. He bought a small Honda with the money from the project, and he was very grateful to me for it. After that we didn't see each other for a while, until he sent me a Christmas card in 1933, in which he wrote that he wouldn't be coming to Japan again because he was eighty-three years old. I missed him quite a bit.
HČ: Was he in fact your American mentor? And later you started work at the firm Sasaki, Dawson & DeMay in Boston, is that right?
NT: I obtained professor Eckbo's signature without any objections, confirming the defence of my thesis. I also consulted him about my future employment. When I told him I'd like to go to the east coast and work in an architecture studio there, he asked me if I'd like to work in the studio of Sasaki Hideo (1919–2000) in Boston. Without hesitation I answered: "Yes". Professor Eckbo immediately picked up the phone and called to Boston. Unfortunately it wasn't a good time, they told him that Mr. Sasaki was currently on a business trip in Japan. But despite that they decided to take me on at the firm, and asked when I could start. And so I resumed my life as an architect.

の時は、タイミングが悪く、ササキ氏は日本へ出張中であると言われたんですが、すぐに入社が決まり、いつから来られるかと聞かれ、私の建築家としての第二の人生が始まりました。

チャプコヴァー： 確か、ササキ・ドーソン事務所で働いていた頃、コンペティションに応募されていますね。

内藤： 『新建築』っていう雑誌が日本にありまして、その雑誌が主催で一年に一度若い人たちのためのコンペティションを開催していたんです。それに、僕と中国人、中国系のアメリカ人で応募して。コンペティションの審査員は冒頭でお話しした吉村先生でした、日本の面積で言うと、240坪のところに6軒家を入れて、それでそれぞれにプライバシーを持ちながら生活をできるような家を造るというようなプランだったかと思います。とても一等になるなんて思っていなかったんですけど、幸か不幸か一等になったんです。大変ありがたかった。

チャプコヴァー： 大変貴重なお話ありがとうございました。

HČ: If I'm correct, then during the time when you were working for the Sasaki-Dawson studio, you also took part in a number of architecture competitions.
NT: The Japanese magazine Shinkenchiku (New Architecture, November 1968) used to announce a competition for young architects once a year. I applied, as well as one Chinese architect and an American of Chinese origin. The aim of the competition, the commission of which initially included the aforementioned professor Yoshimura, was to design six buildings on a land plot of 240 cubo (794.4 m^2), constructed in such a manner as to preserve not only the functionality of the buildings but also the privacy of their inhabitants. Although it wasn't my intention to gain first prize, I was evidently lucky and I won. At that time I was very grateful for that victory.
HČ: Mr. Naitō, thank you very much for the interview.

戦後のプロジェクト (抜粋)

Post-war projects (a selection)

83–85 – アメリカ企業リーダーズダイジェストの日本支社。東京、1951年、のち建て壊し。

Headquarters of the Japanese branch of the American magazine Reader's Digest (Tokyo, 1951, later demolished)

86–88 – 群馬音楽センター。高崎、1961年。

Gunma Music Centre (Takasaki, 1961)

89 – 聖アンセルモ教会の祭壇、側面。
目黒、東京、1956年。

Side view of the altar of St. Anselm's Church
(Meguro, Tokyo, 1956)

90 – 聖アンセルモ教会の模型。目黒、東京、1956年。

Model of St. Anselm's Church (Meguro, Tokyo, 1956)

91–93 – 南山大学。名古屋、1964年。

Nanzan University (Nagoya, 1964)

94–95 – 上智大学。東京、1969年。

Sophia University (Tokyo, 1969)

96 – 南山大学。名古屋、1964年。
Nanzan University (Nagoya, 1964)

北澤興一

北澤興一氏は、1962年からレーモンドの事務所で働いたのち、10年後の1971年に独立し、株式会社北澤建築設計事務所を設立した。この会社は、今日まで存続している。教育面でも精力的に活動をしており、工学院大学などで教鞭を取った。レーモンドの事務所に所属していた頃に手がけたプロジェクトを挙げると、南山大学、立教高校・大学、千代田ハウス、上智大学、CAJ音楽堂、ハワイ国際会議場計画などがある。

Kitazawa Kōichi

Mr. Kitazawa started work at the Raymond Architectural Design Office in 1962. After almost ten years, in 1971, he set up his own Kitazawa Architects studio, which still exists to this day. Mr. Kitazawa is also active as a lecturer, teaching for example at Kogakuin University. Of the projects on which he worked at the Raymond Architectural Design Office we can mention Nanzan University, the Rikkyō University and High School, Chiyoda House, Sophia University, the CAJ (Custom Audio Japan) concert hall and the International Conference Center in Hawaii.

チャプコヴァー: レーモンド事務所に入る前に、工学院大学で学生として他に影響受けた人物はいましたか？

北澤: はい、工学院大学のときにフランクロイドライトのところから帰ってきた天野太郎先生 (1918〜1990)ですね。フランクロイドライトのことを熱心に教えていただいて、私はすっかりライトファンになってしまいました。彼には、卒業の時に遠藤新 (1889〜1951, 6ページを参照)の研究をしなさいと言われ、それがきっかけで天野研究室に残って、遠藤新の研究をしたんです。私がどこに就職するか決め悩んでいたところ、天野先生がアントニン・レーモンド事務所を勧めてくださいました。ただ、天野先生にはコネクションがなかったんですね。困っていたら、たまたま高崎にある井上工業の社長さんの一人息子が清水建設で働いておりまして、彼に紹介してもらってお会いすることができたのです。彼は私の高校からの友人と現場で一緒だったんです。井上さんに私は、レーモンド事務所に入りたいので、父親の房一郎さんに何とかレーモンドさんと話を付けてほしい、というようなお願いをしました。じゃ、高崎に一緒に行こうと言われ、親子でもなかなか会えないとの事でしたが、なんとかコンタクトを取って頂いて、二人で会いに行きました。私は卒業設計を持参して得意に説明をしたら、「そんな絵の説明を受けてもなにもならない。実現した建築はないのか、建築っていうのは生きた芸術で実現しなかったら意味がない。実現した設計図を持ってきなさい。その作品によっては紹介しよう」と言われました。大学生は普通、実現した作品なぞありません。ですが、私には4作品ありまして、その中から住宅の木造とＲＣ造を設計図と写真集にして持参したところ、木造住宅はレーモンドさんに見てもらえそうだ、と言われて紹介してもらえることとなりました。しかし、レーモンドさんにお会いできたものの、その年は入社希望者が40名以上もいたです。そのなかから採用されるのは2名程度。2日間に渡る試験で、学科と外観パースの実技を受け、幸いにも入社を認められた時には感激したことが思い出されます。

97 – 南山大学 コンクリート打設を手伝う北澤。

Kitazawa Kōichi assisting on the construction of Nanzan University (early 1960s)

HČ: Mr. Kitazawa, who influenced you at the time when you were studying at Kogakuin University, before you started working for the Raymond Architectural Design Office?
KK: When I was studying at Kogakuin University it was professor Amano Tarō (1918–1990), who had just returned to the university after finishing his work with Frank Lloyd Wright. He lectured about Wright with such fervour that I became a great admirer of Wright. When I graduated, he advised me to study the work of Endō Arata (1889–1951, see p. 7). And so I decided to remain within the working group of professor Amano and focus on studying the work of Endō Arata. At the time when I was racking my brains in search of work, professor Amano recommended the studio of Antonín Raymond. However, professor Amano didn't have any connections. At the moment I when was beginning to despair, I was introduced to the only son of the director of the company Inoue Kōgyō from Takasaki. The director's son worked at the Shimizu Corporation construction firm, and one of his colleagues was a fellow pupil of mine from secondary school. I told Mr. Inoue that I'd like to work for the Raymond Architectural Design Office, and requested that he ask his father, Mr. Inoue Fusaichirō, if he could arrange a meeting with Mr. Raymond. He proposed that we go to visit his father in Takasaki together. He didn't see his father very often, but he managed to contact him, and so we set out for a meeting with him. I brought my dissertation with me, and when I presented it to Mr. Inoue Fusaichirō in the customary manner, he told me that there was no point in showing him anything of the kind. He asked me whether I had any actually realised work behind me, because architecture is a living art, and unless it is realised it serves no purpose. He recommended that next time I bring source materials for a realised work, and on that basis he would decide whether or not to introduce me to Mr. Raymond. Of course, students don't usually have any actually realised designs behind them, but I already had four. The next time I brought with me diagrams and photographs of a wooden family house and a house made of reinforced concrete. I was told that he might be able to show the wooden house to Mr. Raymond and introduce me. I finally succeeded in meeting Mr.

98 – アントニン・レーモンドと北澤興一。70年代初頭。

Antonín Raymond and Kitazawa Kōichi (early 1970s)

HČ: Helena Čapková
KK: Kitazawa Kōichi
PH: Petr Holý

99 – J.五代、N. レーモンド、F.井上。群馬音楽ホールの建設現場にて。

Godai Yoshiko, Noémi Raymond and Inoue Fusaichirō on the construction of the Gunma Music Centre (early 1970s)

ホリー: 井上工業の社長というのは井上房一郎さんですよね。

北澤: 井上房一郎さんの一人息子は井上健太郎さんという方で、大学を卒業後、清水建設で働いていた後に井上工業の副社長として入社し、五年ぐらいで社長になりました。しかし、突然白血病で倒れてしまい、一年くらいでなくなられてしまったんです。そこで仕方なく房一郎さんが二人の孫が成長するまで、社長として現場に戻られました。

チャプコヴァー: 井上房一郎さんの自邸はこのレーモンドの笄町の事務所に非常に似ていたと伺っています。

北澤: 井上家は高崎における名家中の名家なのです。高崎観音を寄贈された家柄であり、レーモンドさんと親しくて、よく笄町に打ち合わせに来ていました。ちょうどその頃、井上さんの本家が火事で焼けてしまったんですね。新しく造るという事で、レーモンドさんに設計を頼んでいたのですけれどもなかなか完成しない。そこで、井上さんはレーモンドさんの自邸と同じものを造りたいと、レーモンドさんに原図を見せてもらい、ちょっと道路の関係で透かしてみたら、「裏焼きにすればちょうどいい」と言い出して、トレーシングペーパーに裏焼きしてもらった平面図で造りたいと主張されたそうです。それから、棟梁を連れてきて実測して、「もう設計はいいです」と、「これでできます」という事で本当にそのままできちゃったという感じですね。

ホリー: いい時代ですね。

100 – 笄町のレーモンド家邸宅兼建築スタジオ。麻布、東京、1950年。

Raymond's house and architecture studio Kōgaichō (Azabu, Tokyo, 1950)

Raymond, but unfortunately I discovered that there were over forty candidates interested in working for the firm that year, and he was planning to take on only two of them. I underwent a two-day examination in both academic subjects and practical perspective drawing. I recall that when I was told they were going to take me on I was absolutely beside myself with joy.

PH: Was Mr. Inoue Fusaichirō the director of the company Inoue Kōgyō?

KK: The only son of Mr. Inoue Fusaichirō was Mr. Inoue Kentarō. After graduating he worked for the Shimizu Corporation. He later became assistant director at Inoue Kōgyō, and after about five years in the company he became the director. But suddenly he was diagnosed with leukaemia and approximately one year later he died. As a result Mr. Fusaichirō had no choice but to return to the company management, at least until his two grandsons reached adulthood.

101 – F.井上邸。高崎、群馬。

House of Inoue Fusaichirō (Takasaki, Gunma)

HČ: I heard that Mr. Inoue Fusaichirō's villa was very similar to Raymond's studio Kōgaichō studio.

KK: The Inoue family was the most distinguished of all the families in Takasaki. That was the family that gave the city of Takasaki the great statue of the goddess Kannon. Mr. Inoue Fusaichirō was very close to Antonín Raymond, and often visited him in his Kōgaichō studio. It was just at that time that Mr. Inoue's main house burned down. He wanted to rebuild the house, and asked Mr. Raymond for an architectural design, but somehow it didn't get finished. So Mr. Inoue decided that he wanted the same house as Mr. Raymond had, and had the original diagrams presented to him. When he was studying the diagrams thoroughly because of their connection to the road, he declared: "A mirror image would be ideal", and he had a reverse copy of the plans re-

北澤: 二人が特別の関係だったから成立したものと思われます。

ホリー: 今どきなかなか、できないですよね。

北澤: はい。幸いにも、井上家が孫の時代になってから、房一郎さんが生前に作られた高崎哲学堂はいつでも誰でも見学できる状況になっています。財団法人が今も維持しているんですね。高崎美術館と共に使われています

チャプコヴァー: それから笄町のプランについてもお聞かせください。たくさん綺麗な写真 (58〜59ページを参照) もありますので、このデザインについてちょっと、先生の思い出を絡めながらお聞きしたいと思います。

北澤: はい、アトリエ兼自宅という事で、二棟に分かれていて、庭に面した方が自宅でした。パティオのところで、食卓があって、上は藤棚になってて、その前がプールになっていて。左側にはご夫妻の寝室、右側がレーモンドさんのアトリエの自室でした。窓際にはレーモンドさんのテーブルが見えています (137ページを参照)。

ホリー: 貴重な写真ですね。

北澤: はい、そうかもしれません。ご夫妻の寝室は上もオープンだし、戸襖なので全部オープンになるという造りです。日本の民家と同じ造り方ですね。ベッドが縦に並んでるんですね。間に本棚で、右側がミスター、左側がミセスのベッド。昼間はソファー風に使用していました。写真に写っている小さなプールでは (123ページを参照)、夏にミセス・レーモンドが起きるとベッドを出て、どぶんと飛び込んだりしていました。

ホリー: 凄いですね、寝室のすぐ前に大きなプールがあって。

北澤: いえ、小さいんですよ。しかしミセスや孫たちが良く活用していました。まだ冷房設備の無い時代ですから。藤棚もありまして。藤棚っていうのは、日本では古来からあるもので、そこの下で食事ができるっていうのは、幸せな事だな、と。雨でない限りは、ここで朝昼夜食事をしてました。

チャプコヴァー: 笄町のレーモンド事務所は戦後の非常に重要な建築です。時間を遡ると、戦前の時代の重要な作品として、「霊南坂」っていうレーモンドさんの最初の自邸もあります。その話にいきましょう。

北澤: はい。これは霊南坂に最初に造ったレーモンドの自宅兼アトリエですね。内外の壁がコンクリートの打ち放し仕上げになっています。おそらく世界的に言っても、打ち放しで造ったのは、これが一番早かったんじゃないかな。1923年ですから。ただね、私は最初から打ち放しでいこうというつもりで造っ

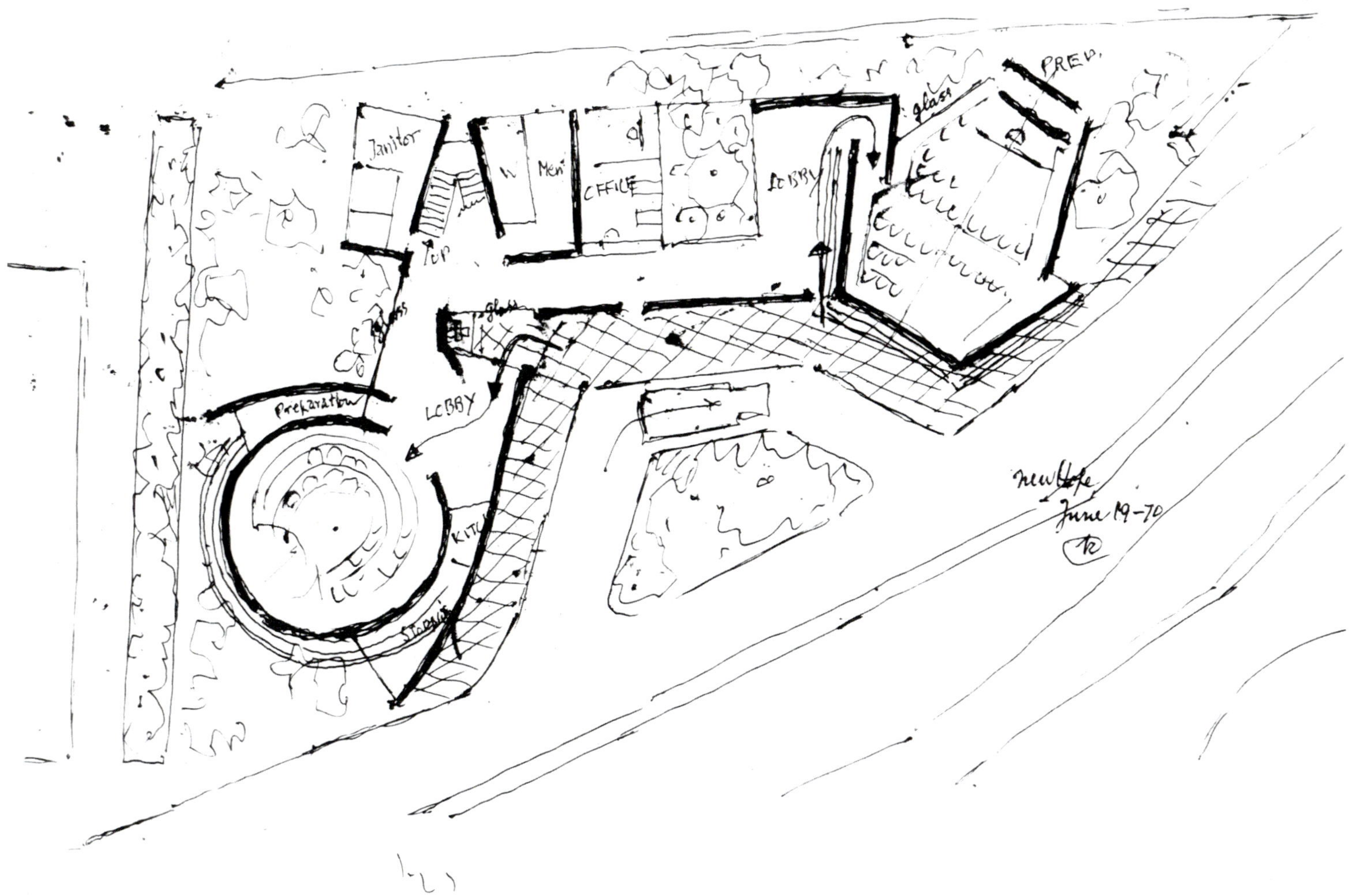

102 – アントニン・レーモンド、哲学ホール図案。高崎。1970年。

Antonín Raymond, Philosophy Study design, Takasaki (1970)

drawn and requested the preparation of the ground plan. He brought a carpenter with him, measured up all the necessary details on site, and declared: "I don't need an architectural design now, I'll make do with this." And he really built it that way.

PH: An amazing time.

KK: I think it was possible only because he had a very special relationship with Mr. Raymond.

PH: It wouldn't be possible today.

KK: You're right. But thankfully while Mr. Fusaichirō's grandsons are at the head of the family, the Philosophy Study in Takasaki[1] is always freely accessible to all those interested in a tour.

The foundation is currently taking charge of the maintenance of the building, but it is also used by the Gallery of the City of Takasaki.

HČ: Please tell us also about the plan for the house in Kōgaichō. We have a series of

01 Former villa of Mr. Inoue.

たかどうか疑問に思ってるんです。たまたま予算が無い中で、コンクリートが綺麗にできたのでこのままでいいんじゃないか、という結論に至ったんじゃないかという風に私は推察してるんです。でもとても綺麗な打ち放しだった。森ビルがこの地域を開発するまで、ずっと保存されていたんですね。レーモンドさんが戦争で帰るときに第百生命の社長さんに譲り、その後は娘さんの住宅として使われていた。1990年の後半まで。我々も何回か見に行っております。吉村順三先生 (73ページを参照) の話によりますと、最初にレーモンドさんは東京でこれを発表しないでフランスの建築雑誌に発表したらしいです。そのフランスの建築雑誌を見て、まだ学生だった吉村先生は、すごく感激して、訪ねて行ったそうです。偶然日曜日だったので、レーモンドご夫妻に会えて、中まで案内してもらって感激して、「私をレーモンド事務所にすぐ雇って下さい」と申し出たそうです。

ホリー: 吉村順三さんとレーモンド夫妻にそんな接点があったんですね。

北澤: 吉村さんはレーモンドのところで約10年仕事して、1941年に設計事務所を設立し、1945年に東京芸大の教授になりました。数多くの建物を設計して日本の建築界をリードした建築家です。その吉村さんが、かつて学生アルバイトとしてレーモンド事務所に入所するきっかけになったのも、この住宅だそうです (56ページを参照)。写真には、ミセス・レーモンドが最初に造ったパイプ椅子の家具が写っていますね。これ、なんでも無いように見えて、実はすごい事なんですよ。1923年という事は、パイプ椅子はまだ造り出される前じゃないかと私は思うんです。正確にはちょっと調べてないですけども、かなり早い時期に、こういうパイプ椅子のアイデアを考案している。この後もこういうデザインは幾つか設計しております。でも、ミセス・レーモンドの家具の中では、スチール製が少ないというのは確かですね。木製が多いんです。それから、暖炉があります。金物で、薪を支えるものをファイヤードックと呼んでいますが、それもミセス・レーモンドがデザインされていました。この自邸は、最初のデザインじゃないかなと、私は思っています。

チャプコヴァー: 戦前の建築としては、軽井沢の夏の家も、大事なプロジェクトだったかと思います。

北澤: はい、これは、コルビュジエが当初計画案で造ったものに非常に似てるという事で、問題になった作品です (10ページを参照)。レーモンド曰く、コルビュジエの資料の中にあったものからヒントを得て、「こういうものを造りたい」という事で、わざわざコルビュジェに手紙を書いて図面を送ったらしいんです。もちろんコルビュジエの計画案は実現しなかった。これは、自分がオーナーですのですぐ実現して、1933年という早い時期に軽井沢にできてるんですね。ちょうど1932年が、軽井沢のセントポール教会の設計だったので、だいたい同じ時期じゃないかと思います。ここから、夏は軽井沢で仕事をするという事が始まったわけです。

103 – 庭の伝説的なプール。笄町、麻布、東京。

Legendary swimming pool in the garden at Kōgaichō (Azabu, Tokio)

photographs available here (pp. 58–59), and for that reason also I'd like to hear what memories you have of the house.

KK: It was half a studio and half a family house, and as a result it was divided into two buildings. The building facing the garden served as a family dwelling. There was a dining table on the terrace, and a wisteria was growing over the pergola. There was a swimming pool in front of the terrace. On the left was the couple's bedroom, and on the right Mr. Raymond's study. In the photograph we can see Mr. Raymond's desk by the window (p. 137).

PH: That's a rare photograph.

KK: Yes, you may be right. The couple's bedroom was open from above. The house was built in such a manner that it was possible to open it up completely with the aid of sliding partitions. It was constructed in the same manner as traditional Japanese houses. The beds were placed parallel to one another, and in the space between them was a bookshelf. Mr. Raymond slept on the right, his wife on the left. At lunchtime they used them as couches. In the photograph you can see the small swimming pool (fig. 103). In the summer Mrs. Raymond often woke up, got out of bed and jumped straight in the pool.

PH: That must be fantastic, having a big swimming pool right in front of the bedroom!

KK: It was small, but Mrs. Raymond and her grandchildren made use of it often. This was at a time when air conditioning didn't yet exist. There was also a pergola with a wisteria in the garden. This kind of pergola and wisteria has been used in Japan since ancient times. It's said to bring luck if you eat your meal beneath it. When it wasn't raining, we had breakfast, lunch and dinner there.

104 – 笄町の自宅中庭で朝食をとるレーモンド夫妻。麻布、東京、50年代初頭。

The Raymonds having breakfast on the patio of their house in Kōgaichō (Azabu, Tokyo, early 1950s)

ホリー: ここでも家具のデザインはミセス・レーモンドが？

北澤: 家具のデザインは、ミセス・レーモンドです。1933年のこの時期、日本には洋風の家具を作る工場が無かったんですね。どこも作ってくれないので、棟梁が作れるようなデザインをして作ったと聞いています。よく見ると、自然の丸太なんですね。自然の丸太を組んで、縄を編んだもので座を作っている。確かにこのデザインだったら、棟梁が造ることができるんですね。その一脚が軽井沢のアトリエに残っております。

チャプコヴァー: アントニン・レーモンドさんとの思い出で、何か心に残っている事とか、お話されたい事などありましたら、お願いいたします。

北澤: 非常に怖い先生でしたね。短気で、怒りっぽい。「雷おやじ」というあだ名がついていまして、怒りだすと止まらないんです。でも私は最初から大変リスペクトしていたので、怒られても平気でした。すごく怒られたのは、南山大学の実施設計を終えて、「現場に行きなさい」と言われた時ですね。現場に行くことになって、2月の初めにレーモンドご夫妻が来るという事で、初めて現場でお会いする事になったんです。けれども、現場を見て歩いているうちにすごく怒り出しまして、上背が僕よりずっと大きい人が、襟首をグーッと持ち上げられましてね、「こんな工事してたら許されないぞ」と。私が赴任する前

105 – アトリエの従業員、軽井沢の別荘前で。30年代。

Employees of the studio in front of the house in Karuizawa (1930s)

HČ: Mr. Raymond's studio in Kōgaichō was very significant in terms of post-war architecture. If we go back in time, to the pre-war period, Mr. Raymond's original house in the Reinanzaka district was also an important structure. Let's talk about that, if we can.
KK: The house in the Reinanzaka district was Mr. Raymond's first headquarters and studio. The interior and exterior walls were produced from unplastered concrete. It's possible, at least I think it is, that this house was the first construction in the world on which rough, unplastered concrete was used. This was back in 1923. However, to be honest I'm not sure if it was the original plan to build a house from rough concrete. I sometimes wonder if it was rather the case that the finances ran out during the construction process, and since concrete was expedient and looked good, then they deci-

の工事なんですけれども、強烈に怒られて。ブリブリ言いながら現場事務所に帰ってきて、「清水建設に電話しろ」と。その当時清水建設は社長よりも副社長の、吉川さんという人が権力を持ってまして、吉川さんに直接「この現場はどうしようもない、現場員を全員取り替えろ、今から私が良いというまで現場は一歩たりとも進めてはいけない」と言うんです。当時は飯場小屋に職人さんが300人以上も宿泊していました。みんな毎日遊んでる。仕事ができない。そういうことでほとんどの社員を入れ替えて、再出発しました。実際、それほどその大きなミスじゃなかった。「こんな事で？」って私は思ったものです。でも、建築家の皆さんならわかると思うんですが、独立基礎で大きな、3メーター角の独立基礎で地中梁が付くところの下に、鉄筋(10mmφ)が２本出てるんですけれども、それが曲がってたり、ずれてたりしたのを見つけたんですね。それで、「鉄筋が非常に悪い」と、「全部調べなさい」と言う。調べて行くと確かにみんな鉄筋が良くなかった。地中梁の主筋なども、間違っていたりして、2か月間ぐらい、現場がストップ。全部造り直したというから、率直に「凄いな」と思いました。「こんなに強く主張できる建築家っているんだな」って。改めてレーモンドの偉大さを、私も身をもって体験しました。

チャプコヴァー: 作業は、レーモンドさんから、こうしなさいと、スケッチで指示をされるのですか、それとも口で指示をされるのでしたか？

北澤: ほとんどがスケッチです。フリーハンドのスケッチで、ノンスケールなんですよ。例えば住宅なんかで考えると、ノンスケールのスケッチを頂いて、「作図しなさい」と。まず100分の1の平面を描かなきゃいけない。そのスケールがわからないので模索しながら、スケールを決めて清書していく。レーモンドさんはその過程でよく見に来られますので、進んでなかったり、良くないところがあると、お叱りになる。私が担当になる前の話ですと、それを横で見ながら、怒ってる事を理解して、家に帰って一所懸命徹夜で、代わりの案を作ってきて、チャンスがあったら見てもらうというような事もやってました。良い提案は、社員が提案しても受け入れてくれる風土はありました。何もかも全部自分で決めるという事じゃないんですね。

チャプコヴァー: レーモンドさんから学んだ事で、大切な事は何でしたか。

北澤: レーモンド事務所では、その設計におけるレーモンドの姿勢として「5原則」というのがありまして。単純・自然・節約・直截・誠実、これが常に設計の基本なんです。常にこの5つの原則に照らし合わせながら、チェックをしていくというのがレーモンドの進め方。これはいまだに私も自分の設計する作品を、こういう事で照らし合わせながらチェックをしています。非常に大切な原則だと思います。レーモンドは非常に素晴らしい幾つもの言葉を残している。例えば、「外部の形は内部の構造の正直な表現でなければならない」、「デザインにおいて表現の手段が単純になればなるほど、その表現は力強くなり真実になり、したがって美しくなる」、「経済性もまた重要で

106 – ニューホープでのノエミ・レーモンドとD.吉村。ペンシルヴァニア、アメリカ合衆国、30年代前半。

Noémi Raymond and Yoshimura Junzō in New Hope (Pennsylvania, USA, late 1930s)

ded to leave the structure as it was. Before the land was bought by the Mori Building Company, the house was preserved in good condition. When Mr. Raymond had to leave Japan because of the war, he left the house to the director of the Daihyaku Mutual Life Insurance Co. The daughter of the company director then lived there until 1990. We also went to take a look at it several times. According to professor Yoshimura Junzō (see. p. 73), Mr. Raymond did not present this architectural design in Tokyo in any way, and first publicised it in a French architecture magazine. Professor Yoshimura saw the house in this magazine when he was still a student, and was captivated by it. He said he went to take a look at it then. It was a Sunday, and he met the Raymonds. They invited him into the house for a tour. Mr. Yoshimura was so moved that he reportedly said: "Please, immediately give me a job at the Raymond Architectural Design Office!"
PH: I didn't know that was how Mr. Yoshimura Junzō met the Raymonds under those circumstances.
KK: Mr. Yoshimura worked for Raymond for approximately ten years, then in 1941 he left and founded his own architecture studio. In 1945 he started teaching at the Tokyo University of the Arts (Tokyo Geidai). He designed a large quantity of constructions and became a leading figure on the Japanese architecture scene. And the reason why Mr. Yoshimura started working at the Raymond Architectural Design Office while still a student was this very house (see p. 56). In the photograph you can see the first tubular chair that was produced by Mrs. Raymond. It may look a little drab, but in fact it's highly significant. You see, this photograph is from 1923. I think that could be before the production of the first tubular chairs was started. I haven't determined

ある」、「これは決して安く作るという事ではない、何事も無駄にしないという事である」など。レーモンドさんの生活を見てると本当に、無駄が無いといいますか、日本人で言ったら「まじめなオヤジ」という感じなんですけれども、お金も遣わない、身なりにはあんまりお金はかけない。でも、ミスターはおしゃれで、けっこう良いお洋服、スーツを常に作ってました。一方、ミセスは自分で織ってきた反物みたいな感じのもので、自分で洋服を作っているというような感じで。ちょっと驚いたのは、これもチェコ風なのかな？ ご夫婦であってもミセス・レーモンドはお金を持たされてないんですね。ミスターが全部持っていて。

ホリー: それはチェコのスタイルですね。

北澤: そうなんですか？ 軽井沢でも、「街に行って、ちょっと買い物をしたいからお金を下さい」って言って一所懸命レーモンドにおねだりするんですね。ミセスが。でも、なかなか渡さない。見ていると、じれったいなって感じなんです。「どういうものを買うんだ？」って聞いて渡すという。日本人はそんな事はできないもんですから、羨ましく思いました (笑)。そういう、おやじ主導の家庭といいますかね、そんなご夫婦でした。でも、お互いに尊敬し合っていました。本来、ミセスも建築をやりたいはずなんです。でも、どうしても建築を一緒に2人でやると喧嘩になるので、ミスターが建築、ミセスが家具・インテリアと、分野を分けていたので仕事がスムーズに進められました。

チャプコヴァー: もともと、ミセス・レーモンドさんはグラフィックデザイナーでしたよね。

北澤: そうですね。二人はニューヨークで結婚して、レーモンドさんの仕事が無い時期はノエミさんが新聞社から頼まれて、グラフィックデザインのものを描いて、新聞に発表してお金を得て生活していた。本当に上手なんですね、絵が。でも、私の働いた10年間、ミセスは1枚も絵を描きませんでした。ですから、ミスターに遠慮して描かないのかな？と、私なぞは思っていました。軽井沢の生活でミスターは「1日1枚描きなさい」と、我々にも要求しました。描きあがったスケッチを、ミスターは壁に画鋲で貼っていくんですね。どんどんそれが増えていく。今でもそういうスケッチ類が本当に沢山保存されてるんです。大変貴重なものですから、私も世にそれを出さなきゃと思いながら、今日まで出さずにいて、申し訳ありません。ぼつぼつどっかで展覧会をやりたいなと企画しています。

チャプコヴァー: 北澤さんが手がけたプロジェクトの中に南山大学があります。

北澤: はい。私は、たまたま恵まれていたんです。1962年に、南山大学の実施設

107 – クロード・レーモンド、軽井沢の別荘にて。30年代。

Claude Raymond in front of the summer residence in Karuizawa (1930s)

108 – 南山大学航空写真。名古屋、60年代中葉。

Nanzan University campus in Nagoya (mid-1960s)

計が始まる直前に参加できてたのですが、そのプロジェクトチームが、基本設計の最後の段階でした。レーモンドさんが現地を一緒に見て行くこととなり、私も同行させてもらいました。新しい敷地は名古屋の町を見下ろす高台にあって、緩やかな起伏があり、低い雑木林が全面的にある広大な敷地でした。そのすばらしい環境の地に大学を新設するという計画で、敷地の中にある細い道を歩くだけでもう楽しくなる光景でした。レーモンドさんは敷地の一番高い尾根の道を南から北に進みながら「これはすばらしい道だからこれを軸線にしよう」と決められたようでした。尾根の左右は斜面で下がっており、そこに建物やグラウンドを造ることになりました。実施設計は順調に進み、完了する前に工期を急ぐため清水建設に見積りを依頼して、着工したんす。約10ヶ月と短期間でまとめられ、着工し始めると2人の若い社員(北澤と大西)は現場に常駐しなさいとの命令を受けました。2月の寒い時から現場監理につき、8棟の建物が完成するまで、とても貴重な経験をいたしました。その現場監理は55年を経た今でも財産となっています。完成した南山大学はすばらしく建築学会賞も受賞されました。しかし、現在の南山大学は増築を何棟も行い、その設計が良くなく、見るに堪えられない状態のため私は見に行きたくない心境なんです（苦笑）。

ホリー: レーモンドさんから授かった大仕事ですね。

北澤: これが完成した時の写真ですね (130ページを参照)。 今でも変わらな

the date exactly, but it's certain that Mrs. Raymond came up with the idea for the design of this chair very early on. Later she produced several more such designs. However, among the furniture designed by Mrs. Raymond there was a minimal amount of metal items, she worked mainly with wood. And then we have the stove on the fireplace. The metal stand which serves as a wood storage bin was also designed by Mrs. Raymond. I think this house is one of Raymond's very first independent designs. The metal stand for firewood in this house is the oldest design of its type.

HČ: I believe that their summer residence in Karuizawa was also a very important project of pre-war architecture.

KK: Yes. But that was a problematic work, because it was very similar to one of Le Corbusier's early designs (see p. 11). Mr. Raymond insisted that he'd merely been inspired by Le Corbusier's work and that he'd used only a few interesting ideas from his diagrams. In fact he even apparently wrote him a letter and sent him the diagrams as an example. This original design by Le Corbusier was never realised. Since Raymond was both the architect and owner, he built his summer residence practically immediately. The house in Karuizawa was completed very quickly, by 1933. In 1932 he was working in Karuizawa on the design of St. Paul's church, and so I believe that this was at approximately the same time. And from then on the custom started to apply that in the summer months works were conducted at Mr. Raymond's summer residence in Karuizawa.

PH: Was the furniture in this house designed by Mrs. Raymond?

KK: Yes, she designed the furniture. In 1933 there was not yet any factory in Japan producing furniture of the Western type. I was told that since nobody manufactured such furniture anywhere, she designed it herself and had it made by a carpenter. If you look carefully, you'll see that she used wooden logs as the material. She bound these logs together with string, and that's how she produced the chair. Furniture designed in that way can also be produced by a carpenter. The chair in the new studio in Karuizawa has been preserved to this day.

HČ: What memories do you have of Antonín Raymond as a person, what could you tell us about his character?

KK: He could be pretty fearsome. He had a fiery temper and was often angry. He was nicknamed "the thunderous grandad", and once he got worked up nobody could stop him. But I always respected Mr. Raymond right from the beginning, and so even if he lost his temper at me I never felt disconcerted by it. He got really angry at me during the time when we were finishing the design for Nanzan University, and he told me to move out onto the building site. At the beginning of February the Raymonds were meant to be coming for an inspection, which would be the first time I'd meet them directly on the construction site. And when Mr. Raymond was walking through the site he went out of his mind with fury and grabbed me by the collar, and because he was much taller than me he pulled me up to his height. "I won't stand for such a building!" The construction was already in that condition before I was assigned to it, but still, he lost his temper at me. He angrily stormed back to the office, which was on the construction site, and said: "Put me through to the Shimizu Corporation!" At that time

109 – 南山大学建設現場にて。左から、野村氏 (清水建設)、アントニン・レーモンド、佐藤氏。60年代前半。

On the construction of Nanzan University, from left: Mr. Nomura (Shimizu construction firm), Antonín Raymond and Mr. Satō (early 1960s)

い。正面が食堂と、右側が図書館。例えば、食堂棟の庇にちょっと変わってる形があるんですけども、これはレーモンドさんの案なんです。「庇を変わった形にしよう」って言って、ちょこちょこっとスケッチを描いて、レーモンドさんが持ってくるんです。でも、私にはなかなか理解できなくて、一所懸命考えて図面化するんですけども、難しい。平面図ができると、断面ができて、側面ができたら、すぐパースにして。パースもすぐ描かないといけないんですね。午後に次の図面が回ってくるまでに描かないと、お叱りを受けるんですね。ですから、本当に一点透視図を短時間で描いて、見てもらい、チェックされていくというような順序を追って形が決まっていくのですね。この写真は図書館で、この時も困難を極めました（130ページを参照）。なかなか難しい図書館で、ちょっと普通では考えられないのですが、柱の中に空調ダクトが組み込まれているんです。フレッシュエアーとリターンダクトが両方組み込まれている。そして、柱の真ん中にどーんっとダクトが入る。それを引っ張り出すところがまた大変なんです。けれども、それによって最も均一な空調ができるんだ、というのがレーモンドさんのアイデアだったんです。構造は苦労しましたけれども、何とかやれた、というような事ですね。この南山大学の思い出としては、そうですね、オーナーが神父さんなんですが、井戸を掘るという事になりまして、その神父さんが「自分たちでどこに掘るか、場所を決めます」って言うんですね。柳の枝の二股をもって敷地の中を歩き回るんです。

ホリー: チェコのやりかたです。そうやって水源を探します。

北澤: 水源があるところになるとその柳の枝が回転するんです。「不思議だな」と思いました。その後、そっと私もやるんですが、私がやっても回転してくれないんです。その水源というのが、図書館の真ん中だったんです。頭を抱えました。「それでは図書館を造るのに困るから、ちょっともう一度やってもらえないか」という事で、違う神父さんにお願いしてやってもらったんですが、2万㎡以上ある敷地でそこしかないんですね。仕方ないので、先に掘って、井戸を造ったんですけれども、本来は井戸っていうのは、真下、真上に、修理修繕のスペースを造らなきゃいけないんですが、それができない。だから、図書館の真ん中に地下室を造り、150Φ位の太さのパイプで掘っていくんですけども、ある時点でどわーっと勢いよく飛び出して、たくさんの水が出たんです。なんとも不思議な体験でした。

ホリー: チェコでは昔からそうやって水源を探し当てるんですよ

北澤: そうなのですね。でも、あれだったら、温泉の水源も見つけられるんじゃないかなって当時、思いました（笑）。神父さんお金持ちになるんじゃないかなあと思ったんですけども、見事ですね。

チャプコヴァー: 南山大学はなかなか大変なプロジェクトだったんですね。

at the Shimizu Corporation it was the assistant director rather than the director himself who made the decisions, a certain Mr. Yoshikawa. Mr. Raymond told Mr. Yoshikawa directly: "This construction site is in an appalling state! Replace all the workers immediately! Until I give you the go-ahead, this construction must not proceed an inch further!" There were about three hundred labourers staying in the accommodation on site. Mr. Raymond insisted that they were all just messing about and were incapable of working. As a result he had almost all the workers replaced. But it seemed to me that no great problem had arisen. "All because of such a trifle?" I thought to myself. The architects will surely understand the seriousness of the problem, which was that in the foundations of the building, in the position where a large, three-metre square beam was to be placed, a concrete reinforcement was protruding, or more precisely two bars with a diameter of 10 mm. They determined that the bars were deformed and misaligned. And that's why Mr. Raymond told me that the "concrete reinforcement was poor", so that I'd recheck everything. And when I checked it, I discovered that all the reinforcement was indeed poor. Even the main reinforcement of the underground beam wasn't right. The construction was then halted for two whole months, because Mr. Raymond decided that everything had to be redone. I truly admired him. I was surprised that there was such an architect who fought so uncompromisingly for his point of view. I experienced for myself once again what an exceptional person Mr. Raymond was.

HČ: Did Mr. Raymond give you working instructions with the aid of sketches, or did he explain them to you verbally?

KK: Mostly with the aid of sketches. They were sketches drawn in freehand, and without scale. For example, in the case of one family house we received a sketch without scale and the strict instruction: "Draw up a diagram!" First of all I had to draft a ground plan on a scale of 1:100, and because I didn't know the required scale, I sought it during the course of the work and progressively compiled a diagram. In this phase of the process Mr. Raymond regularly came to check if I'd made any progress, and if I'd made any mistakes he'd shout at me. – Before I reached the position where I was heading the projects myself I used to observe from a distance how Mr. Raymond got angry at someone, and I tried to understand where the problem was. – Then I went home and worked assiduously all night on a provisional solution. After all, Mr. Raymond was the type of man who accepted proposals from his subordinates if they appeared to be good. It wasn't the case that he always had to come up with everything himself.

HČ: What for you was the most important thing you learned from Mr. Raymond?

KK: In the Raymond Architectural Design Office the "Five Basic Principles" applied, which expressed Raymond's approach to architecture: simplicity, directness, naturalness, economy of means and authenticity.[2] Those were the foundations of all designs. Mr. Raymond always judged everything with the aid of those five principles. I myself make use of these principles to this day when checking my designs. I think they're genuinely important principles. Mr. Raymond left a lot of important ideas in his wake. For example: "The external shape must *authentically* express the internal structure." – "The *simpler* the means of expression of the given design, the more effective, clearer

02 Antonín Raymond defined the principles of his work repeatedly, e. g.: "Simplicity, directness, naturalness, economy of means, perfect material and spiritual function in the creation as a whole and in all its details are the aim." ("Creation and imitation". In: *This is Japan,* 1954, p. 171, 1953. Nine pages, stored in the collection of Kitazawa Kōichi in the New Studio in Karuizawa).

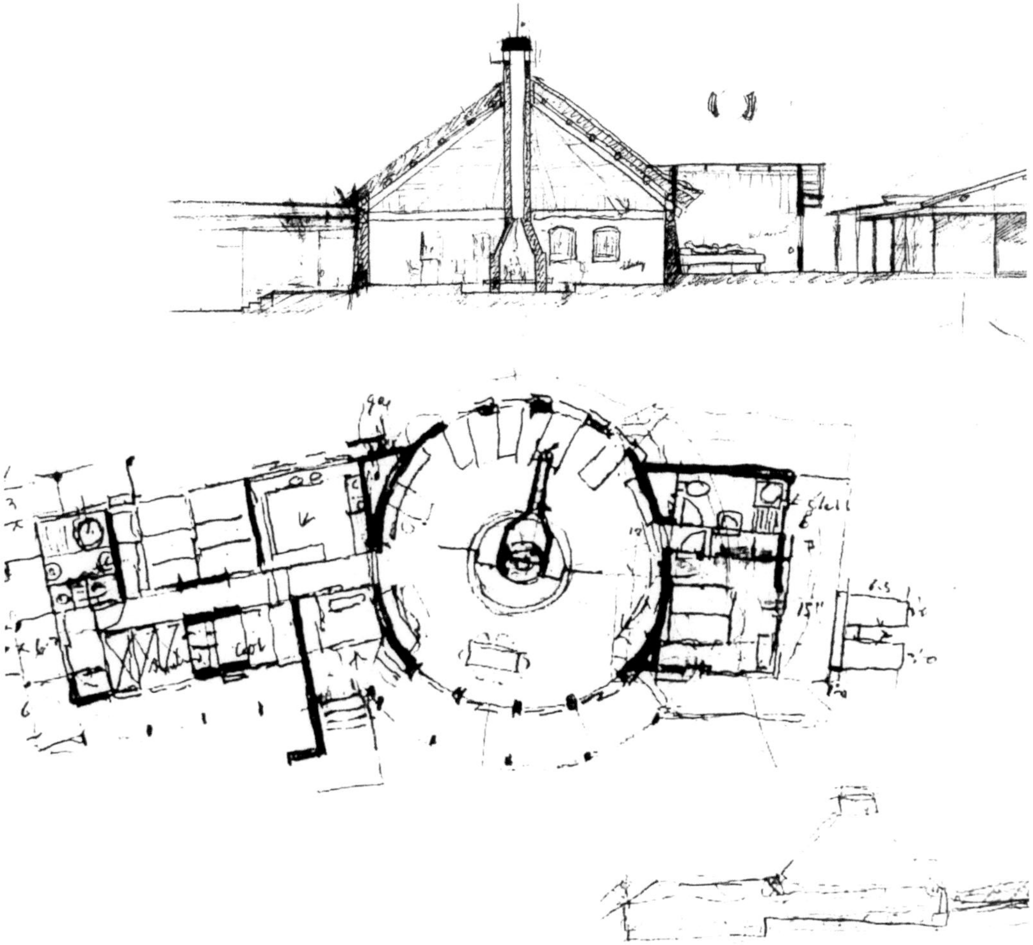

110 – 軽井沢新スタジオの初期スケッチ。50年代末。

One of the first sketches of the design of the New Studio in Karuizawa (late 1950s)

北澤: はい。レーモンドさんに怒られたり、一所懸命現場作業をやったり、大変でした。外壁は、オール打ち放しですから、どうしたら打ち放しが綺麗にできるか、清水建設の社員と議論をしまして。ガラスの仮枠を作って、上からコンクリートを流して、どういう状態でコンクリートを固めていくか話し合いを重ねました。例えば、気泡が出るじゃないですか、それが上まで行かないで止まってしまうと、打ち放しの肌が悪くなるんです。それと、どうしてもわからなかったのが、仮枠に杉板を使うんですけれども、真っ黒くなってしまう杉板が出てくるんです。それを触ってみると、打ち放しの表面がボロボロ取れてしまうんですね。要するに硬化してないコンクリートなんです。不硬化現象って言うんですけれども、その原因を探っていかなきゃいけない。探っていくと、どうも、太陽光の影響じゃないかということがわかって。杉のヤニが表面に出ると、そのコンクリートを固まらせない要素が出るんじゃないかという結論に至ったんです。それで、杉板が何日間、太陽に当たったらそうなるかを現場で実験しました。0日、1日、2日、3日、4日という仮枠の材料を作って。流し込んでみると、それがズバリ当たりまして。太陽光に当てちゃうと、黒くなっ

111 – 南山大学のセミナーホールと教会のスケッチ。名古屋。1960年代初期。

Sketch of seminary and church of Nanzan University in Nagoya (early 1960s)

and ultimately more beautiful it will be." – "Economy is also important." – "We don't have to build cheaply at all costs, but we mustn't be wasteful." When you watched Mr. Raymond it truly seemed that he never wasted anything. He didn't waste money, he didn't spend excessively on his own appearance, but he always wanted to look good, he wore quality suits. Incidentally, Mrs. Raymond's dresses created the impression that she had woven and then sewn the fabric herself. I was a little surprised by the fact that although they were married, Mrs. Raymond never had any money on her, that was always carried exclusively by Mr. Raymond – probably a Czech custom.

PH: Yes, it is a Czech custom.

KK: Seriously? Even in Karuizawa she had to plead with him: "I'm going to town and I'd like to buy something, can you give me some money please." But her husband wouldn't give it to her just like that. When I observed them, he seemed somewhat irritated, handing over the money to his wife with the words: "And what do you want to buy?" The Japanese couldn't do such a thing, and so I envied him a little. *(Laughs)* It was a household in which the man had the final word. Nevertheless, there was a mutual respect. In fact, Mrs. Raymond also wanted to devote herself to architecture, but

112 – 軽井沢新スタジオの玄関。1960～1961年。

Entrance to the New Studio in Karuizawa (1960–1961)

113 – 笄町邸宅のリビング。麻布。1951年。

Living room in Kōgaichō, Azabu (1951)

if both of them had begun designing buildings it would undoubtedly have ended in an almighty argument every time, and so they preferred a division of labour: Mr. Raymond engaged in architecture and Mrs. Raymond designed furniture and interiors. Thanks to this they were able to work together smoothly.

HČ: But Mrs. Raymond was originally a graphic designer.

KK: You're right. They got married in New York at a time when Mr. Raymond was out of work, and Mrs. Noémi sketched for newspapers. Her graphic designs were published, and so both spouses lived off the royalties. Those drawings were truly accomplished. But in the ten years I worked at the firm, Mrs. Noémi did not draw a single picture. It occurred to me that she might be a little too acquiescent to her husband. Mr. Raymond wanted us to produced at least one sketch every day. He then pinned

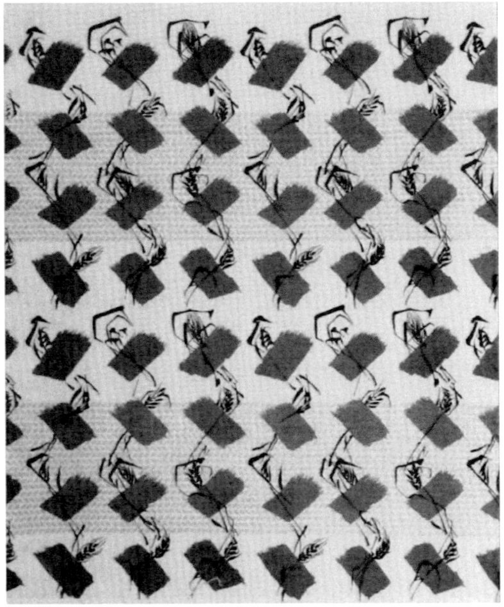

114–115 – ノエミ・レーモンド「絨毯図案」1960年代。

Noémi Raymond, designs of carpets (1960s)

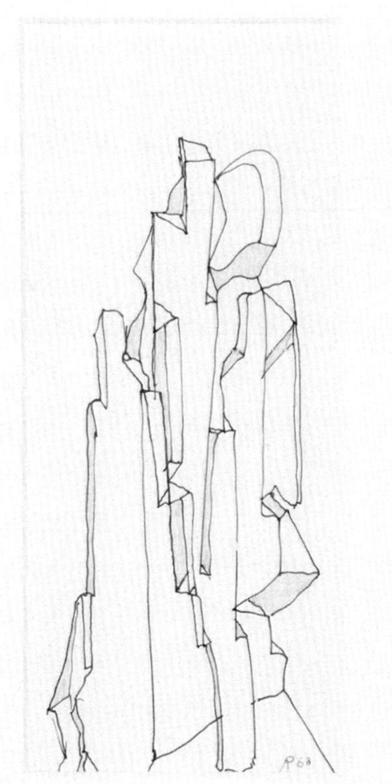

116 – アントニン・レーモンド「軽井沢でのデッサン」1968年。

Antonín Raymond, drawing from Karuizawa (1968)

て、その打ち放しが綺麗な肌にならないという事がわかったんです。そういう研究はそれ以前も以後もなかったものですから、発見でした。南山大学ではそんな事をやって、なんとか造り上げていったんですが、楽しかったのは壁に色をつける作業です。打ち放しのコンクリートでできた校舎を見て、レーモンド夫妻が「ちょっと色が寂しい。どうしようか？」と言うんですね。「腰壁に色を付けたい」と。「どの色にしようか？」と考えてたら、ミセス・レーモンドが道路際にあった、赤い土を拾い上げて「この色がいいです」と言ったんです。「その色に近い色を作りなさい」と。これがまた東京の、ミセスが懇意にしている塗装屋さんでないとできないって言うので、そちらへ頼んで、来ていただいて、コンクリートの打ち放しに塗ってもらう。ただ、あれは水性なんです。だから、染み込ませるんですけど、肌が杉板の木そのままなんです。そんな風に夫婦のやりとりで、色が決まっちゃうというのは、見ていて楽しかったですね。

チャプコヴァー: セントアンセルモ教会の赤も同じ赤でしたか。

北澤: あれは少し違う赤系です。セントアンセルモ教会はまだ目黒にちゃんとありますよね。良い状態で保存されています。あの教会の内部は素晴らしいですね。中央の金箔の天蓋と背面壁画の正円(外側)と内接円が4つで構成されていて、見事な聖壇がデザインされています。壁構造は、壁・屋根ともに三角形の組合せで、内外ともコンクリート打ち放し仕上げとなっています。構造的には折版構造で、この折版が、私は群馬音楽堂につながっているという風に思っております。この二つの折版は、所員の構造家で後に東工大の教授になられた岡本剛さんが解析したんですね。群馬音楽堂の頃はコンピュータなんか無く、手計算と、計算尺で、解析した時代でし

our sketches to the wall. There were more and more of them. Many of them have been preserved to this day. They're rare treasures, and I've been telling myself for a long time that I'll let them see the light of day again. I'm really sorry that to this day I still haven't done it. I'm determined to hold an exhibition.
HČ: The projects you worked on also included Nanzan University.
KK: I was lucky at the time. I joined the project in 1962, shortly before the commencement of the works on the plan for the realisation of the construction. The project team was just in the final stage of the basic design. Mr. Raymond went with the team to look at the construction site, and I was allowed to accompany him. The land plot for the construction was on a slightly undulating raised surface, with a view of Nagoya. It was a large piece of land, and the entire surface was covered with low vegetation. When I was walking along the narrow paths that led to the land plot, I was already beginning to look forward to the construction of the new university. They were ideal conditions. Mr. Raymond went from south to north along the route that led along the highest ridge, and declared: "This is a very good footpath, we'll make it the axis of the entire construction." It appeared that the decision had been made. On both the right and left sides of the ridge was a slope on which we constructed buildings and a playing field. The plan for the realisation proceeded without any difficulties, but in order to accelerate the process we requested that the Shimizu Corporation construction firm compile price quotes, and so we started work on the construction itself. We put the project together within the space of ten months, thus within a fairly short time. As soon as the construction works were commenced, two young employees were sent there as supervisors – Kitazawa and Ōnishi. My work as a construction supervisor began in the cold of February. Before we completed all eight buildings, I gained a wealth of valuable experiences. For example, the experience of construction supervision remains invaluable to me to this day – after fifty-five years. The university was an amazing architectural work. It won a prize, which was awarded by the Architectural Institute of Japan. Of course, now it has been added to within the Nanzan University campus by a number of other buildings which aren't remotely good quality structures. At present I find it unbearable to look at the university, I don't have the slightest inclination to go there. *(Smiles bitterly)*
PH: Mr. Raymond believed in you, he entrusted a very important work to you.
KK: This is a photograph from the completion of the construction (p. 130). Nothing has changed here to this day. At the forefront is the dining hall, on the right is the library. For example, the guttering of the dining room has a somewhat unusual shape, that was Mr. Raymond's idea. He said: "Let's make the shape of the guttering a little unconventional", and he quickly drafted a couple of sketches and handed them to me. But I had no idea what to do with them. I did everything in my power to prepare a diagram, but it was difficult. I made out a ground plan, then a cross-section and a side view, and immediately after that a bird's eye view. I had to do the bird's eye view immediately; if I hadn't drafted it by the afternoon, when further diagrams had to be done, I'd have been in for a tongue-lashing. I really had to prepare the bird's-eye view

117 – アントニン・レーモンド、軽井沢でのデッサン。1968年。

Antonín Raymond, drawings from Karuizawa (1968)

118 – レーモンド夫妻とゲルハルト・シュライバー神父。南山大学建設現場にて。60年代前半。

The Raymonds and Father Gerhard Schreiber on the construction of Nanzan University in Nagoya (early 1960s)

た。ちょっと小話になりますけど、実際に現場が出来上がって「仮枠を外せるようになったので外していいか」と、施工者が岡本さんに聞いたら「まだ駄目だ」と言うんです。「あと1か月、待ってくれ」と。何の意味があるかなと思って後で聞いたら、「毎晩お百度参りした」って言うんですね。岡本剛さんが。「え？ 神頼みなの？」と思いましてね（笑）。そのぐらい大変なんわけですよ。ちょっと驚きました。「壁厚は12インチしか駄目だよ」と言うレーモンドさんの絶対指示は変えられないんですね。ですからそれ以上の厚みのコンクリートにできない、壁構造的には非常に難しいんです。1か月延びて、あらゆるところに下げ振りを下ろして沈下量を測れる準備をして、内部足場を少しずつ外して、沈下量を測定しながら、全部支持足場を外したというわけです。その話をしながら、岡本さんは「コンクリートっていうのは、構造クラックが入って当たり前なんだよ」と言っていました。なかなか理解に苦しむんですけど、ラーメン構造で、あの大きな梁に、縦に構造クラックが入る。それを見て、「ああ、よかった」って岡本さんが言う。その真意は、「鉄筋が入って、それが作用したからこれだけのクラックだけで済んだんだ」っていうこと。「じゃなかったら崩れちゃうんだ」と。「この鉄筋が構造的に作用したという、確証になるんだ」と言うんですね。なかなか理解するのが難しいお話なんですけども、私もよく造ってる建物で、クラックが梁にピッと入ると「ああ、これでいいんだな」と思いながら、満足することもあったりして。そういうものなんですね。

as quickly as possible, have it checked and if necessary correct it. Using this procedure I managed to complete the design of the guttering. – In this photograph is the library (p. 130). I also had a fair amount of problems with that. It's a pretty complicated structure. It wouldn't occur to just anyone, but the ventilation shafts are built into the pillars. There was both inlet of fresh air and discharge. Ventilation shafts in the pillars! It's quite a job to get to it when repairs are needed. But precisely thanks to this the air is ventilated evenly. This was Mr. Raymond's idea. The production was pretty demanding, but finally it worked out somehow. From my other recollections of Nanzan University I also recall that the client was a Catholic priest, and when we wanted to dig a well, he declared: "We'll find the place for digging it ourselves." And then he walked through the entire land plot with a willow branch.

PH: That's also how it's done in the Czech Republic, the source is sought with a divining rod.

KK: When he approached the place where the source was, the willow branch started to bend. It was a strange experience for me. I later tried to do it myself in secret, but the divining rods didn't move at all. Incidentally, that spring was in the middle of the library, which was a problem, and so I asked: "It's going to be quite difficult to build the library like that, can you try it one more time?" I asked another priest, and he tried it once more. But despite the fact that the land plot covers more than 20 000 m^2, he couldn't find any other source. We had no choice. So first of all we dug the well. The well should really have had sufficient free space in its upper and lower sections in order to enable any applicable repairs and maintenance, but unfortunately that wasn't possible. And so we had to build an underground room in the centre of the library, in which we then dug a well with a diameter of 150 cm. During the digging, water suddenly started gushing out of the ground and filled up the well. – A truly strange experience.

PH: In the Czech Republic that method has been used to locate the source for centuries.

KK: Really? At the time I wondered whether it would be possible also to discover hot springs using the same method. *(Laughs)* A wonderful thing! The priests could make a lot of money off it.

HČ: Nanzan University was a demanding project in many respects.

KK: That's true. Besides the fact that the work on the construction site was demanding, I also had to deal with the frequently angry Mr. Raymond. The exterior walls were made of unplastered concrete, and I had to quibble with the employees of the Shimizu Corporation concerning how to make the concrete look good. We produced a glass mould, into which we poured the concrete from above, and then we argued about the state in which we'd leave it to harden. You know that bubbles form in concrete, right? And if those bubbles don't come right to the surface, the quality of the external layer of the concrete will be poor. – There was one more thing I didn't understand very well at the time: the moulds for pouring concrete were produced from cedar panels, and some of them had turned completely black. When I touched them,

チャプコヴァー: 葉山の別荘にも北澤先生は関わっていらっしゃいますね。

北澤: この葉山の海の家っていうのは1957年に、レーモンドさんが、自分の週末の家として造ったものなんですね。非常に変わってまして、丸太と、断面でわかると思うんですが、外の柱が倒れてるんですね。倒れて、7尺5寸の庇を支えている。こうして海の先端に飛び出すような敷地のところに、小さな建物が建てられた。この写真は海岸から撮ったものですね（144ページを参照）。これが2階のリビングです。海岸が見える広いバルコニーがあって、手摺が30cmのテーブルを兼ねていました。2階からは葉山海岸を見渡すことができて、遠くに富士山を望むことができたんです。1階がアトリエになっていて、当時非常に大きな絵を描いていました。一色海岸に突出した敷地で、海がきれいで、非常に使いやすいアトリエでした。私は、レーモンドさんの建物の中では一番好きな建物でした。

ホリー: レーモンド先生も気に入っていらっしゃいましたか？

北澤: 軽井沢新スタジオを造る以前は1年中、週末に行っていました。レーモンドも大いに気に入っていたと考えられます。2階のリビングにある暖炉は、非常によく燃えるんです。レーモンドの暖炉の規格サイズというものがあって、鉄板で造られていました。笄町の自宅も同じ暖炉です。1階は広間で何もないんです。外階段で上がって、玄関があって、リビング、ベッドルームが2つ。中央にバス、トイレ。非常にコンパクトで使いやすい小住宅です。海側のサイドのバルコニーがどーんっと大きくて、そこからの眺めがとても素晴らしいんです。この写真は凄いですね（146ページを参照）。レーモンド自身が作った焼物3点を置いてあって。これはレーモンドさんのネガの中に入ってた1枚なんですけど、レーモンド自身が撮ったとしては凄い良いアングルだなあと思いまして。愛犬もちゃんといますし、富士山もちゃんと写ってます。レーモンドがいよいよ身体を悪くしてニューホープに帰ることになった時に、財産を処分するわけですが、葉山の別荘を最初に処分したんですね。当時、コックさんと秘書役を任せられてたチェイさんという方がいまして、夜電話がかかってきて、「北さん、大変だ。葉山を知らない人に売っちゃうっていうのが今日決まったよ」と言ってきた。今でも覚えています。レーモンドさんに「その話で会いたいけれどいいか」って聞くと、レーモンドが「いいよ」って言うので飛んでいきました。すると、ある弁護士さんが「売ってほしい」と言うから、「売るよ」と約束しちゃった、と言うんです。おいおい、と。そういう訳のわからない人に売るって事は、私は反対なので、これだけの作品はレーモンド事務所が買って保存すべきだと、主張しました。そうでなかったら我々仲間内で買いたいという話もして。「そんな嬉しいことはないから、じゃあ、明日断るよ」と。でも、翌日に断ったら、「不動産っていうのは、口約束で契約が成り立ってる。嫌だと言うんだったらあなたを訴えますと言われた」と。「建物を大切に保存しますと記入するから」と契約者が言い、仕方がないから、売却しました。そうしたら、三ヶ月で壊されて、更地にされた。悔しいってもんじゃあり

I could feel crumbled concrete. In other words, the concrete hadn't hardened sufficiently. I had to find the cause. I investigated the matter, and it occurred to me that it could have been caused by the sun's rays. I discovered that the sun's rays cause the cedar wood to release resin, and it's this that results in insufficient hardening of the concrete. I conducted an experiment on the building site: I left cedar boards in the sun for several days, and then I made them into moulds, which I then classified according to the number of days the wood had been exposed to the sun – 0, 1, 2, 3, 4, 5 – I tried pouring concrete into them, and it showed that my theory truly was correct. I realised that if the moulds were exposed to sunlight, they'd turn black and the surface of the concrete wouldn't look good. No such similar research had ever been done, either before or after, and so it was a great discovery. At the same time when I was dealing with such similar problems, we were proceeding with the construction. I enjoyed the work in connection with choosing the colour of the exterior walls. When the Raymonds saw the school building made of unplastered concrete, they said: "That colour is kind of sad. What are we going to do with it?" We decided to brighten up the lower part of the wall with some kind of paint. When they were contemplating which colour to choose, Mrs. Raymond found some red clay by the path, and declared: "This is a good colour." She ordered me to procure a paint that would be as similar as possible to that clay. I was also told that the paint could only be produced in Mrs. Raymond's favourite paint shop in Tokyo. And so I ordered it from there and arranged for a painter to come and paint the unplastered concrete. But there was a problem: it was a water-based paint, which means that it was absorbed into the material, and so the surface of the concrete remained exactly the same as when it had come out of the cedar mould. I enjoyed watching the Raymonds discussing in order to reach a decision on what colour to choose.

HČ: Did you use the same red colour on St. Anselm's church?

KK: It was a slightly different shade of red. St. Anselm's church is in the district of Meguro. It's survived in good condition. The interior space is superb, what do you think? There's a beautiful altar formed by a golden canopy, behind which there's a composition on the wall of one large and four smaller mutually interlocking circles. The walls and roof are composed of a combination of triangles – all made of unplastered concrete. The construction is made up of concrete slabs. I think that it's a reference to the building of the Gunma Music Centre. The static calculation of both constructions from stacked slabs was prepared by my colleague, Mr. Okamoto Takashi, who later became a professor at the Tokyo Institute of Technology. This was at a time when computers didn't yet exist, and the static calculations were made with the aid of a slide rule. – I've got a story about that. During the work on the construction site, one of the construction workers asked Mr. Okamoto if he could remove the wooden mould from the concrete, because the concrete ought to be ready by now. Mr. Okamoto told him not yet, that he should wait another month. I was interested to know why, and so I asked him about it later. He explained to me that he was performing a Japanese religious ritual and that for a period of one hundred nights he was praying

119 – 聖アンセルモ教会前面。目黒、東京、1956年。

Facade of St. Anselm's church (Meguro, Tokyo, 1956)

120 – 葉山別宅。1957〜1958年。
House in Hayama (1957–1958)

ません。残念極まりない。その一年後には、今度は軽井沢を売ることになりました。購入を申し込んだのは、有名な実業家。金額まで提示してきました。でもその人が維持管理してくれると思えない、しっかりと保存してくれると思えなかった。なので、すぐにレーモンドさんのところにいって、「それはダメだ！」「やはりレーモンド事務所が買って保存するべきだ！」と私は主張しました。レーモンドさんは「じゃあ明日の役員会で許可を得てみる」と言ってくれましたが、結果NOでした。それならば、私が買いましょうと申し出たんです。そこから凄く大変になりまして、私なんぞは４〜５万円の月給取ですか

121 – 葉山別宅。一階アトリエ。
1957〜1958年。

House in Hayama, ground floor studio (1957–1958)

to the gods. We had no other option but to rely on the gods (*laughs*). It really was that arduous at the time. I was fairly surprised by that. Mr. Raymond's instructions were clear: the thickness of the walls must not exceed 12 inches. We therefore couldn't use stronger concrete, and from the perspective of a structural engineer this was very difficult. He gained a deferral of one month. He re-measured the entire structure using a plumb line, and checked that the construction wouldn't sink under its own weight. He gradually removed the internal scaffolding, and while he was still re-measuring the degree of subsidence of the structure, he also removed the supporting scaffolding. He told me this, and added: "A proper concrete construction must have cracks." It's rather difficult to understand, but when a lengthwise crack appeared in a large beam of the frame construction, Mr. Okamoto felt relieved, and said that it was a very good sign. He said that because it meant the steel reinforcement inside the concrete was working, and at the same time nothing worse occurred – it was just a crack in the concrete. Had it been worse, the construction would have collapsed. The crack in fact demonstrated that the steel rods in the concrete were fulfilling their function. It's difficult to explain, but I myself too, when I'm building houses, wait until cracks appear in the beam. When that happens, I finally feel satisfied and think to myself: "This is the way it ought to be!"

PH: Did you also contribute to the design of the summer residence in Hayama?

KK: Mr. Raymond built the house on the beach in Hayama as his weekend cottage in 1957. It was a very peculiar house. You'd understand it from a cross-section of the building. The pillars in the outer facade, the beams, didn't stand upright, but

122 – アントニン・レーモンド作のセラミック彫刻。葉山。1970年代初期。

Ceramic sculptures by Antonín Raymond (Hayama, early 1970s)

ら、その身分で３千万以上の家を買うというのはほぼ不可能なんです。でも、葉山のこともありましたので、どうしても一つは残し保存したかった。だから、私はどうにか建物を残したい一心で手を上げたんです。そのあとの金策が大変でした。しかし、無事に購入できて、今日まで保存できました。レーモンドが使ってた状態を何も改造せず、絵を取り替えたり、焼き物を取り替えたりはしてますけども、ほんとにそのまま保存してます。ですから、私は見学の希望がある人はできるだけ見てもらっています。毎年ですね、３～４組の大きな団体の見学会が今もあるんです。

この写真は玄関のところです (148ページを参照)。プランを見ると、真ん中がアトリエ兼リビングで十二角形なんですね。スケッチを見ると最初は、円で造ろうとしてるのがわかります。壁だけはレンガを積み上げて、円で造ろうというスケッチが元々はあったんですけれども、やっぱり木造で造りたいという事になって。そうすると、柱と建具が問題になります。そこで一辺が7尺5寸のモジュールで、十二辺ができたわけです。奥には和室、これを客間って呼んでました。さらに、ご夫妻の主寝室、洗面バストイレ、それから左側に厨房、ユーティリティ、メイドルーム、というのがあるんですね。これが母屋の方で、左側にある離れという所が、我々スタッフの泊まるところ。驚いたのですが、母屋を造る7年前に、既にスタッフの小屋を先に造ってるんですね。何で7年もかかったのかなという疑問はあるんですけども、金銭的な問題かと思います。この別荘が全て完成した時は、群馬音楽堂の設計料とか南山大学の設計料が入った時なので。建築家って、だいたいがお金持ちになれないんですよ。だからレーモンドさんも同じだったのかなという風に想像してます。離れ手前側が、

123 – 葉山のレーモンド夫妻。60年代末。

The Raymonds in Hayama (late 1960s)

124 – 軽井沢新スタジオ。60年代中葉。

New Studio in Karuizawa (mid-1960s)

were leaning. The pillars were supported by eaves with a length of 7 shaku and 5 sun (227 cm). In this way a small house was constructed on a plot of land running down to the sea. – The photograph was taken from the beach (p. 144). On the second floor there was a living room, a spacious balcony with a view of the beach and a 30 cm wide bar, which also served as a table. There was a good view of the whole of Hayama beach, and in the distance it was possible to see Mount Fuji. The first floor served as a studio. At that time Mr. Raymond was painting some kind of large-scale picture. In the region which ran down to the Isshiki coastline the sea was very beautiful, and so the studio was in the right place. I liked the house in Hayama the most of all Mr. Raymond's constructions.

PH: And was Mr. Raymond also fond of the house?

KK: Before he built the new studio in Karuizawa, he used to go to Hayama every weekend throughout the year. I think Mr. Raymond was very fond of that house. The wood stove on the second floor warmed the place beautifully. It was made of tin and in dimensions which were then the "standard size for Raymond's stove". He had the same stove in the house in Kōgaichō. The house in Kōgaichō had a salon on the ground floor, which was almost empty. An outside staircase led up to the first floor, where the living room and two bedrooms were located. In the middle was a bathroom and toilet. It was a very compact and practical house. On the side facing the sea there was a large side balcony with a beautiful view.

This is a superb photograph (fig. 122). In it are three pieces of pottery produced by Mr. Raymond himself. This photograph was among Mr. Raymond's negatives, if

125 – 軽井沢新スタジオ。1970年代。
New Studio in Karuizawa (1970s)

8畳の洋間で、2段ベッドが2組。そこに男が4人、寝泊りしてました。一番奥には3畳があるんですが、その3畳には女性が2人。合計で6人。加えて、運転手さん、コックさん、メイドさん、建築のスタッフが3人ですね。レーモンドの10年の中で、アメリカに滞在中期間と病気で行けなかった2回を除き、8年位は、軽井沢で7月の第1週の金曜日から、9月の第1週の金曜日まで、丸2か月間、住み込むというか、籠城していました。レーモンドさんは東京にも戻りません。我々は土日は帰ってもいいよという事になってますので、土日飛んで帰って、また戻ったりしてましたけど。

ホリー: という事は、お客さんはわざわざ打合せに東京から来られてた？

北澤: はい、軽井沢に呼んでいました。庭でバーベキューをして、美味しいお肉をご馳走になられて。我々も同席させてもらえるので喜んでいました（笑）。その頃の日本では、牛肉は希少で、食べられなかったんですね。昭和30年後半から40年初めっていうのはそういう時代だったんです。だから、お客さんが来るとご馳走にありつけるな、と。

ホリー: キャンプファイヤーの跡は今もありましたね。

北澤: 全く同じところにあります。写真に写っているのは、ミスター・レーモンドと、次が五代信作さん (157ページを参照)。それから、松原さん、ミセス・レーモンドと、小林さん、富田さん、２枚目の写真の右が私です。レー

he took it himself then he managed to choose a truly excellent angle: in it we see both his beloved dog and at the same time we have a view of Mount Fuji. – When Mr. Raymond's physical condition deteriorated and he decided to return to New Hope in America, he had to get rid of his property. He decided first of all to sell the house in Hayama. At that time I received a phone call from Mr. Raymond's secretary and cook in the middle of the night. She told me: "Mr. Kitazawa, something terrible has happened! Mr. Raymond has decided to sell his house in Hayama to some strange man." I remember it to this day. I contacted Mr. Raymond and asked him if we could meet together to discuss the sale. He agreed, and I immediately set out to see him. He told me that some lawyer wanted to buy the house from him, and that he'd promised to sell it to him. I was against him selling such an important work to someone unknown. I emphasised that the house should be bought by the Raymond Architectural Design Office, which would maintain it as an important monument. In the end my colleagues and I agreed that if that didn't happen, we'd club together and buy the house ourselves. He was very pleased to hear it, and said that the very next day he'd turn down the lawyer's offer. But the next day the buyer apparently told him that in the case of real estate a verbal promise was enough, and that if Mr. Raymond didn't sell the house to him then he'd sue. He promised to include a clause in the contract that he would look after the house well. Mr. Raymond had no other choice but to sell him the house. Three months later the house was demolished and the land was cleared. I can't even express in words how sorry I was. It's an unbelievable shame. A year later he decided also to sell the new studio in Karuizawa. A well-known businessman showed an interest in it. He even came to show the money he had prepared. But I was worried that this businessman wouldn't maintain the building appropriately, and that he wouldn't be capable of keeping it in good condition. I went to Mr. Raymond immediately and told him that this option shouldn't even be considered, and that the house should be bought and subsequently looked after by the Raymond Architectural Design Office. Mr. Raymond replied that the next day he'd try to obtain the consent of the Board of Directors. However, the result was negative. So I told him I'd buy the house myself. By doing so I considerably complicated my life. I was earning approximately forty to fifty thousand yen a month, and so I certainly couldn't afford to buy a house that cost over thirty million yen. It was practically impossible. But I remember the house in Hayama, and I wanted to save at least one of Raymond's constructions. I wanted to salvage it at all costs, and so I registered myself as the buyer. I had a lot of trouble to get sufficient money together, but eventually I succeeded in buying it, and today the house is in good condition. Apart from replacing the pictures and the pottery, I maintain the house in the condition in which Mr. Raymond left it. I try to show this house to the largest possible number of people, and every year three or four large groups of people come to take a tour of it.

In the next photograph you can see the entrance to the house (p. 148). When you look at the diagram you can see the living room in the centre, which also served as

126 – 軽井沢地区の土壌調査。左から、ノエミ・レーモンド、K.北澤、アントニン・レーモンド、松野氏。70年代初頭。

Surveying the terrain of the land plot in Karuizawa. From left: Noémi Raymond, Kitazawa Koichi, Antonín Raymond and Mr. Matsuno (early 1960s)

モンドさんって、写真を撮られることが嫌いな人でして。カメラを向けると怒るんですね。

なので、写真があまり無いんです。あれだけ軽井沢に行っていても、この位しか無くて。散々探して、1枚出てきたのが、これ（151ページを参照)。独立して私が譲り受ける事になった時のスタッフと撮ったものです。右の真ん中が私。それからレーモンドさん。レーモンドさんの写真も当時の牛肉と同じくらい希少です。写真嫌いも困ったもので、そう簡単に撮らせてもらえない。はい。軽井沢では、孫のビッキーが撮ったご夫妻の写真があります。テラスのところの写真が、いい写真だと思いますね。寒い時期に、お孫さんが連れて来られた時に撮った写真らしいんですね。ちゃんと動物愛護のおばあちゃんが犬を連れている。だいたい犬3匹、猫1匹ぐらいは常に飼っていまして、動物を大変愛していたおばあちゃんでした。

ホリー: 以前、お邪魔させていただいた際に、犬の足を洗うためのお部屋があったのを記憶しています。

北澤: それは浴室だと思います。浴室が外から入れるようになってまして。必

a studio. It has a twelve-sided ground plan. It's evident from the original sketches that the first design envisaged a circular ground plan, but because the building was to be constructed out of wood it would have been complicated to place beams and sliding partitions etc. inside a circle. The twelve-sided plan is composed of walls with a length of 7 shaku and 5 sun (227 cm). At the rear was a Japanese room, which they called the "guest room". Also here is the master bedroom of the Raymonds, the bathroom with a washbasin, bath and toilet, on the left is a kitchen, a chamber and room for the servants. Here you can see the neighbouring house (fig. 171, p. 199), which stood to the left of the main building, where the employees slept. I was surprised that the neighbouring house for employees was actually built seven years earlier than the main house. I wondered why the construction of the main house took seven years, but it was most probably due to finances, since the main house was finished at a time when the firm received payment for the construction of the Gunma Music Centre and Nanzan University. Most architects don't become rich, and so I imagine that Mr. Raymond also had financial difficulties. In the front part of the neighbouring house there was a room in Western style with a surface area of 8 tatamis (approximately 13.2 m2), where there were two bunk beds, on which four

127 – アントニン・レーモンド、北澤オフィスの従業員とともに。1972年。

Antonín Raymond with employees from Kitazawa's office (1972)

128 – レーモンド夫妻、軽井沢新スタジオにて。1970年代。

The Raymonds in the New Studio in Karuizawa (1970s)

ず朝夕、散歩しますので、帰って来た時は浴室で足を洗って中に入れるという、そういう習慣でしたね。動物愛護のエピソードとして、こんなことがありました。軽井沢で仕事をしてましたら、虻が飛んで来たんですね。私がスケールを持ってピンってやったら、たまたま当りまして、飛んでいった先がミセスの足元に行っちゃったんです。そしたら、羽を持って私のところに来て、「これ、可哀想でしょう」と。私は可哀想と思わないんですけれども、「なるほどな」と思いましてね。

ホリー: 虻ですよね？

北澤: 虻。刺されると痛いんですよ、腫れて。でも、その後、スプレー持ってきて、「あなた、これを使ってれば、相手が寄ってきませんから」と。

チャプコヴァー: 話がちょっと逸れてしまいましたね。私から質問があります。レーモンドさんの仕事における最も重要な要素とは、何でしょうか。

men slept. At the rear was a room with a surface area of 3 tatamis (4.8 m2) for two women, so six people in total. In addition there was a chauffeur, a cook and a servant. There were three architects here. I worked for Mr. Raymond for ten years, and I spent two months here from the beginning of July to the beginning of September every year, with the exception of the period when Mr. Raymond was in the USA or when I was ill. Mr. Raymond remained in Karuizawa for the whole summer, but we could return to Tokyo at weekends. I sometimes used to leave in a hurry on Saturday, but I returned again after the weekend.

PH: Does that mean that clients from Tokyo had to go to Karuizawa to attend meetings?

KK: Yes, they did, we invited them to Karuizawa. The clients received invitations to a barbecue in the garden. We employees were able to join them, and we were over the moon about it *(laughs)*. At that time beef was a rare treat in Japan, there wasn't often an opportunity to try it. From the late 1930s to the early 1940s, during the Shōwa era, it was that kind of time. Every time a client came they told us not to descend upon the food straight away like locusts.

PH: The marks of the fireplace can still be seen there to this day.

KK: They're in exactly the same place. In the photograph you can see Mr. Raymond with Mr. Godai Shinsaku (p. 157). Also here is Mr. Matsubara, Mrs. Raymond, Mr. Kobayashi and Mr. Tomita. Mr. Raymond didn't like being photographed. He got angry whenever someone pointed a camera at him. That's the reason why I don't have many photographs. Even though I used to go to Karuizawa often, I only have a couple from there. After strenuously searching I found this one (p. 151). It's a photo with employees at the time when I set up my own business. I'm in the second row on the right, Mr. Raymond is at the front. Photographs of Mr. Raymond are even rarer than beef was at that time *(laughs)*. He didn't like photographs at all, and it was simply impossible to take a photo of him. And here are both of the Raymonds in Karuizawa (fig. 128, p. 152), as photographed by their granddaughter Vicky. I think the photo from the terrace is excellent. The grandmother, who was an animal lover, is with her dog; at almost any time they had three dogs and one cat. The grandmother simply loved animals.

PH: I remember that when I visited the house once, there was a room for washing the dogs' paws.

KK: That was probably the bathroom. There was an entrance to it from outside. Mrs. Raymond was in the habit of washing the dogs' paws after every morning and evening walk, before she took them into the house. She was a great animal conservationist. This also relates to the following story. Once when we were working in the house in Karuizawa, a horsefly flew in through the window. I swiped at it with a ruler, and by chance I hit it. It fell right at Mrs. Raymond's legs. She took it by the wings, brought it to me and said: "You don't do that!" I didn't share her opinion, but I understood her.

PH: But surely it was only a horsefly?

KK: Indeed, and if one of them bites you it swells up and it's pretty painful. But then she brought me a spray and said that if I used it, the horseflies would avoid me.

HČ: We've gone off topic a little. I'd like to ask: what was most essential for you in Mr.

129 – アントニン・レーモンド展。松坂屋百貨店にて。東京、1970年。

Exhibition of the work of Antonín Raymond in the exhibition hall of the Matsuzakaya department store (Tokyo, 1970)

そして、現在の建築に、レーモンドさんが与えた最も大きな影響とは一体何なのでしょうか？

北澤: 最近、軽井沢を見学に来る大学も多いんです。団体ではいきなり60人で押しかけてくるとかありまして。ちょっとびっくりしてしまうんですが、それだけレーモンドさんが現在、見直されているという事がわかるんですね。デザインの先生はもちろんなのですが、日本建築史の先生も多いんですね。建築史を教えていくと、どうしてもレーモンドにぶつかる。特に、日本の建築史、近代建築史を追求していくと、必ずそうなる。それで、作品を見たい、生徒に見せたい、と言ってやってくる。それから卒論のテーマとして扱われることも増えているようです。そのため、卒論生も一緒になって見に来るという事が多いんですね。アントニン・レーモンドという人は非常に堅実な建築デザイン手法

Raymond's work? And what in your view was Antonín Raymond biggest contribution to contemporary architecture?

KK: In recent times a lot of university students have been coming for a tour of the house in Karuizawa. I even had a group of sixty people who wanted to view the house. It's surprising, but it's evidence of how the view of Mr. Raymond is changing at present. Not only experts in design, but also historians of architecture are showing an interest. If anyone is teaching the history of architecture in Japan, they can't avoid Raymond. This applies especially in the case of modern architecture. And as a result there's an interest in Raymond, they want to see the house, show it to their students, and so they come to Karuizawa. Moreover, Raymond's work is increasingly appearing as the topic of dissertations. It has occurred repeatedly that a group of students writing their thesis on Raymond come for a tour of the house. Antonín Raymond created stable architecture, he didn't construct buildings that appeared extravagant. Contemporary Japanese architecture makes the opposite impression on me. There's a clear inclination towards excessive extravagance. I say to myself that I'm acting as a bulwark against these tendencies. I long for the work of Antonín Raymond to be re-evaluated. I believe that even in the present day, Raymond's principles are an important component of the theory of architecture.

HČ: I think you're right. Did you ever ask Mr. Raymond what aspects of his own work he considered most important?

KK: At the moment when I sensed that I would have to say goodbye to Mr. Raymond, I resolved to hold an exhibition for him. I also prepared promotional materials for the occasion. I really made an effort, and I prepared everything necessary, including the graphic design and layout of the photographs. When I was preparing the catalogue, right at the beginning I asked Mr. Raymond to advise me on what I should write. Without a moment's hesitation Mr. Raymond wrote the following sentence: "True beauty contains only those things that come from nature, they are simple and at the same time honest, economical and simultaneously functional." I believe that this is the ultimate standpoint that he arrived at. I later asked a famous photographer to take a photograph of Mr. Raymond, who nonetheless protested with all his might (fig. 46, p. 53), because I needed a photograph of him for the catalogue. It was a superb photograph. Mr. Raymond always frowned in photographs, but in this one he had a warm smile on his face.
– That photograph was then exhibited at the memorial service held for Mr. Raymond.
– The photographer in question also took a group photograph. Mr. Raymond is in the centre and we are standing around him. In this photo also he's smiling for a change. I'm standing right behind him, on his left is Mr. Godai Shinsaku, on the right is Mrs. Raymond and in the foreground Messrs Satō, Kosaka, Tanabe and a number of others.

PH: There is a memorial room in the Raymond Architectural Design Office. It was there that I realised that the Kōgaichō building was constructed from thin logs. Was Mr. Raymond particular about constructions made of delicate materials?

KK: Before the studio in Azabu was built, Mr. Raymond had an office on the construction site of the apartments for the employees of the American embassy (see p. 27). It was a temporary building made of logs. He later used a similar procedure also when

130 – アントニン・レーモンド、同僚とともに。笄町の設計スタジオにて。70年代初頭。

Antonín Raymond with colleagues in the drafting office of the studio in Kōgaichō (beginning of 1970s)

で、奇をてらった建物は造らない。どちらかというと今の日本の近代建築は、奇をてらう方に走っている傾向が強いので、そういうものに対する僕は警鐘じゃないかなと思っています。見直しを求めているというかね。ですから、やはり建築の本筋といいますか、建築の哲学には、レーモンドの哲学が未だに私は生きていると思っています。

チャプコヴァー: おっしゃる通りだと思います。生前、レーモンドさんご本人に作品を作り上げている主な要素などについて伺ったことはありますか？

北澤: 私、レーモンドとのお別れが近づいたことを察して、どうしても最後にレーモンドの展覧会をやってお別れをしたかったんです。その際にパンフレットを作成しました。そこには一所懸命、私自身が、写真の割り付けから何もかも、担当しました。パンフレットを作るにあたって、最初にレーモンドさんに「どういう言葉を書いたらいいか、教えてください」って聞いたんです。そうしたらサッサッと、次の言葉を書いてくれたんです。「最も簡素にして直裁、機能的にして経済的、かつ自然なるもののみが、真によき美を有する」と。ですから、これが、レーモンドの最終的な結論なんですね。また、嫌がるレーモンドに、どうしてもパンフレットに載せたいので、「写真を撮らせてくれ」って頼んで、ある有名なカメラマンに写真を撮ってもらいました。素晴らしい写真でした。彼は、いつもしかめっ面でしか写真に写らないんですが、この時ばかりは、にこやかに写りまして。この写真はレーモンドのミサに使いました。その時に

軽井沢新スタジオ（1962年、長野県＝現存）
「戦前の山荘が新軽井沢ゴルフ倶楽部の中程にあって、早朝の散歩の途中に、管理を頼んだ土屋さん（農家）宅でお茶をいただく習慣がありました。その南側に小高い丘があり、そのころから土屋さんに、この場所に夏のアトリエを造りたいと頼んでいたそうです。田園や森、山を広く望める眺望のある敷地であり、その為に建物の床高が三段に分かれ、各々の景色に親しむことができます。アトリエは12角形。杉丸太のトラス組で、中央暖炉の煙突がRC造の構造体であり、12辺のトラスを受けています。スパンが大きい場合に、単に梁成を大きくして架構するのは間違いで、細い部材でトラス状にして美しい骨組を造り、全部を見せてデザインするのがレーモンド調でありました。インテリアは壁がラワンロータリー合板目透かし真鍮釘打、木製建具に椅子付は、築後56年経過した現在でも美しく保存されております。夏は麻布の設計室には冷房がなく、涼しい軽井沢に7月第1週の金曜日に設計スタッフ4名、メイド、コック、運転手、秘書の8名と夫妻が軽井沢に移動し9月第1週の金曜日まで2か月間をこのアトリエで仕事をしておりました。」（北澤）

131 – クライエント（上智大学）との会議。軽井沢新スタジオにて。左から、北澤、西嶋圭子、小林邦子、レーモンド、マーカス、S.五代、松原。60年代後半。

Meeting with client (Sophia University) in the New Studio in Karuizawa.
From left: Kitazawa, Nishijima Keiko, Kobayashi Kuniko, Raymond, Marcus, Godai Shinsaku, Matsubara (late 1960s)

constructing the studio in Azabu. You could also say that there's a connection there with the mountain chalet in Karuziawa (New Studio). When you examine the structure carefully, you find for example that there's a column, a log in the master bedroom, and that it's reinforced with struts (see fig. 59–61). On the left you can see how the strut is connected to the log with an angle brace. If the span is larger, the Japanese use more massive beams in the construction of wooden houses. Mr. Raymond regarded this as a mistake. If the span is large, it's necessary to come up with a suitable structural design. In this case the struts clearly demonstrate their strength. The essence is to reinforce the entire construction of the beam and the log, which supports the roof, using narrow struts in the shape of scissors. As a result, in a number of places the beams are placed close to one another. – Mr. Raymond occasionally used to say that the chief task of architectural design was to create a structure so that it would create a very solid impression even with narrow beams. I greatly respect Mr. Raymond for that opinion. – Over the course of my entire career I've designed several chalets and houses in Karuizawa. The mountain chalets mostly belong to the local landowners. When I've asked them whether they'd like to take a look at Raymond's new studio, all of them replied that they would. And so I show them Raymond's twelve-sided houses, the tour begins, and all of them are surprised by the combination of paper walls, wooden beams and plywood. They all say that if they'd known it was possible to create such an amazing space using those resources, they'd have done the same themselves. At that moment it's decided that when building a chalet they'll use logs. The design is very simple. Usually architecture studios get themselves into debt because

The Raymonds' pre-war summer villa was located on the site of the golf club in New Karuizawa. On their morning walk, the Raymonds were in the habit of going to the house of the caretaker, the farmer Mr. Tsuchiya, for tea. On the southern side of his house was a small hill, on which the couple wished to build a studio. Spreading out around the plot of land are mountains, fields and forests, and so in order to have a good view of everything they divided the house into three parts. The studio is in a dodecagonal shape. In a cedar frame is the chimney of the central fireplace of an RC construction, fixed on 12 sides with a truss. The span of the construction is considerable, but it would have been an error to use a more robust frame. Raymond's design consists in the use of a cluster made of material with a narrow profile, from which he created solid structures in his characteristic style. The walls of the room are made of plywood panels joined together with brass rivets. The wooden construction, including the wooden furniture, remains beautifully preserved even after more than fifty years. – Because the drafting office in Azabu did not have air conditioning, on the Friday of the first week in July four architects, a housemaid, a cook, chauffeur and a secretary moved to the cooler Karuizawa, thus a total of eight people plus the Raymonds. We worked in Karuizawa for two months, and then returned to Tokyo on the Friday of the first week in September. (Kitazawa Kōichi)

132 – 足立別荘。1966年。
Adachi summer villa (1966)

は、集合写真でレーモンドさんを中心にした写真も撮ってもらいましたね。これも笑顔で写っています。珍しくね。レーモンドの真後ろにいるのが私で、その左が五代信作さん、右にミセス、手前に佐藤さん、小坂さん、田辺さん等のメンバーが写っています (157ページを参照)。

ホリー: レーモンド事務所には記念室がありますね。そこでは細い丸太で建物ができあがっていることがわかります。レーモンドさんはそういう細い材料を使って部品を組み立てることについてこだわりをお持ちでしたか？

北澤: 麻布に建設する以前は現場事務所が、赤坂のアメリカ大使館員アパートメントの中にあったんですね。急ごしらえ足場丸太を使って組んだのですが、

133 – 足立別荘、内観。

Interior of the Adachi summer villa (1966)

of designs of chalets and holiday homes. Today it's a long time since the economic bubble burst and there was an exodus of employees from studios, and there's an increase in the number of designs of summer residences and chalets. It's a great pleasure for me to work on these kinds of orders. Logs maintain their attractive appearance even after ten or twenty years. They have only one disadvantage, which is that they're too expensive, but I always try to procure them as cheaply as possible. I always order stripped logs at a sawmill in the Yoshino region in the Nara prefecture, because they sell me slightly damaged logs, which might for example have knots or other minor defects, for a lower price. Thanks to this I can use logs on the construction, while maintaining relatively low costs.

PH: At the time when the studio was being built in Karuizawa, the roofs were thatched.

その方式が麻布のものに繋がっているんですね。さらに言えば、軽井沢の山荘にもつながってる。詳しく見てみますと、例えば夫婦の寝室。柱があって、上り丸太があって、それを方杖で支えてる。左側は、やっぱり方杖と丸太の火打材で組み合わせています。日本人の木造の造り方は、スパンが大きくなれば、梁材を大きくしちゃう。それは間違ってる、とレーモンドさんはお考えになられた。スパンが大きくなったら骨組みを工夫してデザインする。この場合方杖が、非常に力を発揮するんですね。ですから、柱も、あの上り丸太も、細くて鋏方杖で、補強をしてやる、というのが基本なんです。つまるところ、1間ピッチで、丸柱が立っていくわけです。このようにして、非常に細いメンバーで、それを力強く見せるのが、建築家のデザインなんだ、と生前よくおっしゃっていました。私もこの点は、とても尊敬してます。私自身、軽井沢で別荘をたくさん設計していますけれども、軽井沢の山荘って地主さんのオーナーが多いんですね。彼らに「レーモンドの別荘を見られませんか」って尋ねると、「うん、見たい見たい」って言うから、レーモンドの十二角形を見せるんです。打ち合わせはそこからスタートします。皆さん、丸太と障子と、それからラワンベニヤという組み合わせにびっくりされて、「こんな素敵な空間ができるんだったら、同じように造ってほしい」と口をそろえて言います。その瞬間には、丸太を採用するっていうのが決まっている。これデザインとして、非常に楽なんです。普通、設計事務所で別荘設計すると、赤字になっちゃうんです。でも、バブルがはじけて、スタッフが少なくなって別荘も設計できるようになったので、現在は別荘を引き受けるようになって。非常に楽しんでやっています。丸太って10年経っても20年経っても綺麗なままなんですね。ただ欠点は高いので、安く仕入れなきゃいけない。だから、あの磨き丸太を造ってる奈良の吉野の工場に頼んで、跳ね出し品を回してもらうんです。ひび割れが入っちゃった、節が出てきちゃった、えくぼが出ちゃった、という丸太を安く譲ってもらうわけです。そのおかげで、工事費を安く抑えて、丸太を使ったものができるわけです。

ホリー: スタジオを始める時は、屋根が草になってますよね。

北澤: カラマツの枝ですね。

ホリー: あのような屋根の扱いについてお聞かせください。

北澤: この写真は、レーモンドさんが造った最初の竣工写真の一枚です (147ページを参照)。茅葺きで非常に綺麗にできています。実際に今は茅はのってません。もう既にこの時、日本の消防法で変な法律ができて、屋根材は不燃材としなければいけない、となった。茅葺きが造れなくなっちゃったんですね。板葺きもできなくなっちゃった。どうしたかって言うと屋根を瓦棒で造って、鉄板で造って、竣工検査を受けてから、内緒で、茅をのせるんですね（笑）。鉄板屋根の上に丸太を組んで、竹と丸太を茅に結び付けていくという茅葺きの方法ですので、茅がもたないんです。勾配が緩いともう10年で駄目になっち

KK: They were thatched with Japanese larch branches.
PH: Please tell us a little more about those roofs.
KK: This is a photograph of the construction immediately after it was completed (New Studio in Karuizawa, 1963, fig. 124, p. 147). A beautiful thatched (kayabuki) roof. Today it's no longer thatched. Even then there was a special fire law in place that stipulated that roofs had to be made of non-combustible materials. It was no longer possible to continue making thatched roofs. The same applied to shingle roofs. People used to circumvent the law by making roofs out of tiles or tin, and as soon as the building had passed the inspection, surreptitiously converting the roof to kayabuki. *(Laughs)* Logs are attached to a tin roof, and then thatching is tied to the logs using bamboo. However, a roof constructed by this method won't last long. Even on a not very steep roof, the thatching will only survive the weather conditions for a maximum of ten years. The craftsmen who were able to make thatched roofs have virtually disappeared from Japan. If you order a roof from one of the few who've remained, it'll be very expensive. It's virtually impossible to cover a house with a thatched roof in this day and age. That stupid law is ruining traditional Japanese architecture. It's a great shame, kayabuki roofs are wonderful. I wish people would understand. I'd like the state to pass a law that would respect it. For example, thatched roofs have an exceptionally good insulating function against heat, cold and noise. A kayabuki roof is an amazing thing. Today the house in Karuizawa has a tin roof, and when it rains I can't help myself, that noise gets on my nerves. I tell myself that one of the main tasks of architects today is to find an answer to the question of what material to choose for the roof.
HČ: This might be a somewhat unpleasant question, but we know that Mr. Raymond left Japan in 1936 and didn't return until 1948. Did you ever talk to him about that period?
KK: I know very little about that story. At that time Mr. Raymond didn't go directly to America, but spent some time in India. There he built the Golconde, the dormitory of the ashram, together with George Nakashima (1905–1990), who he brought with him as his assistant. I think that it was only afterwards that he went to America. Some critics contend that during the time he was in America he collaborated with the American army, but I'm absolutely convinced that this wasn't the case. By chance he had been in the army, and they assigned him to the intelligence services, and so it's possible that he could have been called in for consultations. I myself belong to the wartime generation, and as a result I know very well the power of those napalm raids. During such an attack houses are immediately engulfed in flames. The idea that Mr. Raymond would actually have proposed such attacks is nonsense. He worshipped Japan, and there is no way he would have approved such a thing. I only know that when he was asked what the houses were like in Japan, he answered that the majority of houses were made of wood. When the Raymonds returned to Japan after the war and saw the devastation following the bombing, they burst into heartfelt tears. Moreover, he made a substantial contribution to the rebuilding of Japan. As you well know, shortly after his return he created the Tokyo headquarters of the Reader's Digest, as well as his house in Azabu, which also served as a studio. – We've already mentioned the Reader's

ゃいます。茅葺きが全体に日本から消えちゃたもんですから、職人がいないのと、数少ない職人にお願いすると非常に高いという事で、現在はなかなか実現できません。そういう変な法律が日本の伝統的な建築を駄目にしている、造れなくしているというのが、非常に残念です。茅葺きっていうのは素晴らしい。そのことをわかってほしい。理解ある法律を国が作ってほしい。音響の面でも、寒暖対策の面でも、茅葺きの方が本当に効果があって素晴らしいんです。現在は軽井沢も、鉄板屋根のままになってますから、雨の音も気になってしかたない。今後は屋根材をどう扱うかが建築家の1つの命題じゃないかなと思っています。

チャプコヴァー: ちょっと聞きにくい事かなとも思うんですが、レーモンドさんは1936年に日本を発って、それから1948年にまた戻ってこられますよね？ その間のことを何かお話しになっていたりしますか？

北澤: 断片的には聞いています。この時、直接アメリカに帰られたんじゃなくて、インドに行っているんですね。それで、修道院の宿舎を造っている。ジョージ・ナカシマさんだけを連れてって、助手にして、立派な建物を造った。その後、アメリカに戻っていった、というのが経緯かと思います。一部の評論家が、戦時中にレーモンドがアメリカ軍に協力したと書いていますが、私はそんなことは絶対になかったと思っています。たまたま軍に所属して、情報機関に配属されたので、確かに相談はあったかもしれません。私も戦中派なので、焼夷弾の威力はよく知っています。爆撃が来ると、家がばぁーっと燃え盛るんです。そんなものをレーモンドさんが提案したなんてバカなことありますか。日本を愛するレーモンドがそんな事を提案するはずがない。知っている限りだと、日本はどういうい家が多いかと聞かれ「木造がほとんどだ」と答えたくらいでしょうか。でも、戦後帰ってきて焼野原になったところを見て、２人で泣いたようです。それから日本の再建に注力するんです。後はみなさんご存知の通り、戦後帰ってきて間もなく、リーダースダイジェスト東京支社や麻布の自邸兼アトリエを造り、拠点を構えたのです。リーダースダイジェストの話が出たのでちょっと説明しますが、あれの何が素晴らしいかっていうと、スチールサッシュの引き違いを初めて造ったということですね。それから有名なのは、Pタイル、アスファルトタイル、床。Pタイルっていうのは、その後になると当たり前になったんですが、アメリカから小さな見本を持ってきて、田島応用化学というアスファルトの会社に、「アスファルトでできているから製品化しなさい」と指示したところから始まったんです。田島応用化学の社長を呼んで話したら一生懸命開発してきて、作ってきてくれた、と。でも、何度も作ってはダメ出しをし、その繰り返しの果てに何とかできるようになった、という経緯があるわけです。あと、忘れてはならないのは、天井の吸音テックス。これもアメリカからサンプルを持ってきて、分析してみると、なんと味の素さんの廃材でできるという事がわかって、味の素さんが開発して吸音テックスを作ったというから驚きです。これらの

134 – リーダーズダイジェスト。東京、1951年。

Reader's Digest (Tokyo, 1951)

素材は輸入しようと思えば簡単にできたと思うんですけども、レーモンドさんは日本企業を育てたいという気持ちが非常に強い方だったので、そうやって戦後間もない頃に企業を巻き込んで再建していったのです。

チャプコヴァー: 貴重なお話しですね。ありがとうございました。

135 – リーダーズダイジェスト。東京、1951年。

Reader's Digest (Tokyo, 1951)

136 – リーダーズダイジェスト。東京、1951年。

Reader's Digest (Tokyo, 1951)

Digest headquarters, and if I were to stress any feature of interest it would be the fact that it was here that sliding windows in steel frames were used. The asphalt and PVC floor is also well-known. At the time he brought a small sample with him from America, and gave instructions to the Tajima company, which was engaged in the manufacture of asphalt products, to start producing these floor coverings, because they were made of asphalt. He called the company director of Tajima, and their conversation led to the firm making a concerted effort to develop and produce this new feature. However, at the outset a lot of mistakes appeared in the production, and it took a while before repeated testing of the manufacturing procedures finally brought about the successful the production of asphalt floor coverings. And I mustn't forget the soundproofing materials used in the roofs. These too he brought as a sample, originally from America. When he subjected this material to analysis, he discovered that it was possible to produce it from the waste products produced by the Ajinomoto company. Back then I was very surprised when I found out that the Ajinomoto company announced that it had developed and produced the soundproofing material itself. If he'd wanted to, Mr. Raymond could easily have imported this material, but he was the type of man who liked to see Japanese companies develop. In fact he applied such a procedure immediately after the war when he engaged Japanese firms in the rebuilding of the country.

HČ: Mr. Kitazawa, thank you very much for your important testimony.

デッサン
絵画
陶芸品

drawings
paintings
ceramics

137 – A.レーモンド、水彩画（無日付け）。

A. Raymond, watercolour (undated)

138 – A.レーモンド、水彩画（無日付け）。

A. Raymond, watercolour (undated)

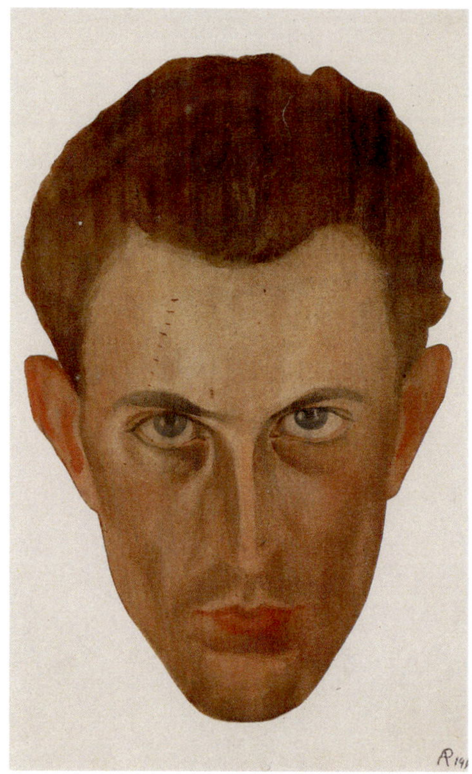

139 – A.レーモンド、自画像、1910年。

A. Raymond, self-portrait (1910)

140 – A.レーモンド、水彩画（無日付け）。
A. Raymond, watercolour (undated)

141 – A.レーモンド、水彩画（無日付け）。
A. Raymond, watercolour (undated)

142 – A.レーモンド、ミクストメディア（無日付け）。

A. Raymond, combined technique (undated)

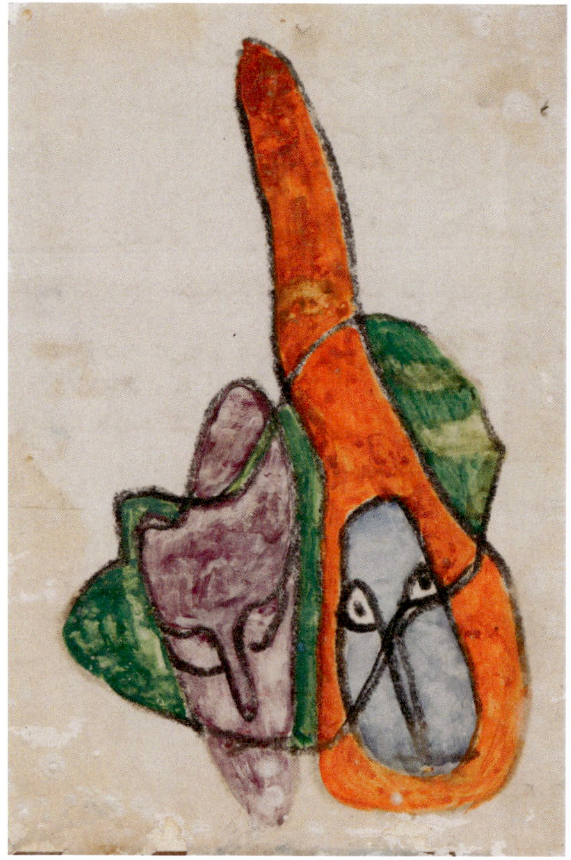

143 – A.レーモンド、水彩画（無日付け）。

A. Raymond, watercolour (undated)

144 – A. レーモンド、デッサン
(無日付け)。

A. Raymond, drawing on paper
(undated)

145 – A. レーモンド、水彩画
(無日付け)。

A. Raymond, watercolour
(undated)

146 – A.レーモンド、帝国ホテルで働く日本人大工たち。1920年。

Japanese carpenters on the construction of the Imperial Hotel (1920)

147 – A.レーモンド、水彩画（無日付け）。

A. Raymond, watercolour (undated)

148 – A.レーモンド、1960年代。

A. Raymond in his studio (1960s)

149–150 – A.レーモンド、陶芸作品、(無日付け)。

A. Raymond, pottery (undated)

151–152 – N.レーモンド、インク デッサン、(n•i•pサイン、無日付け、1918年以前)。

Noémi Raymond (ink drawing, signed n•i•p, undated, before 1918)

153 – 帝国ホテル設計室でN.レーモンドが孔雀をモチーフに描いた壁画の原画 (水彩画、1920年頃)。ライトに採用されて実施設計に進められた。

Noémi Raymond, design of the interior decoration of the Imperial Hotel (colour drawing, approx. 1920). The design was accepted and realised by Frank Lloyd Wright

154 – ノエミ・レーモンド「女騎手」。モデルはフランク・ロイド・ライトの娘。タリアセンでの研究期、ウィスコンシン州、アメリカ合衆国。

Noémi Raymond, the rider. The model was Frank Lloyd Wright's daughter (from the period of her studies in Taliesin, Wisconsin, USA)

155–156 – N.レーモンド、インク デッサン、(n•i•pサイン、無日付け、1918年以前)。

Noémi Raymond (ink drawing, signed n•i•p, undated, before 1918)

157 – 足立別荘。内観。1966年。

Interior of the Adachi villa (1966)

北澤 興一 建築家 (1962~1971)

小林 薫 建築家 (1964~2004)

小林 邦子 ノエミ・レーモンドのアシスタント (1962~1969)

西嶋 泰親 建築家 (1954~2002)

西嶋 圭子 アントニン・レーモンドの秘書 (1966~1970)

Kitazawa Kōichi architect (1962–1971)

Kobayashi Kaoru architect (1964–2004)

Kobayashi Kuniko assistant to Noémi Raymond (1962–1969)

Nishijima Yasuchika architect (1954–2002)

Nishijima Keiko secretary of Antonín Raymond (1966–1970)

北澤： 本日の座談会メンバーはヘレナさんの依頼から私が4人を選ばせていただきました。軽井沢の夏２ヶ月間をレーモンド夫妻とともに過ごした仲間です。西嶋さんは私より先輩で、このチェコ大使館の建設にあたり、施設の設計と施工監理にかかわる責任者として従事されました。

チャプコヴァー： アントニン・レーモンドさん及びノエミ・レーモンドさんと関係が深かった5人に集まっていただきお話を聞きたいと思います。初めに今お話が出ていた、このチェコ大使館の設計について、議論いたしましょう。

ホリー： 私は、過日、この施設のリニューアル工事をした時に、建設当時の設計図を拝見いたしました。レーモンド設計事務所のスタンプがはっきりと押されていて、保存されていたことを確認いたしました。

北澤： 西嶋さんが設計に参画していましたので、建築許可を取得するために東京都等との折衝もしていました。この建物については、全て把握しています。レーモンドさんがアメリカに帰国する前からでしょうか。確か、帰国されたのは1973年ですよね。

西嶋： チェコスロヴァキア国内で行われた設計コンペにより、大使館施設の設計・監理を担当する建築家として選出されたイワン・スカーラさんと在日チェコスロヴァキア大使館から、レーモンドさんにコンタクトがあったのは、帰国された３～４年以前の1969年頃だと思います。

チャプコヴァー： その時、レーモンドさんは、まだお元気でしたか

西嶋： スカーラさん[1] 達がレーモンドさんに、コアーキテクトとしての協力を要請しに来訪されていた頃まではご健在でした。その後、レーモンドさんが体調を崩されて帰米された後で、レーモンド設計事務所がコアーキテクトとして

158 – ゴルフを楽しむアントニン・レーモンド。1970年。

Antonín Raymond on the golf course (ca. 1970)

01 Ivan Skála (1935生まれ)1960年代または1970年代チェコスロバキアの代表的な建築家だった。

Kitazawa: Upon Helena Čapková's suggestion I have taken the liberty of inviting four people to today's discussion. They are my colleagues, who spent the summer months together with the Raymonds in Karuizawa. Mr. Nishijima joined the firm before me, and was responsible for the architectural design and construction supervision of the building of the Czechoslovak embassy in Tokyo, where we are currently seated.
HČ: I invited the five of you to this discussion because you had a deep relationship with Antonín Raymond and his wife Noémi. To start with I'd like to ask you about the architectural design of the building of the Czechoslovak embassy that you've just mentioned.
PH: At the time when the embassy building was undergoing renovation, I had the opportunity to consult the original diagrams, and so I can state that they have been preserved, with a still clearly legible stamp of the Raymond Architectural Design Office.
Kitazawa: Mr. Nishijima contributed to the architectural design of the building directly, and negotiated with the Tokyo authorities concerning their consent for the construction. He knows everything about this building. I believe that this was before Mr. Raymond returned to the USA. If I'm not mistaken, he returned to the USA in 1973?
Nishijima: I think that Mr. Raymond was contacted by Ivan Skála, who won the architectural competition in Czechoslovakia and was appointed chief architect on the project, and by the Czechoslovak embassy in Japan at some time in 1969, thus four years before Mr. Raymond returned to America.
HČ: Was Mr. Raymond still working at that time?
Nishijima: When Mr. Raymond was visited by Ivan Skála,[1] who wanted to request his co-operation in the design of the embassy building, Mr. Raymond was still at his zenith. Afterwards his health deteriorated. The decision that the Raymond Architectural Office would collaborate on the project wasn't taken until he was back in the USA. The first to be sent to Japan was Mr. Hrdlička.

159 – ゴルフを楽しむノエミ・レーモンド。1970年。

Noémi Raymond playing golf (ca. 1970)

Kitazawa: Kitazawa Kōichi
HČ: Helena Čapková
PH: Petr Holý
Nishijima: Nishijima Yasuchika
ET: Eva Takamine, head of Czech Centre Tokyo
Kobayashi: Kobayashi Kaoru

01 Ivan Skála (born 1935) made his name as a designer of Czechoslovak representative architecture in the late 1960s and early 1970s.

協力することが決定されました。最初に、来日・駐在されたのは、ハルドリチカさんでした。

ホリー： それは駐日大使でいらした時ですね。

西嶋： 大使ではなく、ハルドリチカさんは外務省の営繕担当技官です。スカーラさんが来日するまで、ハルドリチカさんは事前準備をすすめていました。大使館の建設用地は、治外法権であるにも拘わらず、東京都では建築許可が不可欠となっているので、東京都の関係部局と折衝を始めました。

ホリー： 東京の許可が必要だったんですね。厳しい。

西嶋： 東京都の指導に基づき、許可申請書を提出しましたが、公徳会を含む審査の結果は、不許可でした。計画施設の面積と高さが、この建設敷地に対して、建築基準法に定められている数値を大幅に超過しており、周辺の環境の阻害が危惧され、さらに近隣の反対が強かったことが理由でした。数ヶ月か後に、スカーラさんが来日し、可能な限り法の規制に沿うため、機能として支障のない施設を地下室に移して地上の高さと床面積を低減した案を作成しました。再度許可申請書を提出し、公聴会を含む審査を経て許可を取得し、実施設計に着手したのです。スカーラさんとハルドリチカさんは、工事が竣工するまで駐在していました。

チャプコヴァー： その時、この外務省の方はどこに住んでいましたか？

西嶋： 港区伊皿子の賃貸マンション住んでいました。

ホリー: この敷地はもともと江戸時代のお屋敷の跡でしたよね。島津家でしたか。大使館の敷地をチェコスロヴァキア国が、どのようにして入手したのか、それはまだ謎なのです。購入したのか、それとも授与されたのか。

西嶋： 多分、購入したのだと思います。昔のことは判りませんが、この敷地を取得した時は私有地でした。名前は忘れましたが有名な方で、住宅一棟の敷地として一区画で所有されていました。

ホリー： 私はいろいろ資料室とかで調べましたが、チェコスロヴァキアの時代のことなので、関係する書類等の資料が保存されていませんでした。この敷地を入手した経緯を知りたいのです。私有地としては結構膨大な敷地ですね。

西嶋： 銀杏の大木が敷地の真中に数本ありましたね。敷地の西側に存在する銀杏の大木はそれを移植したものです。伐採・廃棄するより、移植により造園に役立てる選択でした。

160 – 在東京チェコスロヴァキア大使館建設チーム。前列に外務省のハルドリチカ氏と建築家イワンスカーラ氏。1970年代。

Implementation team of the construction of the Czechoslovak embassy in Tokyo. Mr. Hrdlička from the Ministry of Foreign Affairs and the architect Ivan Skála are seated in the front row (1970s)

161 – 在東京チェコスロヴァキア大使館。1971–1977年。

Building of the Czechoslovak embassy in Tokyo (1971–1977)

PH: Did he come to Japan as the ambassador?
Nishijima: Mr. Hrdlička wasn't the ambassador, but rather the manager of the buildings belonging to the Ministry of Foreign Affairs. He worked on the preparation of the construction before Ivan Skála's arrival. Although the right of extraterritoriality pertained to the land designated for the construction, it was still necessary to arrange a building permit at the Tokyo Metropolitan Government, and it was Mr. Hrdlička who took charge of the negotiations with the authorities.
PH: So the agreement of the Tokyo administration was essential. That's a fairly strict procedure.
Nishijima: According to the instructions of the Tokyo Metropolitan Government I submitted an application for a building permit, but the result of the approval process, which also incorporated a public hearing, was negative. The reason our application was rejected was the fact that the breadth and height of the proposed building markedly exceeded the limits set by the construction law in relation to the size of the land plot. There were concerns that the character of the original development would be impaired. It also generated a sharp reaction from the neighbours and local inhabitants. A few months later Mr. Skála arrived in Japan, and prepared a simplified design, in which he attempted to comply with the prescriptions as far as possible. He transferred those parts of the building whose functions so permitted to the underground area, thereby reducing both the height of the building and the overall size of the area to be built on. We prepared a new application for the building permit and attended a public hearing

高嶺： とても大きな銀杏の木です。毎年、庭師さんに来て頂いて剪定していただいています。

西嶋: レーモンドさんは、敷地にある樹木を大切にし、可能な限り現状維持または移植により活用しました。ここの敷地内の良質の大きな樹木はなるべく移植して残しました。

チャプコヴァー： 設計プロセスについて、チェコでコンペがありましたね。どの様にしてこの建物を建てたのでしょうか

西嶋： オリジナルの構想をもとにして設計し直して、この実施案ができました。

北澤： その時にはコンペティションの建築家も一緒に計画しましたか。

西嶋： 先ほど話したように、スカーラさんは、二度目の許可申請に使用する設計図の基本計画を作成しました。実施設計の図面は、スカーラさんと協議しながら、レーモンド設計事務所が全て作成したのです。

ホリー： それでは、実施設計図は、もうプラハのものではなくて、全部レーモンド設計事務所で作成されたのですね。

チャプコヴァー： このディーテイル、この階段とか、このカーブとかは、スカーラさんのアイディアですね。

西嶋： 私はコアーキテクトとして、スカーラさんのアイディアをできるだけ実現するように協力しました。建築に関する法規制・建設工法・技術と建築資材等にかかる情報・説明・提案、施工にかかる問題点を協議・解決することにより、高品質の建物の竣工と順調な工事の進展をサポートしたのです。しかし“設計者の意図を尊重して”とは、レーモンドさんとしては、絶対容認できることでなく、スカラさんの手摺は拒否されていたでしょう。レーモンドさんは、視覚的に軽快な表現を求めた方で、重苦しい表現の作品は皆無です。

ホリー： 重圧感のある大使館は、やはりレーモンドさんのスタイルとは違いますね。

西嶋： そのご指摘通りで、お断りしときたかったのです。多分大使館を見たら、あれっ？ レーモンドさんの作品と遥かに違う作品じゃないか、と思います。それは大使館の設計にレーモンドさんが全く関与していなかった結果です。過去に、レーモンドさんに、コアーキテクトのオファーがありましたが、見解の相違で喧嘩別れとなりました。

高嶺：チェコセンター東京所長 高嶺エヴァ。

162 – 在東京チェコスロヴァキア大使館入り口。

Entrance to the Czechoslovak embassy in Tokyo (1977)

and approval process. We obtained the permit and commenced the construction. Messrs. Skála and Hrdlička remained in Japan until the completion of the project.
HČ: Where did the employees of the Foreign Ministry live during that time?
Nishijima: They rented flats in the Minatoku district of Tokyo, specifically in the place called Isaragu.
PH: Wasn't there previously some seat of the nobility on the land where the embassy now stands? I think it belonged to the house of Shimazu. It remains a mystery to me as to the manner in which Czechoslovakia obtained the land. Did the state buy it? Or did it obtain it as a gift?
Nishijima: I think the land was bought by Czechoslovakia. I don't know what it was like before, but when we obtained the land plot it was private land with one residential building, which belonged to some kind of relatively well known personage whose name I unfortunately can't remember now.
PH: I've looked through various archives, and I think that due to the fact that these events took place during the time of socialist Czechoslovakia, no source materials have been preserved. I'd like to know the full story of the change of the owner of that land, since I think it's too big a plot to be private land.
Nishijima: There used to be a number of fully grown ginkgos in the middle of the land. That large tree that's now on the western side of the land plot is one of them, we replanted it. We were able to make use of the trees in the landscaping of the garden, it was a better option to replant them than to cut them down.

163 – 在東京チェコスロヴァキア大使館を代表する階段。

Staircase of the prestigious premises of the Czechoslovak embassy in Tokyo (1977)

164 – 西嶋氏とスカーラ氏。在東京チェコスロヴァキア大使館の庭園にて。1970年代。

Mr. Nishijima and Mr. Skála in the garden of the Czechoslovak embassy in Tokyo (1970s)

西嶋： レーモンドさんは、デザインに関して絶対に妥協を許しませんでした。
ホリー： そうですね。レーモンドさんの建築を見ますと軽快ながら堂々としています。この手摺のデザインは、レーモンドさんと意見交換があったのかなと、実はちょっと不思議でした。

西嶋： そのヘヴィーな手摺は、レーモンドさんの嗜好から考えたら、もう信じられないでしょうね。この断面で造りたいというスカラさんの提案の実現に苦労しました。ストレートな部分はまだしも、特にカーブで更に捩れている部分を作製するのは大変なスキルが求められましたから。ウォルナットの積層材で基本の形状を整え、カーブの部分はさらに現場で、職人がカンナで削りながら求められた形状に整えられました。

ホリー： それでは、チェコスロヴァキアから持ってきたのですか。

西嶋： いいえ、日本の工場で製作されました。日本の国内のトップクラスの内装業者である内外木材が作製しました。その工場と職人のスキル・レベルは抜群で、素晴らしい仕事をしてくれます。

ホリー： 内外木材は、まだありますか。

西嶋： あると思います。本当に秀逸な仕事をします。それ故に、手摺の綺麗で滑らかな曲線が表現されています。

165 – 在東京チェコスロヴァキア大使館を代表する階段（地下）。1977年。

Staircase in the basement of the prestigious premises of the Czechoslovak embassy in Tokyo (1977)

ET: That really is a big tree. Every year we get a professional gardener in to prune it.
Nishijima: Mr. Raymond appreciated those fully grown trees on the land, and as far as possible tried to preserve or replant them. So we replanted and maintained the majority of the healthy trees that were growing there.
HČ: The architectural design of the Czechoslovak embassy was decided by a competition. How did the construction itself take place?
Nishijima: We had to revise the original designs in order to comply with the construction prescriptions and "fit into" the budget.
Kitazawa: Did the author of the original design also co-operate with you on the new diagrams?
Nishijima: As I mentioned earlier, Mr. Skála created the basis for the new, reworked design for the second attempt to obtain the building permit. We prepared the final diagrams in the Raymond Architectural Design Office and consulted Mr. Skála on them.
PH: So that means the final design didn't originate from Prague. Was everything finished in the Raymond Architectural Design Office?
HČ: But some individual elements, for example the staircases, are designs by Ivan Skála, aren't they?
Nishijima: As a fellow architect I tried to implement Skála's designs as far as this was possible. I provided information, an interpretation of the construction laws and legislative prescriptions relating to architecture. I proposed construction procedures and technical solutions, discussed the use of building materials or solved

小林： 内外木材は、皇居などのハイ・グレードのクオリティーを求められる工事を請けている内装工事専門の企業です。

西嶋： 大使館の建設工事に使用されたチェコスロヴァキアの製品はステンドグラスだけです。

小林： ここの建物の設備関係の作業は全部チェコの職人を使用したのではありませんでしたか？

西嶋： いいえ。それは、通信関係の設備に限定されます。通信関係の資機材とそれらの設置と配線工事に従事する職人は、全てチェコから送り込まれ、厳しく管理されていました。また工事中にセキュリティ監視官が駐在して、常時工事現場を巡回していました。特に盗聴対策だと感じました。

検査のため工事現場を回っていますと、すーっと現れるので、どんな業務なのか察せられましたが、あまり気分の好いことではありませんでしたね。

高嶺： 怖い時代でしたね。

西嶋： 社会主義共和国の時代でしたから、非常に厳しくて。こちらに駐在した方達のお子さんは、日本の学校に通学することは許されませんでした。

ホリー： そうでしたね。確かロシアン・スクールに。

西嶋： 他国のインターナショナル・スクールも許されず、ロシアン・スクールだけが許されました。だから、プライベートの家庭教師をつけるか、ロシアン・スクールに行くかの選択を求められました。また、大使館のスタッフもできる限り館内での生活を求められていました。それ故に宿舎・娯楽施設等が大使館内に併設されているのです。

ホリー： 教室も地下にありまして、未だに黒板があります。窓がない部屋なんですよね。

西嶋： シネマは、大使館のスタッフのための娯楽施設で、映写機室には、普通の映画館と同じ機材を備え、シネマ・スコープ対応のスクリーンも設置されています。素晴らしい機材を備えてありました。

高嶺： 今でもありますけど、ほとんど使用していませんね。

ホリー： 映写機はそのままで、現役でまだ作動しています。

西嶋： 客席が72人くらいの、映画館で使うような本格的な映写機を２台設置してあり、交互で連続して投影できます。

166 – 在東京チェコスロヴァキア大使館のメインホール。1977年。

Main hall of the Czechoslovak embassy in Tokyo (1977)

problems that arose during the construction. All so I could ensure the smooth running and high quality of the construction. Among other factors, the design of the railings is an example of respect for the original design of my colleague. Mr. Raymond would undoubtedly have refused to realise such a design. He liked his structures to create a light visual impression, you don't find any heavy elements in his work.

PH: The embassy building creates a fairly monumental impression, does this therefore differ from Raymond's style?

Nishijima: It's exactly as you say. He wanted to reject it. I think that when you look at the embassy building, it's quite surprising that it doesn't resemble the other works of Antonín Raymond in any way. And this is because Mr. Raymond didn't contribute whatsoever to the design of the building. At one point they offered him the opportunity to take on the role of co-architect, but due to their different views on the issue they weren't able to agree and their co-operation never took place. With regard to designs, Mr. Raymond never made any compromises.

PH: Mr. Raymond's designs evoke a feeling of lightness in me, but at the same time also respect. The design of the banisters always struck me as somewhat peculiar, I thought to myself that it probably resulted from a compromise between the ideas of Mr. Raymond and the other architects.

Nishijima: If I were to take Mr. Raymond's taste into consideration, then such a robust banister would be something unthinkable. I had a lot of work trying to realise Skála's design and produce a banister with the required profile. The straight

高嶺： 贅沢な作りですね。

西嶋： 贅沢なのですが、実際当時は、そういう生活をせざるを得ないから他の諸々の施設を揃えたわけです。

ホリー： 船舶の様に自由に外に出られないのですから、全ての生活をこの館内で済ませるという時代があったのです。

高嶺： この施設は地下二階まであってすごく深いんですよね。そこには何か意味があったのですか。地下室が多いような気がします。

小林：高さ制限もありましたね。

西嶋：地下階に配置して機能的に支障のない施設を、極力地階に配置することにより、建物の地上部分の、床面積を縮小して高さを低く抑えたことで、周辺地域の環境に配慮して建築関連の法令による規制を踏まえた都庁の指示に対応することができました。当時は、日影規制の法令が間もなく施行される時期でしたので、日影規制による制約も踏まえて設計しました。

高嶺： 地下は広くて迷路みたいで、初めての人は迷子になりそうなんですよね。地下室は、防衛だとかシェルター的な役割もありましたか。

西嶋： それは、ありませんでした。しかし当時は，ロシアの統制下でしたので、来日または帰国する際に空路を経由する場合は、ロシアまたはチェコのエアラインのみを利用するよう制約がありました。それで一つ悲劇が起きたんです。ハルドリチカさんは、大使館の竣工まで駐在して担当業務を完了させたんですが、シンガポールからプラハまでのチェコ航空のシートがなかなか確保できず、２ヶ月待たされました。やっと帰国の途に就きましたが、不運なことに、シンガポールまで利用した JALの航空機がクアラルンプールで墜落し、ハルドリチカさんは奥様と共に不帰の人となられました。出発する前日に挨拶に来られて握手した時の、ハルドリチカさんの満面の笑顔が、今でも忘れられません。

北澤： そういうことがあったんですね。西嶋圭子さんは、五代美子さんのあとを引き継いで、レーモンドさんの秘書に。何ヶ月か五代さんと一緒にしていましたよね。

西嶋圭子： そうですね、引き継期間が３ヶ月で、その間色々ご指導いただきました。

小林邦子： 彼女に最初に会ったのは軽井沢のアトリエでしたね。[2] レーモンドさんが執筆をしていらした時でした。

02 軽井沢新スタジオ。1962年竣工。

section didn't present any problems, but the curvature of the banister required a considerable amount of skill. The basic shape came from laminated walnut boards and the bent passages were shaped by a specialist directly on site.
PH: So the banisters don't originate from Czechoslovakia?
Nishijima: No, they produced them in a Japanese factory. It's the work of a first-class Japanese manufacturer of interiors, the firm Naigai Mokuzai. Their factory and craftsmen were of a very high standard, and they produced excellent work.
PH: Does the Naigai Mokuzai company still exist?
Nishijima: I think so. They accomplished truly superb work, thanks to which the banisters have attractive, delicate curves.
Kobayashi: Naigai Mokuzai is a firm that is engaged in interior design and works for clients that demand only the highest quality, for example for the Emperor's palace.
Nishijima: The only Czechoslovak product that we used in the construction of the embassy building was the stained glass.
Kobayashi: Didn't Czech craftsmen do all the work in connection with the furnishing of the building?
Nishijima: No, they only worked on the telecommunications equipment. All the components of this equipment and the craftsmen who installed it and were in charge of the wiring were from Czechoslovakia. And they were under strict supervision. Members of the security services also worked there throughout the entire period of the construction in Japan, they were ever-present and inspected everything. I think it was their job to be vigilant mainly due to the possibility of bugging. Whenever I was walking around the building site on an inspection, one of them always appeared so unexpectedly that I could immediately guess the type of occupation they were engaged in. It wasn't a very pleasant experience for me.
ET: It was a scary time.
Nishijima: The Czechoslovakia of "real socialism". The children of the employees working there weren't allowed to attend Japanese schools.
PH: You're right. I suspect they had to go to Soviet schools.
Nishijima: They weren't allowed to attend international schools of other states either. Only Russian ones. So they had two options: a private teacher or attend the Russian school. Moreover, it was demanded of the embassy employees that they leave the embassy building as little as possible, because it contained not only their accommodation but also leisure time facilities.
PH: There's also a classroom in the basement, to this day it still contains a blackboard. It's that room without windows.
Nishijima: There's also a cinema for embassy employees. The projection cabin contains the same equipment as in a professional cinema, and the canvas is suitable also for wide-screen films. It's top class technology.
ET: The equipment's still there now, but it isn't used much these days.
PH: The projector is original and still fully functional.

西嶋圭子： そうですね。

小林邦子： 圭子さんが来て、始まったのがあの自叙伝でしたか。[3]

西嶋圭子： いいえ、あの時は『私と日本建築』です。黒い表紙の本ですね。[4] 当時、私は二十歳で、津田スクールオブビジネスの学生でした。レーモンド事務所から、「1966年の夏休みの１ヶ月半くらい軽井沢で秘書の仕事」の求人依頼が学校に来まして、私は応募しました。校内での選抜試験（英文タイプ、英文速記等）の結果、幸運にも採用されました。当時、勉強不足で、レーモンドさんが、世界的に著名な建築家だということは、全く知りませんでした。まだ学生ですから、仕事をした経験もなく、私に務まるのだろうかと、不安一杯で、軽井沢に行きました。軽井沢駅に着きましたら、レーモンドさんの運転手さんが、迎えに来てくれましたのを覚えています。

西嶋圭子： 別荘に到着しましたら、レーモンドさんご夫妻、3匹の犬、2匹の猫、建築家の方々、邦子さん、コックさんとメイドさんが出迎えてくれました。1か月半、どれだけお役に立てたかは、分かりませんが、通常の秘書業務に加え、岡本太郎さんのご来訪の接客や、本の原稿のタイプも順調に仕上がり、貴重な経験をさせていただきました。有意義で、楽しくて、夢のような1か月半でした。いよいよ、東京に帰る前日、レーモンドさんが、バーベキュー用の焚火を燃やしながら、来年、卒業したら、私の秘書になりませんかとお仕事のオファーをしてくださったのです。

ホリー： 貴重なことばっかりですね。

北澤： ですから、私と邦子さん・圭子さんの二人とは軽井沢で何年か夏を一緒に過ごしていました。若い時ですから楽しかったです。

チャプコヴァー： 軽井沢での毎日の仕事のリズムはどのようなものでしたか。

西嶋圭子： あの素敵な暖炉のあるアトリエで、皆で仕事をしていました。

北澤： 東京の事務所と同じで朝９時から夕方５時半まで。我々スタッフは、母屋ではなく、裏にある小屋と呼んでいる細長い建物で生活していました。

チャプコヴァー： 離れですね。

北澤： そうですね。彼女ら二人は奥の３畳のせまい部屋で寝泊まりして。

小林邦子： 自炊生活でしたね。

03 自伝 アントニン・レーモンド，アントニン レーモンド (著), Antonin Raymond (原著), 三沢 浩 (翻訳) 鹿島出版会; 新装版 (2007/9/1), Antonin Raymond: an Autobiography by Antonin Raymond. (Charles E. Tuttle Company; 1st edition, 1973)。

04 アントニン レーモンド (著), 三沢 浩 (翻訳), 私と日本建築、SD選書17、鹿島出版会、(1967/6/1) 。

167 – 在東京チェコスロヴァキア大使館の映写室。1977年。

Cinema room of the Czechoslovak embassy in Tokyo (1977)

Nishijima: The cinema contains approximately 72 seats and two professional projection machines, which are used regularly in cinemas. It was possible to alternate the projectors during screening.
ET: That's fairly top class equipment, isn't it?
Nishijima: It is high quality, but only because at that time the employees had no choice, they had to live inside the embassy, and as a result they at least prepared some kind of "attractions" for them.
PH: The age they were living in required that they didn't "abandon ship", they had to live within the confines of the embassy.
ET: The building has two underground floors, it reaches down to a considerable depth. Was there a reason for this? It seems to me that there's an excess of these underground rooms.
Kobayashi: That was because the height of the building was restricted.
Nishijima: By locating the maximum possible number of parts of the building whose functions allowed it in the basement, it was possible to reduce both the surface area of the construction and its height. Thanks to this it was possible to comply with the conditions of the construction law, adherence to which was demanded by the Tokyo Metropolitan Government. At that time it was expected that a "shade regulation" would soon come into force, and so when designing the building we also took this regulation into account.
ET: The basement is expansive and reminiscent of a labyrinth. Someone unfami-

168 – 在東京チェコスロヴァキア大使館建設チーム。二列目左から、西嶋さん、ハルドリチカ氏、スカーラ氏。

Implementation team of the construction of the embassy. Standing in the second row from the left are Mr. Nishijima, Mr. Hrdlička and Mr. Skála

ホリー： 自炊していたのですか。３畳部屋というのは、台所の奥の部屋でしょうか？

北澤： はい、台所の奥の部屋です。離れの３畳部屋に彼女が、我々は居間に二段ベッドが２台配置されているので４人で就寝できました。離れに、男４人と３畳に女２人の６人が合宿していました。もう朝・昼・晩と自炊で。コックさんはいましたが、レーモンドさん夫妻のためだけですから、我々スタッフのものは作ってくれませんでした。

ホリー： 上下関係が守られていたということですね。

北澤： しかし、たまにお客さんが来訪されると、庭でバーベキュー・パーティーをしました。バーベキューの時は、我々スタッフも、美味しいものをいただけましたので、楽しみにしていました。

チャプコヴァー： レーモンドさんとの、コミュニケーションは英語ですか。

西嶋圭子： 英語ですね。

ホリー： ノエミさんも英語とフランス語ですか。

169 – 軽井沢新スタジオ、1960〜1961年。

New Studio in Karuizawa (1960–1961)

liar with the place could easily get lost there. Did the basement also have a defence function, like a bunker or something similar?

Nishijima: The underground rooms didn't have any such function. But at that time Czechoslovakia was under Russian domination, and the regulation applied that the air transport of the embassy employees between Japan and Czechoslovakia could be provided exclusively by Russian or Czech airlines. This played its part in a tragedy. Mr. Hrdlička remained in Japan until the completion of the construction, but once he had fulfilled all his obligations he was unable to obtain a flight to Prague via Singapore, and he had to wait another two months for his departure. Then he eventually flew out with JAL (Japan Air Lines), and on the flight to Singapore the plane crashed over Kuala Lumpur. Mr. Hrdlička and his wife were killed in the accident. To this day I can't forget Mr. Hrdlička's satisfied smile the last time we shook hands before he left.

Kitazawa: So that also took place at that time... Mrs. Nishijima Keiko became Mr. Raymond's assistant after Mrs. Godai Yoshiko. But you worked together with Mrs. Godai for a number of months, didn't you?

Nishijima Keiko: Yes, that's right. There was a period of three months before the position was fully transferred to me, and during that time I learned a great deal from Mrs. Godai.

Kobayashi Kuniko: The first time we met was in the studio in Karuizawa.[2] At that time Mr. Raymond was working on his book.

02 New studio in Karuizawa, completed in 1962.

小林邦子： 私は、最初の頃はなんでわからないの！“Don't you understand?”って言われましたけど。だいたい英語で。

ホリー： きつい。それではノエミさんは、日本語をあまりお使いにならない？

小林邦子： ノエミさんは、日本語が比較的お上手で達者だったと思います。

西嶋圭子： 日本語検定の２級くらいではないですか。よく、レーモンドさんの別荘の管理をしていただいていたお隣の土屋さんに、“あなたはね、田舎者でしょう”とか言ったりしていました。また、身分の高い日本の方々とのお付き合いが多く、お上品な言葉を多数記憶されており、「土屋さんのおみ足はいかがですか？」とか、気品の高い言葉を交えた会話もしていました。一方で、レーモンドさんは、どちらかというと、日本語を積極的に勉強していません。片言はわかりますが、日本語での会話は無理でした。

170 – 軽井沢新スタジオの設計室。1960年代。

In the drafting office of the New Studio in Karuizawa (1960s)

小林邦子： 下手ではありませんでしたよ。とても効果的な使い方をなさいましたね。

西嶋： 図面のレタリングに誤りを見つけると「you should use ジビキ(dictionary)」と叱られました。全部が日本語では、コミュニケーションできませんでした。ノエミさんは、日本語によるコンタクトは、比較的よくできました。丁寧な言葉と、とんでもない言葉がよく混ざるのです。

北澤： ノエミさんは、散歩しているとき、畑の仕事しているお年寄りに必ず声をかけていました。「天気がいいですね」とか「頑張っていますね」のような会話を交わしていました。

小林邦子： そのお散歩なのですけれど、ちょっとの散歩じゃないんですよ、２時間くらい。軽井沢から下仁田の方まで歩くんですよ。ですから皆ついていけなくなて。

チャプコヴァー： 毎日ではないですよね？

小林邦子： ほとんど毎日です。

北澤： 私たちは無理でしたので、遠慮しましたが、彼女達は一生懸命ついて行きました。

ホリー： 確かに、犬とか猫とか、動物・虫の命を大切に扱う夫人だったと聞いていました。

Nishijima Keiko: That's right.
Kobayashi Kuniko: Was he working on his autobiography?[3]
Nishijima Keiko: No, at that time he was working on the book *Myself and Japanese Architecture*. It's a book with a black cover.[4] I was twenty years old and I was studying at the Tsuda School of Business. An advertisement appeared at the school entitled "Position of secretary in Karuizawa for one and a half months during the summer holidays of 1966", and I applied. I was lucky and did well in the entrance test – written English and English shorthand – and the firm took me on. At that time I had no idea that Mr. Raymond was an internationally renowned architect. I was studying and I had no experience of employment, and so I set out for Karuizawa full of doubts as to whether I'd be able manage the work at all. I remember that Mr. Raymond's chauffeur came to pick me up at the station in Karuizawa.
When I arrived at the summer residence, both of the Raymonds came to welcome me with their three dogs, two cats, the architects, Mrs. Kuniko, the cook and the housemaid. I don't know how useful I was for that month and a half, but in addition to the usual work of a secretary I also looked after visitors, for example when Okamoto Tarō came to Karuizawa, and I also transcribed the manuscript of Mr. Raymond's book. They were all valuable experiences. I spent a very purposeful and pleasant month and a half there. It was like a dream come true. The day before I returned to Tokyo, during a barbecue in the garden, Mr. Raymond asked me whether I'd like to work as his secretary the following year, once I'd completed my studies.
PH: Truly a valuable experience.
Kitazawa: And as a result Kuniko, Keiko and myself spent the summer months in Karuizawa together for a number of years. We were still young. I have fond memories of that time.
HČ: What was a usual day like in Karuizawa?
Nishijima Keiko: We all worked in the studio with that beautiful fireplace.
Kitazawa: We worked from nine in the morning until half past five, just as in the office in Tokyo. The accommodation for us employees was in the long building at the rear, behind the main house.
HČ: Aha, so not in the main building, but the adjacent one.
Kitazawa: Yes, exactly. Kuniko and Keiko slept in the small room at the back, with a size of approximately three tatamis (5 m^2).
Kobayashi Kuniko: We cooked for ourselves.
PH: You cooked? That room with a size of three tatamis, was that the room at the back behind the kitchen?
Kitazawa: Yes, that room was at the back behind the kitchen. The two women slept in the small room and we four men slept on two bunk beds in the living room. There were six of us in total living in that adjacent house. We prepared breakfast, lunch and dinner ourselves. There was a cook there, but he cooked only for the Raymonds, he didn't prepare food for the employees.

03 Antonin Raymond: an Autobiography by Antonin Raymond. (Charles E. Tuttle Company; 1st edition, 1973).
04 Antonín Raymond: Myself and Japanese Architecture. (Translated by Misawa Hiroshi; SD, separate issue no. 17, 1. 6. 1967, Kashima, Tokyo).

小林邦子： そうです。

チャプコヴァー： スカーラさんとのコミュニケーションは、英語で通じましたか。

西嶋： スカーラさんとは英語でコミュニケーションをとっていました。なんとか通じました。

西嶋圭子： 日本語も少しお話しされましたね。

チャプコヴァー： 西嶋さんは芸大出身ですよね。

西嶋： はい。

チャプコヴァー： どうやってレーモンド設計事務所に入りましたか。

西嶋： 洋画家の兄の関係で、美術評論家の山田智三郎先生の、知遇を得ていました。山田先生はレーモンドさんと昵懇の間柄でしたので、私をレーモンドさんに紹介して下さったのです。私の時代は就職難でしたから、非常にありがたかったです。

ホリー： 芸大に入学されたのは、何年でしたでしょうか。

西嶋： 入学したのは、1950年です。1954年に卒業しています。

チャプコヴァー： レーモンド設計事務所に入るのは結構大変だと聞いたのですが。テストもあったりとか？

西嶋： 私の数年後くらいまで、入社試験は実施されていなく、紹介されて入社した人ばかりです。

北澤： 私の入社は1962年だったのですが、前の年までは試験がなくて、レーモンド設計事務所は募集もしてなく、縁故採用だけでした。それで縁故を一生懸命探していたら、私の時は希望者が４０人もいたので、試験を行うことになったのです。それで私と大西さん(芸大)の２人だけが選抜されました。その年に、小林邦子さんも一緒に入られました。試験じゃない方で。

小林邦子： 私は試験無しでした。朝日新聞に齊藤虎郎さんという建築家がいらして、レーモンドさんと親しくしていらっしゃった。その方から「俺の事務所に入りたかったらレーモンドさんのところで修行をしてこい」って言われ、紹介していただきました。緊張してレーモンド設計事務所にうかがうと、ミセ

171 – 軽井沢新スタジオの離れ。夏のあいだ従業員たちはここに住んだ。軽井沢。

Adjacent house (hanare) where employees of the studio lived during the summer (New Studio in Karuizawa)

PH: So the relationship of subordinates to superiors was adhered to.
Kitazawa: Of course. If guests visited, we held celebrations in the garden, barbecue parties. We always looked forward to barbecues, because it meant that we employees could also have something good.
HČ: Did you speak to Mr. Raymond in English?
Nishijima Keiko: Yes, English.
PH: And what about with Mrs. Noémi Raymond, did you communicate in English and French?
Kobayashi Kuniko: At the beginning she used to ask me: "Why don't you understand?", but yes, we communicated primarily in English.
PH: That sounds somewhat harsh. So Mrs. Noémi didn't speak Japanese?
Kobayashi Kuniko: I think Mrs. Noémi spoke Japanese relatively well.
Nishijima Keiko: I'd say she'd passed at least the second level of the JLPT (Japanese-Language Proficiency Test). Occasionally she conversed in Japanese without any problems with Mr. Tsuchiya from the neighbourhood, who looked after Mr. Raymond's summer residence. She often met together with very high-ranking personages, and she memorised words from very formal Japanese, which she then used in conversation. On the other hand, Mr. Raymond never made any effort to learn Japanese. He knew a few words, but it was impossible to have any conversation with him in Japanese.
Kobayashi Kuniko: But it wasn't the case that he couldn't learn Japanese, he used it quite effectively.

ス・レーモンドが「私のところにいらっしゃい」と。私は住宅の設計をしたかったので、インテリアを勉強する素晴らしい機会に恵まれました。

北澤： その時は、先任の伊藤京子さんがいた時ですか。

小林邦子： はい、いらっしゃいました。2年後でしょうか。京子さんがお辞めになるまで。庭に面したミセスのお部屋で色々と教えて頂きました。

チャプコヴァー： ３人でインテリアを中心に設計をしたんですか？ インテリアデザインとか家具とか。

小林邦子： 住宅の造付家具、カーペット、カーテンそに家具でしたね。大きな建物をつくる時に家具が必要になりますでしょう？　そうすると建築担当の方がノエミさんのところにいらして、「ここの家具どうしましょう」っておっしゃるんですよね、大体ね「これデザインしてください」とか。

ホリー： 家具までオーダーメイドっていうのは素敵ですね。

北澤： 南山大学の家具も手がけたんでしたっけ？ ものすごいボリュームになりましたよね？

小林邦子： 写真を見てください。これは南山大学ライブラリーのカラースキームです (図175を参照)。ノエミさんは、床タイルのパターンや家具の張り地のカラースキームも作りました。

北澤： Ｐタイルのデザインですね。

小林邦子： はい。家具はミセスのラフなスケッチから製図しました。スケールは日本の尺でした。これをｃｍに直して製図して、建築家の方にお渡しすると、大きな図面の中にこの家具がトレースされて。

西嶋： 伊藤忠商事関係の方と記憶しています。

北澤： 昔はこのような、青図しかなかったのですね。白黒で焼けるようになったのはずっと後になります。

小林邦子： それで、これを家具屋さんに渡してまず原寸図を作ってもらいます。何回もチェックをして、物件によっては建築の担当者にも原寸のチェックをしていただきました。ＯＫがでると家具屋さんが作ったモデルを直して、家具屋さんまで行っては細かい指示をしました。
ホリー： これなんて、カーペットのデザインだ。本当にコラージュみたいに作っているんですね。

172 – レーモンド夫妻とアトリエの従業員、1960年代。

The Raymonds with their employees in the studio (1960s)

Nishijima: When he found a mistake in the descriptions for the diagrams, then he reprimanded me: "You should use a *jibiki*" (dictionary). But if there was a whole conversation conducted in Japanese, he didn't understand. Mrs. Noémi spoke Japanese relatively well. Even if she often mixed up formal and colloquial Japanese.
Kitazawa: When Mrs. Noémi was out on a walk, she always exchanged a few words about the weather or work with the older people who were working in the fields.
Kobayashi Kuniko: And they weren't short walks, Mrs. Noémi went out for two hours at a time. She used to walk from Karuizawa all the way to Shimonita, and none of us could keep up with her.
HČ: But weren't they everyday walks?
Kobayashi Kuniko: She went out for a walk almost every day.
Kitazawa: We men couldn't have managed it, and so every time we made excuses, but the girls did their utmost to keep pace with her.
PH: I heard she had great respect for all life, including animals – dogs, cats, even insects.
Kobayashi Kuniko: Yes, that's true.
HČ: Did you speak to Mr. Skála in English?
Nishijima: Yes, we communicated with Mr. Skála in English. We were more or less able to get by.
Nishijima Keiko: He also spoke a little Japanese.
HČ: Mr. Nishijima, you studied at the Tokyo University of the Arts (Tokyo Geidai), is that right?
Nishijima: Yes.
HČ: How did you come to work at the Raymond Architectural Design Office?
Nishijima: Thanks to my brother, who was a painter, I knew the art critic Yamada Tomosaburō. Mr. Yamada and Mr. Raymond got along very well, and as a result he was able to introduce me to Mr. Raymond. At that time it was pretty difficult to find work, and so I was very grateful to him for it.
PH: When did they accept you at the Tokyo Geidai?
Nishijima: I started my first year in 1950 and I finished the school in 1954.
HČ: I believe it was difficult to get into the Raymond Architectural Design Office. Did you have to take entrance exams?
Nishijima: They didn't introduce entrance exams at the firm until a couple of years later, when I'd already been working there for a few years. Until that time they took on employees on the basis of a recommendation.
Kitazawa: I joined the firm in 1962, and up until the previous year there hadn't been any entrance exams. At that time they didn't announce the recruitment of new employees at the Raymond Architectural Design Office, everything was just on recommendation. I tried to get into the firm through my connections, but it was just that year that they had more than forty candidates, and so they eventually decided to hold entrance examinations. In the end only myself and Mr. Ōnishi, a

173 – 軽井沢を散歩中のノエミ・レーモンドと西嶋さん。1970年頃。

Noémi Raymond and Mrs. Nishijima on a walk in Karuizawa (ca. 1970)

小林邦子： これは私が貼っています。建築の図面にミセス・レーモンドが色鉛筆でデザインされます。それを描き直して。家具を含めてオリジナルスケッチは殆ど残っていません。とても残念です。

チャプコヴァー： デザイン方法がはっきりとわかりますね。

小林邦子： これはミセス・レーモンドデザインのカーテン地です。建築担当者の図面から全てのインテリアをデザインします。これはプライス邸のリビングですね (209ページを参照)。こういう布地も殆ど全部織らせました。

ホリー： 織物工場に発注して？

小林邦子： 当時、佐々木織物や川島織物に頼みました。

チャプコヴァー： このテキスタイル。京都ですか？

小林邦子： はい、京都の本社からです。色サンプルを持ってきて、その色の糸で作りました。

北澤： これらは、全部フリーハンドでノエミさんが描いたのを一生懸命縮尺して図面化するんですね。あと、昔から使っている家具も使われます。

ホリー： 当時のデザインはいいですね。現代のものと比べてもはっきりと良さがわかる。

西嶋： 当時は、デザインと品質に納得できる既製家具は、市場になかったんですよ。

小林邦子： 初めの頃のお話しではリーダーズダイジェストの家具も全部作ったとか。

西嶋： あれも、全部作らせました。

小林邦子： あの家具デザインをスタンダード化しようという働きがあったようですね。でも、できなかった。

西嶋： 松坂屋社長の伊藤さんの自宅の設計を担当したのですが。1957年〜1958年の時代は、デザインも含めて高品質の家具が市場に何もなかったので、家具および造り付け家具を全部デザインして造らせました。抽斗のハンドルなど小さいものまで、何から何までデザインして。ここまで徹底できたのは稀な例だと思います。それもこれも、そのときの工事費が潤沢でしたので実行できたのです。

graduate from the Tokyo Geidai, were chosen. Also that year Mrs. Kobayashi Kuniko joined the company, although they accepted her without any exams.
Kobayashi Kuniko: I didn't take any exams. The architect Saitō Torao worked at the Asahi newspaper, and he knew Mr. Raymond very well. Mr. Saitō said that if I wanted to work with him, I'd first of all have to gain experience under Mr. Raymond. When I visited the Raymond Architectural Design Office, my nerves completely on edge, Mrs. Raymond told me I should work for her. I initially wanted to build family houses, but eventually I gained an amazing opportunity to learn to design interiors.
Kitazawa: Was your predecessor, Mrs. Itō Kyōko, still working there at the time?
Kobayashi Kuniko: Yes, at that time she was still there. For about two years. Before Mrs. Kyōko finished working there I learned a great deal from her in that room with a view of the garden that belonged to Mrs. Noémi.
HČ: Did the three of you focus primarily on interior designs, furniture design and so on?
Kobayashi Kuniko: We also did family houses, but above all furniture. When you're constructing a large building, then of course you need furniture, such as built-in furniture, carpets, curtains. In those situations one of the architects came to Mrs. Noémi and said: "How are we going to solve the furniture in this house?", or: "Please can you put together such and such a design."
PH: Even the furniture was made to order.
Kitazawa: Did you also design the furniture for Nanzan University?
Kobayashi Kuniko: Please take a look at this photograph (fig. 175, p. 205). That's the colour scheme of the university library. Mrs. Noémi also designed the patterns for the tiled floor and the colour schemes for the furniture covers.
Kitazawa: Is that the floor made of plastic tiles?
Kobayashi Kuniko: Yes. I created the technical diagrams according to Mrs. Noémi's sketch. The scale was originally in Japanese units, "shaku", which I then converted into centimetres and prepared a diagram. Then I handed the diagram to the architect, and he sketched the furniture into the overall architectural design.
Nishijima: I remember, it was an order for someone from the Itōchū company.
Kitazawa: Before they were just kind of blue copies of the diagrams. They started to make the black and white ones much later.
Kobayashi Kuniko: Then the diagrams were handed over to a furniture making firm, which prepared the technical documentation on a scale of 1:1. This was checked several times. In the case of some houses the designs for the furniture were also checked by the chief architect of the project. When a design was approved, I took the design with comments to the carpenter, and handed him detailed instructions.
PH: Is that the design of the carpet? That design is reminiscent of a collage.
Kobayashi Kuniko: I stuck that together. Mrs. Raymond sketched her designs into the architectural plans in coloured pencil. I then redrafted them. Unfortunately the original diagrams, including the designs of the furniture, haven't been preserved.

174 – 南山大学の内観。名古屋、60年代。

Interior of the library of Nanzan University in Nagoya (1960s)

北澤： 邦子さん、このオリジナルの布地は、ノエミさんが保存していたのですか。

小林邦子： これは織らせた物のサンプルだったと思います。

チャプコヴァー： 川島織物ですか。

小林邦子： 佐々木織物か川島織物のいずれかです。カーペットも、この様な毛玉のサンプルがありまして、1尺角のサンプルを確かオリエンタルカーペットに作らせたと思います。

ホリー： カーペットまで残ってるんですか。大変貴重です。

小林邦子： お風呂のタイルも。完全に一つの部屋でカラースキームが決まって綺麗にできていたという。なかなかできないですよね。

ホリー： ノエミさんの美的センスは素晴らしいと思っていまして。日本の織物から色々な影響を受けていらしたかたですか。

小林邦子： そうですね、来日前にコロンビア大学で勉強されていますね。

チャプコヴァー： ティーチャーズカレッジで。

小林邦子： アーサー・ダウ(1857〜1922)。フェノロサ(1853〜1908)門下の。

チャプコヴァー： そうですね。アーサー・ダウ。日本に滞在して新しいデザイン教育、つまるところ、アート教育を始めた方ですね。

小林邦子： その頃から、日本の古美術をかなりアメリカに紹介していました

175 – ノエミ・レーモンド、南山大学の内観、カラー・スキーム図案（コラージュ）。名古屋、60年代前半。

Noémi Raymond, interior design and colour scheme for the library of Nanzan University in Nagoya (collage, early 1960s)

HČ: It's wonderful to see the manner in which it was designed.
Kobayashi Kuniko: This is the material for the curtains, which was designed by Mrs. Raymond. On the basis of the diagrams prepared by the architect, she designed the whole interior. Here we can see the living room in the Price villa (fig. 178, p. 209). We had almost all the materials woven.
PH: Did you order them from a textile factory?
Kobayashi Kuniko: At that time we used to use the services of the textile firms Sasaki Orimono and Kawajima Orimono.
HČ: Are the textiles from Kyoto?
Kobayashi Kuniko: Yes, they're from the head office in Kyoto. We brought samples of colour and then we produced them from yarn of the same colour.
Kitazawa: Here are the designs drafted by Mrs. Noémi, we did our utmost to convert

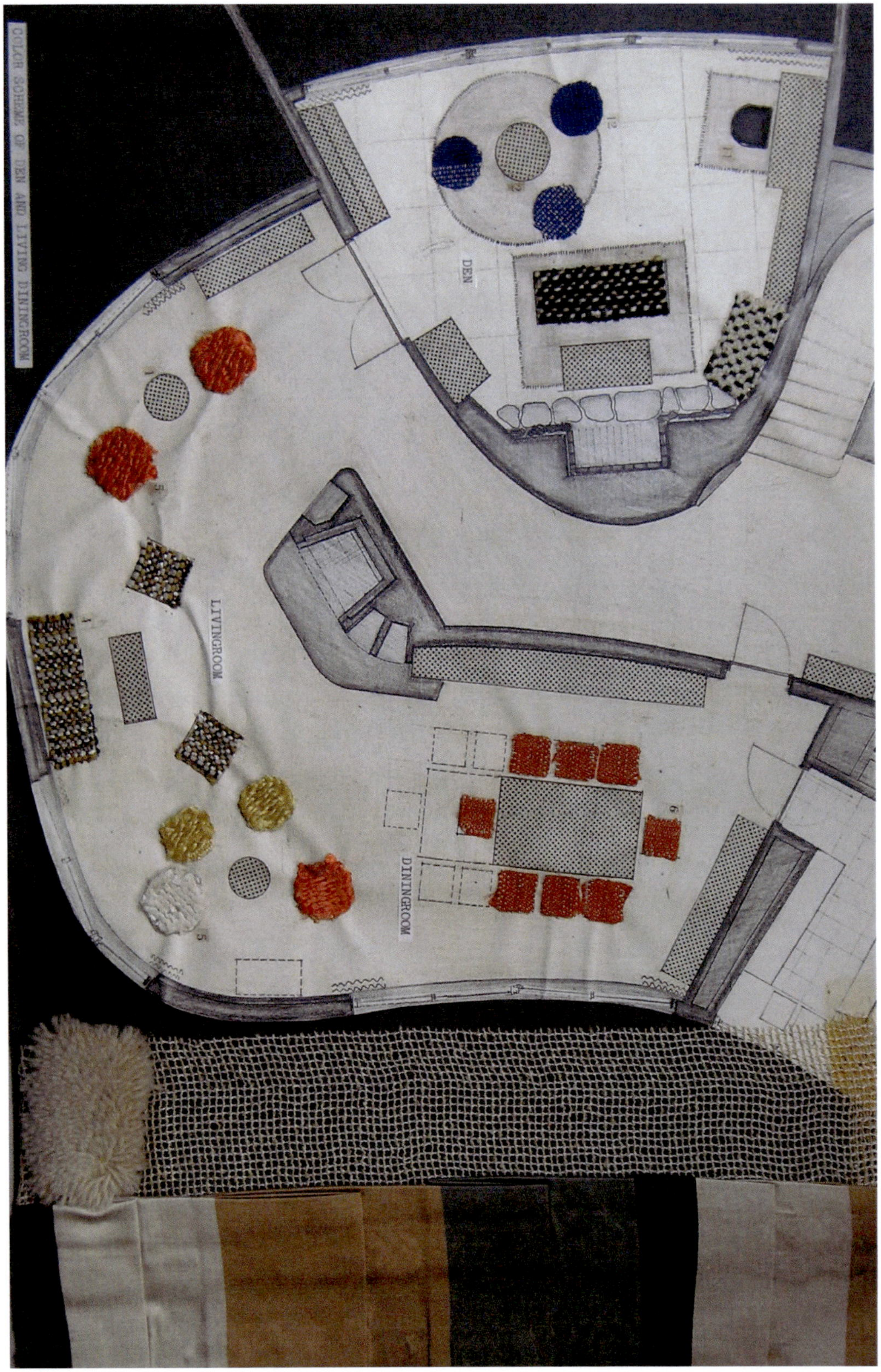

176 – ノエミ・レーモンド、プライス邸インテリア。コラージュ、1962〜1964年。

Noémi Raymond, interior of the residential house of the Price family villa (collage, 1962–1964)

177 – プライス邸インテリア。1960年代。

Interior of the residential house of the Price family villa (1960s)

them to scale and prepare diagrams based on them. We also used the design of the furniture we had available.

PH: At that time the design was of a high standard. In comparison with modern items you can clearly distinguish the difference in quality.

Nishijima: Back then there was no ready made furniture on the market that we could have considered satisfactory in terms of its design and quality.

Kobayashi Kuniko: I heard that when the firm started, it also manufactured all the furniture for the Reader's Digest offices.

Nishijima: Yes, we also had all of that produced.

Kobayashi Kuniko: You reportedly endeavoured to manufacture furniture in larger series, but it didn't work out.

Nishijima: I designed a house for Mr. Itō, the director of the Matsuzakaya company. In 1957 and 1958 there was no quality furniture on the market that looked good, and so we had to have both free-standing and inbuilt furniture produced. We designed everything, including even small details such as the handles on the drawers. However, I think such a detailed design was rather the exception. It was possible to implement all of that only because we had a very generous budget.

Kitazawa: Mrs. Kuniko, those original fabrics that Mrs. Noémi designed, have they also survived?

ね。フランク・ロイド・ライトが日本に来るかって言われた時に、直ぐ承知されたわけです。ライトも随分日本の美術を持ってらして。

チャプコヴァー： そうですね。コレクターもされたり。アートディーラーの仕事なんかもやりました。

北澤： ライトの奥さんとノエミさんがお友達だったんでしょ。

チャプコヴァー： そうですね。ウィリアム・ノエル。ノエミ・レーモンドさんは、ティーチャーズカレッジでアートやグラフィックデザインを勉強したのではないでしょうか。その時にアーティストの仕事を引き受けて、デッサンとかしたりしたのではないかと思います。戦後になると、北澤先生から聞いた通り、レーモンドさんと結婚して、ご自分でデッサンをすることはなくなりました。レーモンドさんは逆に毎日描きましたね。

軽井沢ではレーモンドさんは絵を描いていたけれども、ノエミさんが描いたのは見たことがない。

小林邦子： ノエミさんは描いてないですね。

北澤： レーモンドさんに遠慮していたのではないかなと僕は想像しているのだけど。描いたら本当に上手だからね。

小林邦子： ノエミさんのスケッチはたった一つ、これ (215ページを参照)。

北澤： ノエミさんのタッチだね。

小林邦子： 何の絵だったか全然覚えてないんですけど。これ一つだけです。あとは全て、家具等のスケッチはレーモンド事務所に置いてきました。それらはもう無いと聞きます。ニューホープに帰られたり、旅行されたりした時に頂く手紙には時折スケッチがありました。旅行中も計画を何時も気になさって、図面を送って下さいとか、良いアイデアがありますかとか。詳細な御指示がありました。

ホリー： 北澤先生から前に拝聴したのですけれども、ノエミさんはお召し物に和製の布地をお使いになっていたとか。

小林邦子： レーモンドの叙勲のお祝いの写真では、シルク紬のグレーのシンプルなスーツを着てらっしゃいましたね (52ページを参照)。[5] 普段着は木綿のワンピースが多かったと思います。

北澤： 僕から見ると服装はちょっと地味だったかな。

05 旭日中綬章（1964年)。勲三等。

178 – ノエミ・レーモンド、プライス邸インテリア。コラージュ。コラージュ、1962～1964年。

Noémi Raymond, interiors of the Price family villa (collage, 1962–1964)

Kobayashi Kuniko: I think this is a pattern that we had woven.
HČ: Is this from the textile firm Kawajima Orimono?
Kobayashi Kuniko: From the textile factories Sasaki or Kawajima. We also had balls of woollen thread and samples of carpets. If I remember rightly, we had we had an "oriental rug" made out of samples approximately thirty centimetres square.
PH: Was the rug also preserved? That's a rare treasure.
Kobayashi Kuniko: The tiles in the bathroom too. One colour scheme for the whole room. The result looked very good. Something like that takes a lot of work in order to succeed.
PH: Mrs. Noémi had an extraordinary aesthetic sense. Was her work influenced by the Japanese weaving tradition?
Kobayashi Kuniko: Probably, yes. Before she came to Japan she studied at Columbia University.

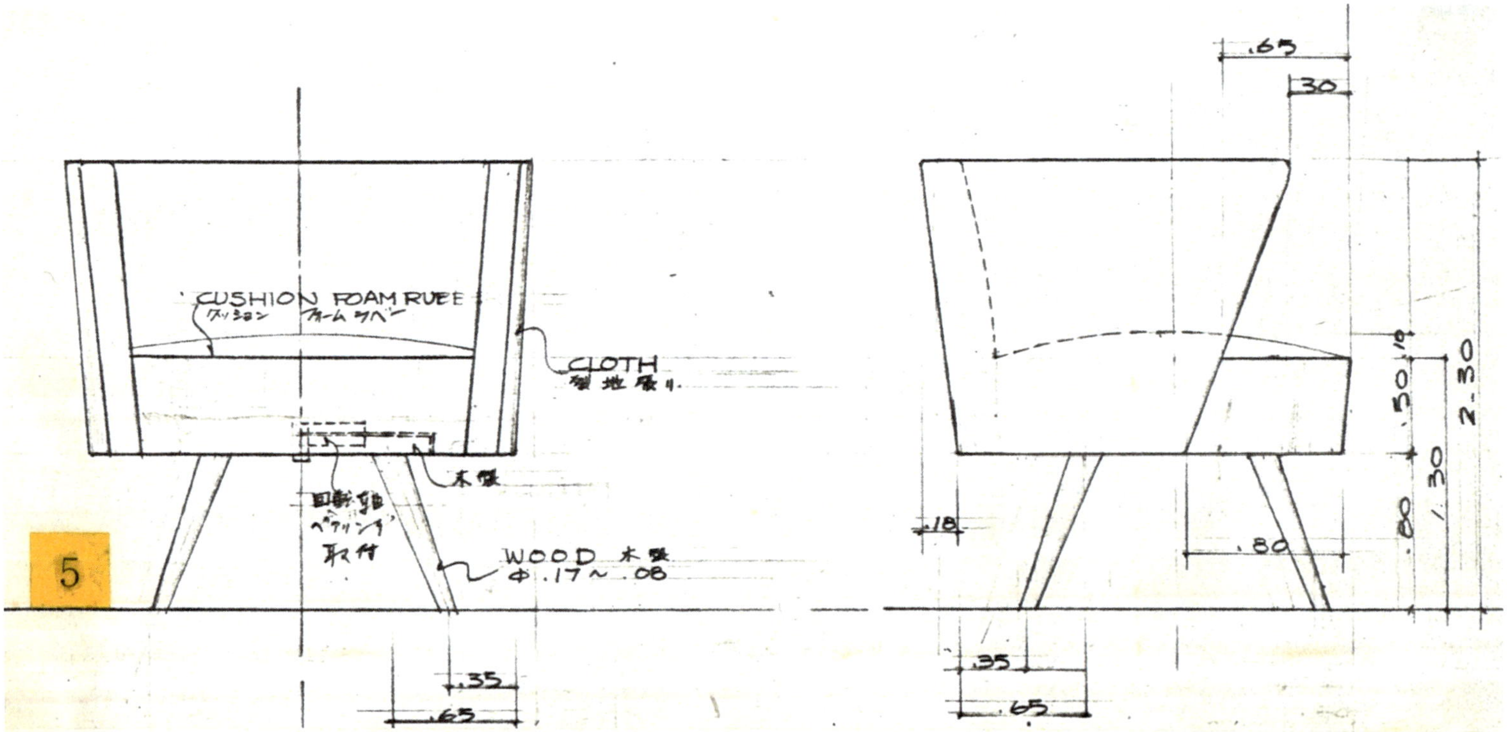

179 – プライス邸の椅子図案。1960年代。

Chair design for the Price family villa (1960s)

小林邦子： 金色のネックレスをいつも身につけておいででした。古いものが好き、新しいものは嫌いですとはっきりおっしゃっていて。ミスターはウイスキーがお好きでしたね。

ホリー： オン・ザ・ロックですか？

小林邦子： そうそう。カランカランって音がすると、今日はご機嫌よさそうだなって。

北澤： 食事の前は必ずお飲みになっていましたね。

ホリー： ウイスキーどんなブランドがお好みで？

小林： 日本のやつは好きじゃなかったみたい。スコッチは好きでした。

北澤： 僕の前ではサントリーのダルマだった。

チャプコヴァー： 小林先生はどういう経緯でレーモンド設計事務所に入社されたんですか？

小林： 私は不思議な形で。私の先輩がレーモンド事務所にいまして。ちょうどオリンピックの年だったかしら、銀座松坂屋をクライアントとして手がけてい

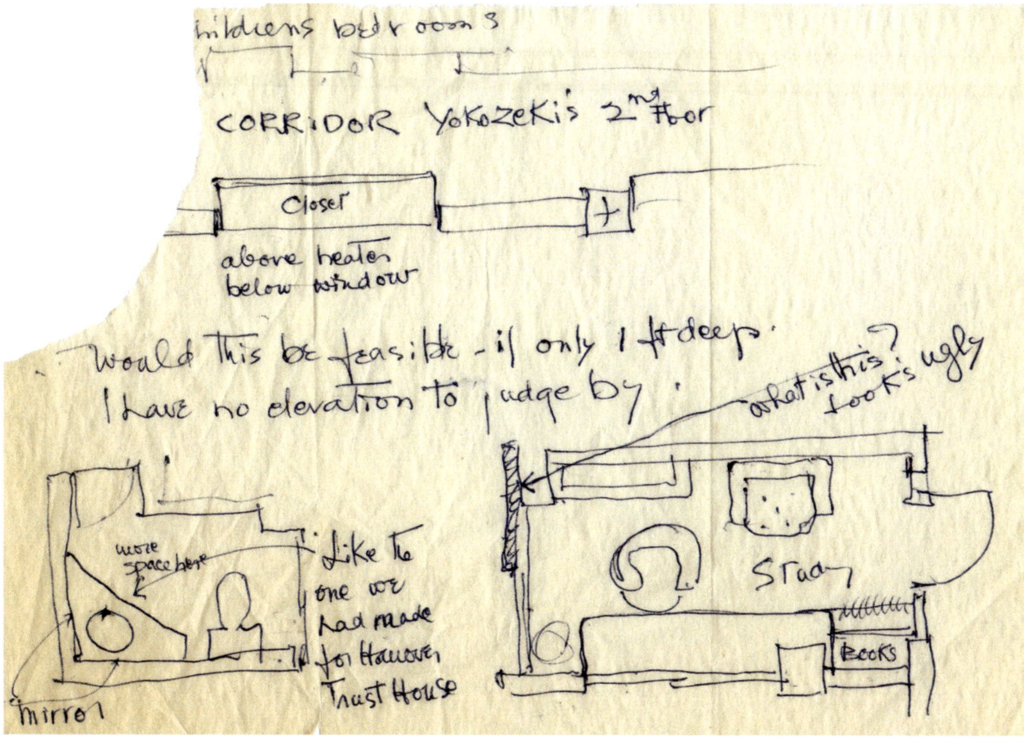

180 – ノエミ・レーモンド、ヨコゼキ家宅内観図。60年代前半。

Noémi Raymond, layout of the interior of the villa for the Yokozeki family (early 1960s)

HČ: At the Teachers College.
Kobayashi Kuniko: She was taught by Arthur Wesley Dow (1857–1922) and Ernest Francisco Fe nollosa (1853–1908).
HČ: Arthur Dow, who also visited Japan, was a pioneer of a new teaching method for designers and graphic artists.
Kobayashi Kuniko: And in addition to that, at the time there was a growing fashion for Japanese antiques in America. This was also the reason why Frank Lloyd Wright immediately agreed when we asked him if he'd like to come to Japan. Incidentally, Wright owned several Japanese artworks.
HČ: Yes, he was also an art collector and trader.
Kitazawa: Was Wright's wife a friend of Mrs. Noémi?
HČ: Yes, she was. Her name was Miriam Noël. – Noémi Raymond studied art and graphic design at the Teachers College. Mr. Kitazawa told me that after the war and after her marriage to Antonín Raymond she stopped drawing, but apparently Mr. Raymond drew every day.
Kitazawa: Mr. Raymond used to draw in Karuizawa. I never saw Mrs. Noémi draw.
Kobayashi Kuniko: It's true, Mrs. Noémi didn't draw.
Kitazawa: I wonder if this was some kind of capitulation to Mr. Raymond, because she was excellent at drawing.
Kobayashi Kuniko: This is the only preserved sketch by Mrs. Noémi Raymond (fig. 181, p. 215).

らしたんですね。現場事務所で、私はアルバイトとして模型作りを手伝うことになって。松坂屋の現場が終わってから松岡保夫さんからお電話がかかってきて、大使館の仕事が大変だから手伝ってくれないかって。それで、そのままレーモンド事務所に居続けることに。

北澤： 松岡保夫さんは、レーモンドさんのお気に入りのスタッフでした。いくつもの作品を担当していました。松坂屋も担当していまして、大村取締役のもとで現場監理をしていたはずです。軽井沢新スタジオの現場監理も松岡さんです。

西嶋： 松岡さんは、白石建設の紹介でした。

北澤： ああ、そういうことか。白石多士良さん、白石宗城さんは、昔からレーモンドさんをお世話をしてくれていた人達です。
　白石多士良さんのパシフィックコンサルタントは、初代の社長がレーモンドさんです。白石建設もレーモンドさんに言わせると、「俺がアドバイスして作った会社だ」って。それは事実で、ずっと付き合ってたからね。レーモンドさんは日本で生活を続ける上で、三井家とか、白石家とか、昔からの名門を大切にされていたのですね。で、その筋がオーナーになって、仕事を依頼してくれる。だから、アメリカ大使館アパートとか、あの辺の土地の世話をすることになったのも、三井家が持っていたものをレーモンドさんが間に入って世話したという経緯。

チャプコヴァー： 笄町のレーモンドさんの自邸と設計事務所（1950年竣工）の敷地は、どなたが所有者でしたか？

西嶋： あの土地は、服部セイコーの服部さんが所有者でした。

チャプコヴァー： 1923年にＲＣ造打ちっ放しで作られたレーモンドさんの最初の自邸である霊南坂のお家も同じく？

北澤： 霊南坂は違います。1957年に建築された葉山の海の家は、三井家の中の一番いいところを譲り受けたと聞いています。大きい屋敷の、海岸に飛び出ている部分の恵まれたところの、小さい面積を譲り受けたのです。あのようないいロケーションの敷地を入手できたのは、三井さんと永年にわたり続いたご縁があったからでした。

ホリー： レーモンドさんは歌舞伎に知悉していたというお話を聞いたことがあるのですが。

北澤： 高崎の井上房一郎さんが、歌舞伎が好きな人だったんです。彼は歌舞伎役者との交際がありました。レーモンドさんご自身は、どうかな。

Kitazawa: Yes, that's her style.

Kobayashi Kuniko: I don't recall any longer which painting it was used as a basis for, only the sketch has survived. All the sketches of furniture and other items remained at the Raymond Architectural Design Office. I heard that they no longer exist. – When she was on her travels, she used to return to New Hope, and she sent me letters, some of which had drawings enclosed in them. Even on her travels she showed an interest in projects that were under way, and she wanted me to send her diagrams. She also asked if I had any good ideas and so on. I had detailed instructions.

PH: Mr. Kitazawa told me that Mrs. Noémi used to wear clothes made of Japanese fabrics.

Kobayashi Kuniko: In the photograph from the ceremony (fig. 44, p. 52) when Mr. Raymond was presented with his award for services to Japanese architecture, Mrs. Noémi is wearing a simple suit made of Japanese silk.[5] However, I think she usually wore cotton dresses.

Kitazawa: Today it strikes us that she dressed rather inconspicuously.

Kobayashi Kuniko: She always wore a gold necklace. She liked old things, she wasn't keen on new things, she said that quite clearly. And Mr. Raymond liked whisky.

PH: With ice?

Kobayashi Kuniko: Exactly! When I heard him mixing whisky with ice in the glass, I knew he'd be in a good mood.

Kitazawa: He always had a glass before dinner.

PH: What was his favourite brand of whisky?

Kobayashi: I don't think he liked Japanese whisky. His favourite was Scotch.

Kitazawa: I saw him drinking Suntory Old Whisky.

HČ: Mr. Kobayashi, how did you come to work at the Raymond Architectural Design Office?

Kobayashi: I came to Mr. Raymond's firm in a somewhat unusual way. One of my older fellow pupils was already working for Mr. Raymond. This was during the time of the Olympic Games, and Mr. Raymond was working on a project for the Ginza Matsuzakaya department store. I got a temporary job in the office directly on the construction site, and I produced architectural models. When the construction finished, I got a phone call from Mr. Matsuoka Yasuo, who told me that the project for the building of the Czechoslovak embassy was fairly demanding, and asked if I would help them with it. And so I stayed with Raymond.

Kitazawa: Matsuoka Yasuo was a favourite of Raymond's. He was in charge of several architectural projects at a time. He was also responsible for the Matsuzakaya project, and supervised the construction as the direct superior of the director, Mr. Ōmura. Mr. Matsuoka also supervised the project on the construction of the New Studio in Karuizawa.

Nishijima: Mr. Matsuoka was introduced to Raymond by people from the Shiraishi Kensetsu firm.

05 On 21 April 1964 Antonín Raymond received the award of the Third Class Order of the Rising Sun from Emperor Hirohito (Shōwa).

西嶋： 高崎の群馬音楽センターの設計に着手したとき、レーモンドさんの最初の案は、円形のホールでした。その案を、このお仕事をご依頼された井上房一郎さんに披露したら、即座に、「このステージでは歌舞伎はできないよ。富士山をどこに置くのだね」って言われて。それで円形の計画案は、断念されました。井上さんは、レーモンドさんにズケズケ何でも言える方でしたね。レーモンドさんは、あえてそういった発言には反発されませんでした。

西嶋圭子： 井上さんは、キャデラックで、レーモンドさんによく会いに来ていました。中で寝られるようにしていて。

北澤： そうでしたね、軽井沢の時、井上さんは大型のキャデラックでよく見えました。

西嶋圭子： ツカツカツカと、アトリエに入ってこられて、「レーモンドさん、これ頂戴！」って。アトリエに置いてあるレーモンドさんの作品を貰っていかれるんですよ（笑）。

北澤： だから高崎の自宅に行くと、レーモンドさんの作品があるわけ。

西嶋圭子： 現在は高崎美術館の1部で公開されている井上さんの自宅は、レーモンドさんの笄町の自邸と同じように造られた建物ですね。キッチンが違うぐらいで。井上さんのお家のキッチンは大きいですよ。

ホリー： 間取りは、確か左右反対なんですよね。

西嶋： そうです。レーモンド邸の平面図を井上さんがアレンジして造った住宅です。

北澤： 井上さんが、設計原図を裏返して見たら、道路と関係良くなることに気づいて。それで、裏焼きしてくださいって。

ホリー： その井上邸ではローテーブルのヘリが高く上がっていますね。何かをこぼしたときに、畳にこぼれないようにって。

小林邦子： はい、この円テーブルは、軽くするために、薄くなっています。

ホリー： そうですね、薄いですね。とても貴重です。若いデザイナーにとっては大変な衝撃になるかと思います。どこを訪ねても見る機会がもうないものですから。

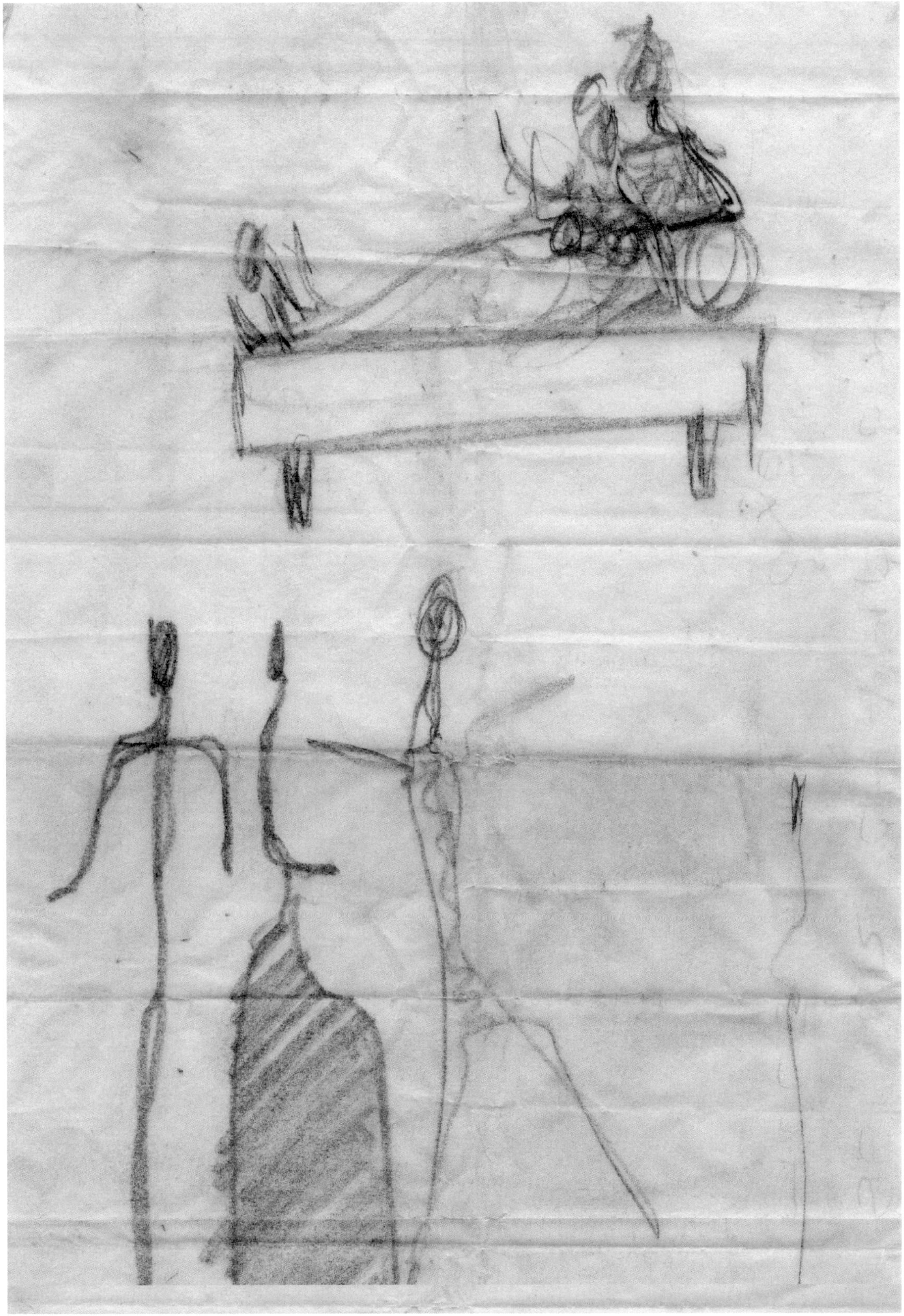

181 – ノエミ・レーモンド、戦後のフリー・スケッチ（おそらくこの時期に損傷を免れたもの）。

Noémi Raymond, freehand sketch from the post-war period (probably the only surviving sketch from this period)

182 – 西嶋圭子氏 小林氏と北澤氏。

Mrs. Nishijima Mr. Kobayashi and Mr. Kitazawa

183 – アントニン・レーモンド、ウイスキーのグラス片手に。1962年。

Antonín Raymond with a glass of whisky (1962)

小林邦子： ノエミさんのデザインで、今作らせようと思うと、なかなかできません。

チャプコヴァー： それは、技術の問題ですか？

小林邦子： 周辺部分を作製する高度なスキルが必要です。こういう襖のデザインも、いちいちノエミさんのスケッチから、和紙を使っておこして。この頃はいい和紙がありましたね。

北澤： 自分で漉いてきたんですよね。美濃まで行って漉いてたんだと思います。

チャプコヴァー： 貴重な資料または写真をありがとうございます。パーティーの写真がありますよね。

北澤： 庭でバーベキューをしてる写真ですね。

西嶋圭子： バーベキューはよくやりました。レーモンドさんは必ず毎日お昼寝してましたね。

小林邦子： 寝室の方を覗くと、足だけ見えるんですよ。
北澤： 大きな足がね。

Kitazawa: Aha, so that's the way it was! Messrs. Shiraishi Tashirō and Shiraishi Munenari had often assisted Mr. Raymond in the past. – The first director of the Pacific Consultants company, which belonged to Shiraishi Taširō, was Antonín Raymond. Also in the case of Shiraishi Kensetsu, Mr. Raymond would tell you: "I advised them on how to establish the company." That's true, and it's a document of their long-term good relations. As long as Mr. Raymond lived in Japan, he was greatly respected by the members of the old and distinguished Shiraishi and Mitsui families. If anyone from those families became the owner of a company or land plot, they placed an order with us. For example, when the Mitsui family obtained the flats of the American embassy and the surrounding lands, Mr. Raymond took care of them.
HČ: Who owned the land in Kōgaichō, where Raymond's house and office were located? (Completed 1950)
Nishijima: The land belonged to Mr. Hattori from the Hattori Seikō company.
HČ: Did that also apply to Mr. Raymond's pre-war reinforced concrete house in the Reinanzaka district from 1923?
Kitazawa: It was different in the case of the house in Reinanzaka. I found out that he obtained the best land for the house on the beach in Hayama, which he built in 1957, from the Mitsui family. They left him a small part of a large residence, the part overlooking the coast. He could only have obtained such a good piece of land thanks to his long-term relationship with Mr. Mitsui.
PH: Is it true that Mr. Raymond was exceptionally well acquainted with kabuki?
Kitazawa: Inoue Fusaichirō Inoue of Takasaki was very fond of kabuki, and he was also friendly with the actors. But it doesn't seem likely to me in the case of Mr. Raymond himself.
Nishijima: When we started work on the project of the Gunma Music Centre, Mr. Raymond originally designed a hall with a circular ground plan. When we presented this design to the client, who was Mr. Inoue Fusaichirō, he told us without hesitation: "It's not possible to play kabuki theatre on such a stage. Where would we put Mount Fuji?" And so we had to abandon the idea of the circular floor plan. Mr. Inoue was the type of man who wasn't afraid to tell Mr. Raymond everything without any embellishment – and Mr. Raymond was unable to oppose him.
Nishijima Keiko: Mr. Inoue often came to visit Mr. Raymond in his Cadillac, which he had customised so that he could sleep in it.
Kitazawa: You're right, I often used to see Mr. Inoue in his big Cadillac at Karuizawa.
Nishijima Keiko: He came into the studio and said: "Mr. Raymond, I'll take this, all right?" and he took one of Mr. Raymond's works that had been stored in the studio away with him *(laughs)*.
Kitazawa: So that's why! When I came to Mr. Inoue's house in Takasaki, he had things belonging to Mr. Raymond there.
Nishijima Keiko: Today Mr. Inoue's house is part of the art museum of the city of Takasaki. Mr. Inoue's house was built identically to Mr. Raymond's Kōgaichō villa.

184 – ノエミ・レーモンド。1962年。
Noémi Raymond (1962)

チャプコヴァー： 遅くまで仕事をされていたんですか？

西嶋圭子： 5時半までです。その後、みんなで自炊をしていましたよね。

小林邦子： 料理しなきゃいけませんから。

北澤： 大変ですよ、女性二人がいろいろ考えてくれて。我々男は使い物にならないですから。お手伝いだけですから。皿洗いくらいしかできない。

ホリー： チェロをなさってたとか。

西嶋圭子： チェロはよく弾かれていましたが、ピアノを弾かれたことはありませんでした。居間の暖炉のそばに置いてあったヤマハのピアノは、レーモンドさんがデザインされたものです。

北澤： やっぱり、建築家・レーモンドのデザインだって感じがしますね。建築的デザインとでも言いましょうか。ピアノっていう感じではないですね。

高嶺： インテリアのために作られたのですか？

北澤： いや、あれはヤマハの銀座ビルを設計した1951年に、ヤマハから正式に設計を依頼されてデザインしています。レーモンドさんの自伝に詳しく書かれています[6]。

チャプコヴァー： 焼き物も製作されていましたね。軽井沢でもされていましたか。

北澤： ええ、別荘で一生懸命粘土をこねて製作されていました。レーモンドさんのその頃の焼き物の先生は濱田庄司さんです。

ホリー： 益子の濱田庄司さんですか。

北澤： はい、そうです。粘土はいつでも手元においてありました。

ホリー： 焼成はどうされてたんですか？

北澤： 窯は麻布の自宅にありました。粘土で作って自然乾燥させたものを持ち帰って、麻布の窯で焼いていました。焼成を手伝う人がいました。

小林： 窯の燃料は、プロパンガスでしたね。

ホリー： 岡本太郎さんとすごく仲が良かったとか。

185 – アントニン・レーモンド、群馬音楽センターの模型を前に。60年代初頭。

Antonín Raymond with a model of the Gunma Music Centre (early 1960s)

06 188頁、注03を参照。

The only difference is their kitchens – the one in Mr. Inoue's house was very spacious.

PH: And the layout of the rooms was a mirror image.

Nishijima: Yes. Mr. Inoue had his house built on the basis of the modified construction plans of Raymond's villa.

Kitazawa: When Mr. Inoue tried inverting the original diagrams, he found that this would improve the connection to the road, and so he asked us for a design with an inverted layout of the rooms.

PH: I noticed that the edge of the coffee table in Inoue's villa is curved upwards. I was told that this was so that the tatamis wouldn't be soiled if something was spilt on the table.

Kobayashi Kuniko: The paper table top is thin, so as to create a light impression.

PH: You're right, it's thin paper. A rare treasure! I think it must be an inspiration for young designers. You don't often see that these days.

Kobayashi Kuniko: That circular table was designed by Mrs. Noémi. Today it's not so easy to make a table like that, it would be very demanding.

HČ: Technically demanding?

Kobayashi Kuniko: It takes considerably advanced craftsmanship skills to produce those kind of edges of a circular table. The same applies also to the design of the paper panel. I redrafted Mrs. Noémi's designs for traditional Japanese paper, which is then used as the filling. – At that time very high quality Japanese paper was still available.

Kitazawa: Did Mrs. Noémi produce the paper herself? I recall that she used to go all the way to Mino to have the paper manufactured.

HČ: These are all very valuable photographs and documents – thank you very much. But you have the photograph from the celebration.

Kitazawa: Do you mean the garden party with the barbecue? (Fig. 172, p. 200)

Nishijima Keiko: We used to barbecue very often. Among other things, Mr. Raymond liked to doze off in the afternoons.

Kobayashi Kuniko: When I looked into the bedroom, I could always only see his legs *(laughs)*.

Kitazawa: Long legs! *(Laughs)*

HČ: Did you work late in the evenings?

Nishijima Keiko: Until half past five. Then we all used to cook.

Kobayashi Kuniko: We had to prepare our own food.

Kitazawa: It was pretty tough for the women. We men were useless to them. We only helped them a little, we were just about able to wash the dishes.

PH: Did Mr. Raymond play the cello?

Nishijima Keiko: He played the cello often, but he didn't even once play the piano that he designed for Yamaha, which stood next to the fireplace in the living room.

Kitazawa: We can truly distinguish Raymond's signature as an "architect" in the design of that piano. He even said that it was an architectural design. It doesn't look like a classic piano to me.

186 – ノエミ・レーモンド、和紙を使った作品。襖と障子のデザイン。1966年。

Noémi Raymond, work with traditional Japanese paper, design of sliding doors fusuma and shōji (1966)

西嶋： よく事務所に遊びに来ていましたよ。岡本さんは、井上さんの様にレーモンドさんに遠慮なくはっきりものを言われる方でした。

チャプコヴァー： 岡本さんや濱田さんだけではなく、その他のアーティストとも関わりがあったのではないでしょうか。

西嶋： 陶芸の荒川豊蔵さん、家具のジョージ・ナカジマさん、彫刻のイサム・ノグチさんとかかな。

ホリー： イサム・ノグチさんとは親しかったですね。リーダーズダイジェストの前庭にはノグチさんの彫刻がありました。

ET: Was the piano produced as an interior furnishing?
Kitazawa: No, the Yamaha company ordered the design of the piano when Mr. Raymond was preparing an architectural design of their building in Ginza in 1951. Mr. Raymond described it in detail in his autobiography.[6]
HČ: He also produced pottery. Did he also focus on this in Karuizawa?
Kitazawa: Yes, he did. In the summer residence he threw himself passionately into kneading clay and producing pottery. At that time his teacher was Mr. Hamada Shōji.
PH: Mr. Hamada Shōji of Mashiko?
Kitazawa: Yes, the very same. He always had some clay at hand.
PH: How did he fire the pottery?
Kitazawa: He had an oven in his house in the Azabu district. He let the clay products dry and then brought them home to fire them. He had an assistant in the firing process.
Nishijima Keiko: By the house in Azabu there was a warehouse where Mr. Raymond used to store antiques and a number of works by famous artists. We used to make an inventory in that depositary with Mr. Raymond twice a year.
ET: Were you checking if everything was in order and nothing was missing?
Nishijima Keiko: Precisely. We checked if the inventory corresponded with the actual collection.
HČ: Where is the collection today?
Kitazawa: Before Mr. Raymond returned to the USA, he asked Mr. Inoue to sell most of it.
Nishijima Keiko: He had a lot of rare treasures. Artworks by Mr. Hamada, an ancient terracotta haniwa statue in the shape of a horse, porcelain and several other things.
HČ: He sent that haniwa statue to the USA. In one letter he wrote that he wanted to keep it.
Nishijima Keiko: In fact that haniwa statue was knocked over and broken by the housemaid when she was cleaning. A shocking event.
Kobayashi Kuniko: That depositary contained a considerable number of rolls of material with patterns that we had designed. We used them as chair covers or bedspreads.
Kitazawa: What happened to those materials?
Kobayashi Kuniko: I have no idea. – Please allow me to change the subject: when Mr. Raymond was away from the Kōgaichō villa, Mrs. Noémi used to invite us to dine together, just us women. Mrs. Noémi was a vegetarian, and so for example we had a big portion of asparagus with butter and garlic. I remember that it was excellent.
Nishijima Keiko: She used black ceramic dishes from Mashiko, which made the food look superb. Mrs. Noémi used to have a lot of guests. I think that this was thanks to her contacts from the Animal Conservation Society, because she visited

187 – 軽井沢新スタジオ内観。1960〜1963年。

Interior of the New Studio in Karuizawa (1960–1963)

06 See note 03, p. 189.

北澤： ノグチさんには、造園計画も手伝ってもらったようです。その前庭の池と彫刻は、ノグチさんの作品です。

西嶋圭子： 西麻布の家の横に蔵がありまして、そこに有名な方々の作品や古美術品が、数多く所蔵されていました。1年に一回、レーモンドさんと二人で棚卸しをしました。

高嶺： 棚卸しをされるときに所蔵品が揃っているかどうか、全部チェックされるのですか？

西嶋圭子： はい、リストに照らし合わせて、全ての所蔵物をチェックいたしました。

チャプコヴァー： 所蔵品は今どこにあるんでしょうか。

北澤： 帰国される前に、井上さんに依頼して、かなり売却されました。

西嶋圭子： 貴重な宝物が沢山ありました。濱田さんの作品とか、埴輪の馬、陶磁器等です。

チャプコヴァー： 埴輪はアメリカに送られました。レーモンドさんが、埴輪などをご自身でキープしたいと決められたという旨が手紙に書いてあります。

西嶋圭子： あの埴輪、実は、メイドさんがお掃除している時に、落として破損してしまったんです。ショックな出来事で、とても困りました。

小林邦子： その蔵にはデザインされた布地の太いロールが沢山保存されていました。椅子の張地とか、ベッドスプレッドなどに使用されていたものです。

北澤： その布地などはどこに行ったのでしょうか。

小林邦子： 私も実は分からないんですよ。話は変わりますが、笄町ではレーモンドさんがお出かけになると、ノエミさんに女性だけお食事に誘っていただきましたね。ミセスはベジタリアンですから、長いままのアスパラをね、バターとガーリックをいっぱいかけて大きいお皿に山盛りに。とても美味しかったのを思い出します。

西嶋圭子： 益子焼の黒い食器でした。お料理がはえて、とても素敵でした。ノエミさんにはよく来客がありましたね。動物福祉協会の関係だと思いますが、有名な方々がノエミさんを訪ねて来られました。李紅蘭の山口淑子さん、麻生和子さん、乗馬ズボンにブーツの堀口大学の妹さん、三井家の三井サキさんと

188 – アントニン・レーモンドの案によるヤマハのピアノ。

Piano from the Yamaha company, built according to a design by Antonín Raymond (1951)

a lot of famous people. For example the actress Yamaguchi Yoshiko, known as Ran Rikō, or the essayist Asō Kazuko, also the younger sister of the poet Horiguchi Daigaku, who used to wear riding trousers and boots, or Mrs. Saki from the Mitsui family.

PH: I see she was friendly with high society.

Nishijima: Before the war Mr. Raymond had friends among the higher social echelons, he associated with the nobility or members of business concerns, the so-called "zaibatsu". These people often ordered designs for houses from Mr. Raymond. Before the war more than half of his orders came precisely from these types of clients. After the war many of them changed their status, and more clients from diverse backgrounds appeared.

PH: Did the good relationships that Mr. Raymond established before the war continue?

Nishijima: Only some of them, but yes.

Kobayashi Kuniko: Mr. Raymond was different from a large number of other foreign architects, who built in classic Western style in post-war Japan.

HČ: Was that because his designs were rather within the realm of hybrid architecture?

PH: You're right, he took into account the needs of the Japanese.

Kobayashi Kuniko: He implemented ideas of modernist architecture. Raymond studied in Prague at a time when houses in the Czech lands had several rooms, which created the impression that there were nothing but doors everywhere. By using sliding paper partitions in his later designs, he managed to enlarge and open up the interior space of buildings.

189 – チェロを弾くアントニン・レーモンド。

Antonín Raymond with his cello

HČ: To this we must also add the beautiful design of the sliding paper partitions by Mrs. Noémi.

Kobayashi Kuniko: I think that the result was a typically Japanese open space.

Nishijima: I heard that Mr. Raymond was very surprised when he saw Japanese architecture for the first time. At that time Le Corbusier and other architects were adherents of the theory of modules, but Raymond noticed that all Japanese houses had already long been designed using a composition of traditional modules. The ground plan of houses in Japanese style is traditionally composed of the following modules: ken (6 shaku), tatami (6 x 3 shaku), cubo (6 x 6 shaku). To this we further add flexible work with the light and open space with the aid of sliding paper doors. For Mr. Raymond this was a completely new world.

Kobayashi Kuniko: At school I learned how to use centimetres. I didn't learn how to measure in feet, shaku and inches until I started working at the Raymond Architectural Design Office.

PH: So Mr. Raymond strictly adhered to shaku in his measurements.

Nishijima: When I joined the firm, the prevailing tendency worldwide was to convert to the metric system, but in the Raymond Architectural Design Office the unit of shaku was used. One shaku is 0.3030 metres, and one foot is 0.3048 metres, thus

いうような方々です。

ホリー： すごいですね。上流階級の方々と交流されていらしたのですね

西嶋： 戦前レーモンドさんは、華族とか財閥等の上流階級の方々の知遇を得ていました。そういった方々から自宅などの設計を依頼されるんです。終戦前の、レーモンドさんの作品の過半数は、彼らがクライアントでした。戦後は、ステータスが変わられた方も少なからずいて、依頼主のバックグラウンドは広くなり多様化しました。

ホリー： 以前のご縁は、続いていましたか。

西嶋： 多少は、続いていましたね。

小林邦子： 終戦後に日本で活躍した外人の建築家の多くが古典的な洋風建築を建てる中で、レーモンドさんは違っていたのですね。

チャプコヴァー： ハイブリット的な建築を設計したわけですね。

ホリー： そうですね。日本の皆さんのニーズに合わせていましたから。

小林邦子： モダニズム建築を実現された。レーモンドはもちろんプラハで学生時代を過ごしたんですが、当時のチェコでは部屋が重なっていて、ドアばかりだったわけですね。それを襖にする事で、もう空間がぱぁーと広がるわけです。

チャプコヴァー： 加えて、ノエミさんの素敵な障子デザインがあったわけですね。

小林邦子： その結果、日本的に開放された空間ができたのだと思います。

西嶋： レーモンドさんが、初めて日本の建築を見た時、相当なショックを受けたそうです。当時、コルビジェ等が建築にかかるモジュール論を提唱していましたが、日本の建物は全て、固有のモジュールにより計画されていることに気が付かれました。日本家屋の平面計画は、昔から使われている間（6尺)、畳(6尺x3尺)・坪（6尺x6尺)のモジュールに基づいています。それと引き戸・襖の間仕切りによるフレキシブルで開放的な空間と、マイルドな採光機能も備えた障子等は、レーモンドさんにとっては、全く新鮮な世界でした。

小林邦子： 私も学校ではセンチでずっと勉強してきて、レーモンド設計事務所に入って、フィート・尺・インチといった尺寸を教わりました。

190 – ろくろに手を伸ばすアントニン・レーモンド。葉山のアトリエ。

Antonín Raymond at his potter's wheel (studio in Hayama)

191 – 陶芸家の濱田庄司宅を訪れるレーモンド夫妻。益子、1960年代。

The Raymonds visiting the ceramic artist Hamada Shōji in Mashiko (1960s)

both units are very similar and it was no problem to measure in shaku. If we also take into account the fact that the material used in construction in Japan was in units of shaku, then we can infer that measurement in these units also corresponded to one of Raymond's architectural principles, namely the principle of economy.

PH: Was Mr. Raymond particular about the original Japanese division into construction modules?

Nishijima: Shaku is further divided into sun – a tenth of a shaku, bu – a tenth of a sun, so it's a decimal system. But in the case of feet it's much more complicated, because an inch is a twelfth of a foot, and this is followed by an eighth of an inch and so on. Unless a special ruler with measurements in feet is used, it's not possible to create diagrams, or to check a finished diagram. When creating diagrams, shaku was often used on a reduced scale: 1:50, 1:100, 1:200 and so on. In comparison with this, in the case of feet the system would be as follows: $^1/_4$ inch = 1 foot (1:48), $^1/_8$ inch = 1 foot (1:96), $^1/_{16}$ inch = 1 foot (1:192). In comparison with shaku in the decimal system, a foot was highly impractical.

Kobayashi Kuniko: A pair of compasses was also essential. Whenever Mr. Raymond

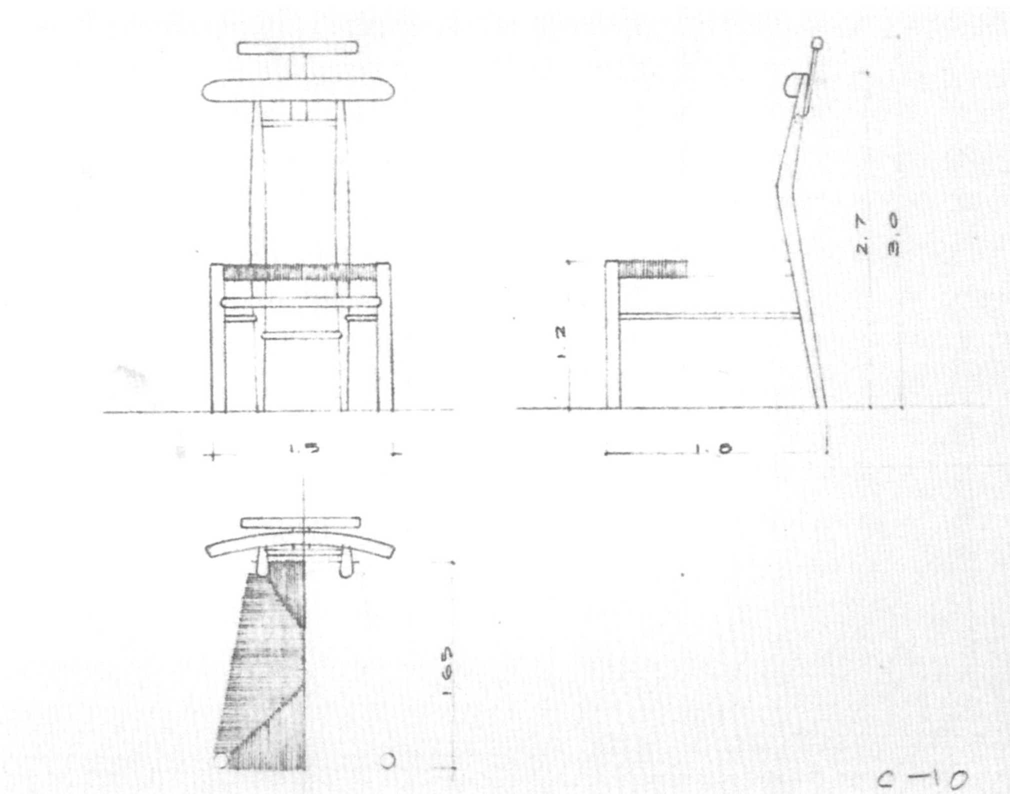

192 – ノエミ・レーモンド、椅子図案。(尺スケール)。

Noémi Raymond, design of chair (in shaku)

ホリー： レーモンドさんはしっかり尺でやってらっしゃったのですね。

西嶋： 私が入社した当時は、世間はメトリックに移行しつつある時期でしたが、レーモンド設計事務所では尺を使用していました。1尺は0.3030mであり1フィートは0.3048mと非常に近似の数値ですので、尺を使用することに支障もなく決断されたんだと思います。また日本の建築用資材は、尺を踏まえた規格の寸法により生産されていることを考慮すると、レーモンドさんの設計理念の一つである“エコノミカル”に踏まえた選択だったんだと推測されます。

ホリー： それだけレーモンドさんは日本の本来のモジュールに留意されていましたか。

西嶋： 尺の単位は、尺、寸(尺/10)、分(寸/10)の１０進法ですが、フィートの場合は、フィート、吋(フィート/12)、吋/8といった具合に非常に複雑な構成です。フィートのメジャー（物指）を所持していないと、設計図を作製することも、図上の寸法を確認することもできません。設計図に使用される縮尺は、尺の場合は、1/50、1/100、1/200等が良く使われていますが、それに対応するフィートの場合は、1/4吋=1フィート(1/48)、1/8吋=1フィート（1/96），

193 – 軽井沢新スタジオを掃除をするノエミ・レーモンド。

Noémi Raymond cleaning in the New Studio in Karuizawa

194 – 笄町宅の内観。麻布、東京、1950〜1952年。

Interior of Kōgaichō in Azabu (Tokyo, 1950–1952)

came into the office, he sat down and the first thing he said was: "Where's the compasses?"

Nishijima: As soon as I sat down to work on a design, Mr. Raymond immediately started to check the diagram with a pair of compasses and give me instructions. Once he reprimanded me: "For an architect a pair of compasses is absolutely indispensable!"

HČ: I have one last question. Mrs. Keiko mentioned that at the time when she started work at the firm, Mr. Raymond was already a renowned architect. How did his fame manifest itself?

Nishijima Keiko: Mr. Raymond was famous not only in Japan, but worldwide. He was awarded the Order of the Rising Sun for his services to Japanese architecture. For him this was the highest honour. I became clearly aware of this later when I was working on the editing of Mr. Raymond's aforementioned biography. As regards his social contacts, he was regularly visited in the office by American or British ambassadors – the entire situation seemed to me as if I were in a dream. It was an honour for me to attend to such guests. During the British Queen's birthday celebrations, Mr. Raymond rode in the ceremonial procession in a Rolls-Royce together with the British ambassador. I heard that even Mr. Shōda and his wife (the parents of the Empress Michiko) attended a concert held at the Raymond Architectural Design Office.

1/16吋=1フィート(1/192)と表示されるので、１０進法の尺に較べると扱いづらいのです。

小林邦子： それと、デバイダーは必須です。レーモンドさんが事務所に来てどんと座ると、デバイダーどこだって。

西嶋： レーモンドさんは、私が作図中の席に着かれると、すぐデバイダーで図面をチェックされ、いろいろ指示されました。デバイダーは、建築家として不可欠の必需品だと叱られたこともありました。

チャプコヴァー： 最後の質問です。先ほど、圭子さんが、事務所に入った時には既にレーモンドさんはとても有名な建築家だったと仰いましたが，その時はどのように有名だったのですか？

西嶋圭子： レーモンドさんは、建築家として、日本国内のみならず、世界にその名が知られていたんです。日本の建築界に多大な貢献をされたことにより勲三等旭日章も授与されていて。それが何よりも素晴らしかった。自叙伝の編纂に携わったことで、さらにその認識を深めました。交流関係で言えば、アメリカ大使とか、イギリス大使が、気軽にレーモンドさんの事務所に来られて、私からしてみれば夢を見ているような状況。そんな中で、彼らを接客応対する機会をいただき、とても光栄に思いました。女王陛下のお誕生日には、レーモンドさんは、イギリス大使とロールスロイスに同乗され、一緒にパレードに参加されていました。正田様ご夫妻が、レーモンド事務所で開催されたコンサートに臨席された、というお話も伺いました。

チャプコヴァー： 新聞にも度々取り上げられていましたし。

西嶋圭子： そうですね。「ジャパンタイムズ」に数十年にわたりコラムを書いていた著名なコラムニストのジーン・ピアースさんが、頻繁にレーモンドご夫妻に会いに来られました。よく、居間のソファーに座って、静かに本を読んでいるお姿をお見かけしました。まるで自宅にいるようにリラックスされている様子が思い出されます。コラムを通じて、訪日されている外国の方々に日本をより深く知ってもらうことに多大な貢献をされた方でしたので、日本の文化をこの上なく愛したレーモンドご夫妻と相通じるものがあったのだと思います。

チャプコヴァー： 時間となりました。これで本日の座談会を終わりにしたいと思います。

195 – ノエミとアントニン・レーモンド。70年代前半。

Noémi and Antonín Raymond (early 1960s)

HČ: His name occasionally also appeared in the press.
Nishijima Keiko: That's true. Jean Pierce, who wrote columns for the Japan Times for several decades, visited the Raymonds very often. I saw her sitting on the couch in the living room, silently reading a book. I remember that she seemed relaxed, as if she were at home. By writing her columns for foreigners living in Japan she made a significant contribution to a deeper understanding of Japanese culture. I think that she got on well with the Raymonds also because of their common interest and love for Japan.
HČ: Unfortunately our allotted time is up, I'll have to conclude our meeting here. – Thank you all very much for your contributions.

アントニン・レーモンド、戦後の母国との接点

1945年以降のアントニン・レーモンドとチェコ人との交友関係を把握する試みは、探偵による捜査を思い起こさせる。なにしろ彼が国境を越えて祖国を去ってからは第二次世界大戦終結時点ですでに35年が経過していたうえ、ヨーロッパの地図は再び書き換えられてしまっていた。

アントニン・レーモンドは戦間期にチェコスロヴァキアを幾度か訪れていたものの、1945年以降国へ帰ることはなかった。彼は1919年にアメリカ陸軍の将校エマニュエル・ヴォスカ[1]の秘書の一人としてプラハを再訪した。1920年代に芸術家連盟マーネス[2]で行った講義については、自伝[3]では言及されていないが、東京での名誉領事職[4]の指名推薦をプラハで受けた時期のことだと推測できる。

次の祖国訪問は1932年のズリーンであり、これについては自伝[5]に記されているように、かつての従業員フランチシェク・サマー[6]に向けた手紙の中で回想している。

確認できる最後のチェコスロヴァキア滞在は、レーモンドの家族が日本からアメリカへ戻った1938年まで下る。この時がプラハで兄弟に会った最後であった。彼らはその数年後にホロコースト[7]で殺された。それによりアントニン・レーモンドは出生地へのつながりが絶たれてしまったのである。

戦後ヨーロッパは鉄の壁によって分断され、特に50年代において東西の交流は限定的な外交レベルにとどまるものであった。レーモンドは事実上、故郷と個人的につながる可能性を失っていた。

1960年代なかば、東側地域の政治状況はいくらか緩和した。チェコで暮らしていたフランチシェク・サマーはかつての上司へ連絡することに決めた。最初の手紙はレーモンドの家族を大変喜ばせた[8]。「親愛なるフランチシェク、これはまさに復活だ。私たちはこの数年、君はもう同じ世界にはいないと思っていた。どうして手紙をよこさなかったんだ？　私たちがどこに住んでいるかは知っていただろ。ポンディシェリ[9]から、私たちはスイスのジュネーヴに向かった。そこで私はベネシュ[10]や松岡洋右[11]に本気で会おうとしたんだ」

アントニン・レーモンドは自伝の中でフランチシェク・サマーについて数

01 エマニュエル・ヴォスカ(1875〜1960)、チェコ系アメリカ人、元は石工、後に採石場の経営者、アメリカ合衆国のスパイ、1917年以降アメリカ陸軍の将校、チェコスロヴァキア軍団とアメリカ陸軍の間の連絡将校として職務を果たした。

02 『スティル』6(11)、プラハの建築家協会、1925〜1926、コラム「ニュースと評論」、68〜69頁。

03 Antonin Raymond, An Autobiography. (Charles E. Tuttle Comp., Rutland, Vermont, Tokyo, Japan, 1973)。

04 名誉領事職は1926年秋から1937年末まで務めた。祖国のための職務が評価され1928年に国から表彰 (白獅子勲章第四位) された。

05 Antonin Raymond, An Autobiography. (1973, p. 124)。

06 フランチシェク・サマー(1907〜1973)、建築家、ル・コルビュジエの弟子、モスクワ地下鉄建設に参加、プルゼン市スロヴァニーの住宅地を共同建設。

07 アントニンはクラドノのユダヤ系商人アロイス・レイマンとルジェナ（旧姓タウスィゴヴァー）の第3子として生まれた。兄弟はイルマ (結婚後ロハティーノヴァー)、1886〜1942)、エルサ（結婚後シュチェドラー)、1887〜1942)、フランチシェク(1890〜1943)、エゴン(1892〜1944)、ヴィクトル(1894〜1942)。家族については以下を参照。Irena Veverková, Antonín Raymond a Reimannové. Osud židovské rodiny ve XX. Století. (Společnost Patria, [Kladno] 2006)。

08 プルゼン市文書館、フランチチェク・サマー

Antonín Raymond's post-war contacts with his native country

The task of mapping Antonín Raymond's contacts with Czechs after 1945 resembles a detective investigation. Indeed, by the end of the Second World War thirty-five years had passed since his departure from his native land, and the map of Europe had once again been redrawn.

Though Antonín Raymond visited Czechoslovakia several times in the inter-war period, after 1945 he never returned to his homeland. In 1919 he came to Prague as an officer in the American army, one of the secretaries of Emanuel Voska.[1] Although the lecture that he gave in the Mánes Union of Fine Arts in the 1920s[2] is not mentioned in his autobiography,[3] we may assume that it took place at the time when he was in Prague to receive his appointment documents for the post of honorary consul in Tokyo.[4]

Another visit, this time to Zlín in 1932, is commemorated both in his aforementioned autobiography,[5] and in a letter to his former employee František Sammer.[6]

His last documented visit to Czechoslovakia took place in 1938, when Raymond was returning with his family from Japan to America. That occasion in Prague was also the last time he saw his siblings, who a few years later were murdered in the Holocaust.[7] Antonín Raymond's ties to his native land were severed thereafter.

In the post-war period Europe was divided by the "Iron Curtain", and as a result contacts between the West and East, especially in the 1950s, took place only rarely and on the level of diplomacy. Raymond thus de facto lost the possibility of personal contact with his homeland.

In the mid-1960s the political relations relaxed somewhat in the Eastern Bloc. František Sammer, then living in Czechoslovakia, decided to contact his former boss. His first letter was warmly received by the Raymond family:[8] "Dear František, this is a true "resurrection". For years we believed that you were no longer in our world. My friend, why didn't you write? Surely you knew where we were. From Pondicherry[9] we travelled to Geneva in Switzerland. There we desperately tried to bring Beneš[10] and Matsuoka together."[11]

Although Antonín Raymond devotes only a few lines in his autobiography to František Sammer,[12] they clearly show the author's affection for this young and talented

01 Emanuel Voska (1875–1960), Czech-American, originally a stonemason by trade, later the owner of quarries, agent of the US secret service, from 1917 a captain in the US army, operating as a liaison officer between the Czechoslovak legions and the USA.

02 In: *Styl*, annual. 6 (11), Society of architects in Prague, 1925–1926, column Zprávy a poznámky, pp. 68–69.

03 Antonin Raymond, *An Autobiography.* (Charles E. Tuttle Comp., Rutland, Vermont, Tokyo, Japan, 1973.)

04 Raymond was in the post of honorary consul from the autumn of 1926 until the end of 1937. For services to his native country he was awarded the Order of the White Lion, class IV, in 1928.

05 Antonin Raymond, *An Autobiography* (Op. cit., p. 124).

06 František Sammer (1907–1973), architect, pupil of Le Corbusier, who among other projects contributed to the construction of the Moscow metro, co-designer of the Plzeň-Slovany housing estate.

07 Antonín was born as the third child of the Jewish trader from Kladno Alois Reimann and his wife Růžena, née Taussigová. His siblings were Irma, married as Rohatýnová (1886–1942); Elsa, married as Štědrá (1887–1942); František (1890–1943); Egon (1892–1944) and Viktor (1894–1942). – On the family of Antonín Raymond see: Irena Veverková, *Antonín Raymond a Reimannové. Osud židovské rodiny ve XX. století.* (Společnost Patria, [Kladno] 2006).

行[12]しか割いていないにものの、そこには若く優秀な建築家への明らかな思いやりがある。次のような言葉もまた、その確信を裏づけるものだ。「ノエミと私は君を本当に愛してきて、その気持ちはちっとも変わることがなかった。手紙を読み終える時には、君のことをもっともっと愛するようになっていた。とても素敵な手紙だ」[13]

1966年から1973年のサマーの死まで、毎年何通かずつ、海を越えて手紙が行き来した（サマーは東京あるいはニューヨークへ手紙を出した）。

現存するレーモンドの手紙の中に、かつてポンディシェリで一緒にした仕事の思い出と、このインドの町についての記述を目にすることができる。「ポンディシェリはいつでも大きくなっていく。彼らは真新しい町を建てるというアイディアを持っている。それを『オーロヴィル』と呼んで、若いフランス人の建築家が取り組んでいる。彼らは私を必要としたのだが、私はというと、もう望んでいないんだ。とても暑いし、他の面でも色々と。それでも一応スケッチを提案した…」[14]。そして東京のレーモンド事務所の近況についても言及されている。

レーモンドのいくつかの言葉から窺い知ることができるのは、彼が社会主義下のチェコスロヴァキアにおける生活を全く想像できなかったという点だ。「夏の間エダ[15]が遊びに来てくれてとても楽しかった。私たちはよく彼女のことを考えているよ。エダと哲学的やりとりをすることを、私はほとんど恐れていた。彼女は昔のチェコでの生活を知らず、私は新しいチェコでの生活を知らない。私たちの人生は根本的に違っているんだ。彼女は君に似ているよ。理想主義的な二人、物質社会における精神的気質だね」[16]。また、この手紙においてレーモンドは政治的影響に屈した建築の芸術史的な評価についても理解できていなかった。「私は自伝で、ズリーン訪問について言及した…。ズリーンは、私からすれば、チェコでのこの種の建築の中で最もよい作例だったが、エダが言うには、私の本にはチェコスロヴァキアの建築についてなど一言も書かれていない、とのことだった」[17]

現存する手紙は、彼が死ぬまでずっと故郷に関心を持ち、魅せられていたことを記録している。彼は可能な限り、特に1968年などには、チェコスロヴァキアでの出来事について情報を集めていた。しかしながら彼が故郷とその将来に抱く心配は、中欧の政治状況への無知から、誤った見解を導き出してしまった。「君が書いたチェコを、プラハを、モラヴィア地方を見に行くことはきっととても楽しく興味深いことになるだろう。けれども思い切って行ってみる気にはならない、もう私自身恐れている、この自分の発言をも…。日々チェコで何が起こっているか注目していると、少し怖いんだ、ハンガリーのことも忘れたことはないし」[18]

これについては次のように考えることができる。「自分の発言を」という言い方は、レーモンドにしばしば起こる問題を象徴するものだ。つまり、社会や世界の出来事に対する自らの言葉と判断によって不都合が引き起こされるという問題だ。

専門的な文脈においてレーモンドの作品は有名であったので、60年代の自由な気風のもとで若い建築家たちは彼にプラハでの展示企画を持ちかけていた。

資料、建築家、グループ２―往復書簡、手紙、1966年8月30日付。

09 フランチシェク・サマーは1930年代にインドの町ポンディシェリでレイモンドの建築事務所が手がけたアシュラム寮計画のために働いた。このアシュラムは哲学者で詩人、神秘家、（いわゆるインテグラルヨガの）グルであったシュリー・オーロビンド(1872〜1950)が創始した。詳細は以下を参照。Helena Čapková, “Dormitář Golconde”. In: Hubert Guzik (ed.), Bydlet spolu. Kolektivní domy v českých zemích a Evropě ve 20. století. (Arbor Vitae, Praha 2017, pp. 134〜143)。

10 エドヴァルト・ベネシュ (1884〜1948)、政治家、国会議員、1935〜1938年および1945〜〜1948年の期間はチェコスロヴァキア大統領。

11 松岡洋右 (1880〜1946)、日本の外交官、第二次世界大戦期の外務省大臣。

12 Antonin Raymond, An Autobiography. (1973, p.160)。

13 プルゼン市文書館、フランチチェク・サマー資料、建築家、グループ２―往復書簡、手紙、1968年5月13日付。

14 前掲。手紙、1966年12月9日付。

15 エダ。この文脈においてはフランチシェク・サマーの娘だのことだと思われる。

16 プルゼン市文書館、フランチチェク・サマー資料、建築家、グループ２―往復書簡、手紙、1966年12月9日付。

17 前掲。Oldřich Starý (et al.), Československá architektura od nejstarší doby po současnost (NČSVU, Praha 1962)。

18 前掲。手紙、1968年5月13日。

architect. This is supported also by the following words from their correspondence: "Noémi and I truly loved you, and nothing has changed. Now I've finally read your letter, we love you more and more. It's so wonderful to read your correspondence."[13]

From 1966 until Sammer's death in 1973 they exchanged letters across the ocean (Sammer wrote either to Tokyo or New York) several times a year.

In Raymond's preserved correspondence we find both recollections of their collaboration in Pondicherry and news from the Indian town: "Pondicherry is getting bigger and bigger. Now they have the idea of building an entire new city – they call it 'Auroville' – and some young French architect is working on it – They wanted me, but I don't want to go there any more – it's too hot – in several senses of the word. But I just provided a sketch..."[14] The letters also contain news from Raymond's Tokyo office.

Some of Raymond's writing indirectly shows that he was completely unable to imagine life in socialist Czechoslovakia: "It was a great pleasure for us to have Eda[15] here with us in the summer, and we think of her often. I was almost afraid to start philosophising with her. She doesn't know life in her homeland as it used to be, and I don't know life there as it is now. Those lives differ fundamentally. She's similar to you. Both of you idealists – spiritually grounded in a materialist world."[16] Within this context he was unable to understand that even art-historical evaluation in architecture was subject to political influence: "In my autobiography I also mention my visit to Zlín... I think that Zlín was the best work of its type in the country, but there's not a single word about it in that book *Československá architektura* (Czechoslovak Architecture) that Eda brought me."[17]

The preserved letters document that his native land continued to interest and attract him until the end of his life. Where possible he followed events in Czechoslovakia, in particular the events of 1968. However, his fears for his homeland and its future betrayed his lack of awareness concerning the political situation in the heart of Europe: "We would be hugely gratified and interested to see for ourselves Bohemia, Prague and that Moravian region you write about – but I do not dare – I now fear myself – and my big mouth... Every day we follow the events in the Czech lands and we are a little worried, after all we have not forgotten the times of the Hungarian Empire.."[18]

We may surmise that by using the phrase "my big mouth" Raymond was referring to the occasional problems he caused in society and the surrounding world through his pronouncements and judgements of events.

In academic circles Raymond's work was well known, and so in the liberalised atmosphere of the 1960s he was addressed by young architects who wished for him to hold an exhibition in Prague. This plan, which emerged in 1965, was also supported by his native town of Kladno. "On the basis of a resolution of the council of the Municipal National Committee of Kladno on the day of 9 December 1965, your employee Mr. Jaroslav Pergl – a member of our cultural and educational commission and the museum council – has been authorised with the task of preparing an exhibition of the natives of Kladno – the internationally renowned architect Antonín Raymond,

08 Archive of the city of Plzeň, file Sammer František, architect, group 2 – correspondence, letter dated 30. 8. 1966.

09 In the 1930s František Sammer worked for Raymond's architectural office in the Indian city of Pondicherry on the project of the dormitory of the ashram, established by the philosopher, poet, mystic and guru (of "integral yoga") Sri Aurobindo (1872–1950). – For further details see: Helena Čapková, "Dormitář Golconde". In: Hubert Guzik (ed.), *Bydlet spolu. Kolektivní domy v českých zemích a Evropě ve 20. století.* (Arbor Vitae, Praha 2017, pp. 134–143).

10 Edvard Beneš (1884–1948), politician and statesman, President of Czechoslovakia in the years 1935–1938 and 1945–1948.

11 Matsuoka Yosuke (1880–1946), Japanese diplomat and Minister of Foreign Affairs at the time of the Second World War.

12 Antonin Raymond, *An Autobiography*. Op. cit., p. 160.

13 Archive of the city of Plzeň, file Sammer František, architect, group 2 – correspondence, letter dated 13. 5. 1968.

14 Ibid., letter dated 9. 12. 1966.

15 Eda – based on the context probably the daughter of František Sammer.

16 Archive of the city of Plzeň, file Sammer František, architect, group 2 – correspondence, letter dated 9. 12. 1966.

17 Ibid. – Oldřich Starý (et al.), *Československá architektura od nejstarší doby po současnost* (NČSVU, Praha 1962).

18 Ibid., letter dated 13. 5. 1968.

この企画は1965年に動き始め、彼の出身地クラドノでも同意を得た。「クラドノ市人民議会の実行委員会会議に基づき、1965年12月9日、貴殿の従業員——我々の文化教育委員会および美術館委員会のヤロスラフ・ペルグル委員は、クラドノが輩出した世界的建築家アントニン・レーモンドおよびツィリル・ボウドの展覧会を行なうことを許可された」

展覧会は1966年クラドノで共産党の地方議会や市議会による文化政策の一環として企画されたものだった。[19]

省庁の許可が下りた内容以外の展覧会開催は不可能であり、レーモンドがその点について同意しなかったことから、彼の作品は以降長期に渡って、広く一般に公開されることはなかった。レーモンドは申し出について次のように記している。「若いチェコの建築家たちがプラハで私の展覧会を開きたいと連絡してきた。もちろん私はやる気になり、楽しみだったのだが、次の手紙に、この件に関してプライベートに許可が下りることはありえないので省庁の誰かの承認が必要だと書いてあった。それで私は省庁に支援を求めたのだが、残念なことに…」[20]

1960年代、アントニン・レーモンドには、いまだクラドノでの実科学校時代の同窓生カレル・ノイマン[21]とつながりがあった。これについてはチェコの政党からの強い影響もあった。カレル・ノイマンはチェコスロヴァキア大使館を通じてレーモンドの日本の住所を聞き出し、公的に何度か手紙のやりとりをした[22]。残念なことに、この往復書簡は現存しておらず、ノイマンがズデニェク・トマ[23]に宛てた手紙から間接的に知ることができるのみである。この交友関係について、唯一のはっきりした手がかりは、カレル・ノイマンへの手書きの献辞が残った自伝の存在だけだ。[24]

1970年代、おそらく広まりはしなかったのだが、レーモンドの創作について認知度を高めようとする動きがあった。最初の記事は雑誌『青年の科学と技術』に掲載されたのだが、概して別の文脈のものであり、ストラホフスキースタジアム改修工事の必要性について論じていた(236ページを参照)。3枚の写真が付けられた短い雑誌記事の結びの文章に、次のような記述があった。「スタジアムの未来として想定される別の例はレーモンドとラドの建築モデルである。これは99000人を収容するスタジアムである」[25]。1973年には、レーモンドの85歳を遅ればせながら記念して、比較的包括的でよく練られた記事が出版された。[26]

その2年後の1975年に、先にも紹介した大の親日家ズデニェク・トマ[27]は、レーモンドと連絡が取れるようになった。この時レーモンドはすでに最晩年にさしかかっていたにもかかわらず、写真家・ジャーナリスト・旅行家であるトマと短い間連絡を取り合った。現存する英語の手紙で、レーモンドは東京の事務所での出来事をまとめ、当時事務所を取り仕切っていた木村氏を称えている。また、チェコスロヴァキアで作品がほとんど知られていないのにもかかわらず「アメリカ人物事典」や「世界人物事典」に自身が取り上げられているという事実への驚きを率直に示していた。

ズデニェク・トマの個人アーカイヴにも、チェコ語で書かれた短い手紙が残っている。日付は1975年10月10日、2枚の写真が封入されている。この手紙か

19 クラドノ地方委員会の書簡、1965年12月15日付、ソコル・クラドノ常任監督の運営管理官J.スラーデク氏宛、ヤロスラフ・ペルグル個人アーカイブ、ブシュチェフラット。

20 プルゼン市文書館、フランチチェク・サマー資料、建築家、グループ2—往復書簡、手紙、1966年8月30日付。

21 カレル・ノイマン(1889〜1979)、プラハで技術を学び、家族はクラドノで運送業の会社を経営していた。

22 この往復書簡はカレル・ノイマンの死後、公的に破棄された。

23 カレル・ノイマンがズデニェク・トマに宛てた手紙、1975年1月10日付。ズデニェク・トマの私的アーカイヴ。

24 現物の本は国立技術博物館(NTM)の建築部門に収蔵されている。

25 In: Věda a technika mládeži, no. 11, 1960, 26. 5. 1960, p. 331. 筆者による注記：この時代、専門家にでもならない限り、彼らがチェコやスロヴァキア出身の建築家であると気づくことは誰にもできなかった。

26 Prokop H. Toma, „Český architekt v Japonsku“. In: Lidová demokracie, 1973, XXIX, No. 278, p. 6。レーモンドはジェヴニチョフで生まれたという誤記がある。

27 ズデニェク・トマ(1938)、写真家、ジャーナリスト、旅行家であり元々は科学者。1970年以降体系的にアジアで写真を撮影している。

196 – 『ヴェダ・ア・テフニカ・ムラーデェジ』誌の複写。下の写真はA.レーモンドとL.L.ラドによるプロジェクト・モデル。

Studio of A. Raymond, Golconde dormitory, ashram of Sri Aurobindo (Pondicherry, India, present state)

and Cyril Bouda. / According to the cultural plan of the District Committee of the Communist Party of Czechoslovakia, the District National Committee and the Municipal National Committee, the exhibition is to be held in Kladno in 1966."[19]

Since it was not possible to organise the exhibition otherwise than with the permission of the ministry, with which Antonín Raymond disagreed, his work remained concealed from the wider public in Czechoslovakia for many years to come. With regard to the offer, Raymond stated the following: "Some young Czech architects wrote to me – they want to hold an exhibition of my work in Prague – I was willing – naturally – I would have been pleased – I had it organised – Then a letter arrived – such an enterprise cannot be permitted privately – it has to be under the auspices of the ministry of something – and so I wrote to the ministry to leave me alone – a shame."[20]

In the 1960s Antonín Raymond was also contacted by his fellow pupil from grammar school in Kladno, Karel Neumann.[21] In this case also, the impulse came from the Czech side. Karel Neumann requested Raymond's address in Japan via the Czechoslovak embassy in Tokyo. They probably exchanged a number of letters[22] but their correspondence was not preserved, and we learn about it only indirectly in the form of Neumann's letter addressed to Zdeněk Thoma.[23] The only tangible evidence of these contacts is a copy of Raymond's autobiography with a handwritten dedication to Karel Neumann.[24]

In the 1970s there were only rather isolated attempts to popularise Raymond's work. The first mention appeared in the magazine *Věda a technika mládeži* (Science and Technology for Youth), but within entirely different contexts (see fig. 197, p. 236).

19 Letterfrom the Council of the Municipal National Committee Kladno, ref. no. j. RA/126/65, dated 15. 12. 1965, addressed to J. Sládek, commercial secretary to the company director of SONP Kladno. Private archive of Jaroslav Pergl of Buštěhrad.

20 Archive of the city of Plzeň, file Sammer František, architect, group 2 – correspondence, letter dated 30. 8. 1966.

21 Karel Neumann (1889 1979), studied technology in Prague, his family in Kladno owned and operated a forwarding business.

22 The mentioned correspondence was evidently destroyed after the death of Karel Neumann.

23 Letter from Karel Neumann addressed to Zdeněk Thoma dated 10. 1. 1975. Private archive of Zdeněk Thoma.

24 The book is stored in the National Technical Museum, department of architecture and civil engineering. The book contains a dedication with the following wording: "New Hope / December / 1973 / Prosinec/ Mému drahému / a / věrnému příteli / Karlovi / také s věrností a vděčností / Antonín Raymond".

らは、1910年から長年外国で暮らしてきたにもかかわらず、いかに深くレーモンドの内面に母語とその言語に対する敬意が根付いていたかがわかる。

ズデニェク・トマはアントニン・レーモンドについて得られた情報と、1978年までの外国での建築作品について積極的に論じた。既にアントニンは亡くなっていたが、「アントニン・レーモンド——異国日本のチェコ人建築家[28]」という題の記事でより多くの読者に、少なくとも故国では忘れられた男についての情報を伝えた。『技術雑誌』は、1975年4月の手紙に付いていた写真を除いて出版された。

この伝記的評論の冒頭で、1945年以降、建築家レーモンドはどの程度祖国とのつながりを保っていられたのかという問いを設定したが、これについて次のように述べることができる。頻繁なやりとりは在日チェコスロヴァキア大使館を通じて行われ、1960年代以降はフランチシェク・サマー、カレル・ノイマンと書簡を往復した。アントニン・レーモンドにとって戦後のチェコスロヴァキアでの生活は未知な面があった。一度もチェコのルーツを捨てることはなく、チェコ人とチェコ語でやりとりすることを自らの義務と捉えていた（手紙の多くには文法の間違いの弁明が添えられた）。

アントニン・レーモンドは次のような理由においても私たちの賞賛を受けるにふさわしい人物である。すなわち母語の知識を、60年以上も祖国を離れていたにもかかわらず生きているかぎりずっと、保持したことである。しかしながら、第二次世界大戦後の祖国の政治的変遷については、あれほど長く鉄のカーテンの反対側で生きてきた者の視点からでは、完全に理解することは到底できなかった。

イレナ・ヴェヴェルコヴァー

SPARTAKIÁDA V BUDOUCNOSTI

K TITULNÍ STRANĚ OBÁLKY

Spartakiáda se stává stále masovější záležitostí našich pracujících. Počet cvičenců s každou spartakiádou stoupá o desítky tisíc. Zamysleli jsme se nad problémem, který vzniká tímto přílivem účastníků i diváků. Je to otázka stadiónu, jenž pojme tak velké množství cvičenců a ještě větší množství diváků. V budoucnu patrně nebude dostačovat ani náš největší – Strahovský stadión. Nehledíme-li už na plochu a počet diváků, jež stadión pojme, máme zde ještě další otázku: závislost úspěchu spartakiády na počasí. Dosud nemáme tak velký krytý stadión, jenž by umožnil cvičencům i divákům provoz za každého počasí.

Proto jsme na obálce našeho časopisu přinesli jednu ukázku, jak by mohl vypadat krytý stadión budoucnosti. Je to zatím model projektu inž. L. Zetlina. Tento krytý stadión by pojal až 200 000 diváků. Konstrukci stadiónu tvoří železobetonové podpěry, jdoucí od základů zešikmeně ke spodní části stadiónu, kde jsou umístěny tribuny. Tyto podpěry jsou značně vychýlené ven od základů a tvoří jakousi „misu". Ve vrchní části této „misy" jsou železobetonové podpěry zachyceny ocelovými táhly do ocelového prstence ve středu stadiónu. Ve spodní části stadiónu jsou železobetonové rampy pro příchod diváků k tribunám. Po těchto rampách lze dokonce přijet vozem. Celá konstrukce stadiónu je zastřešena mohutnou kopulí z průhledné umělé hmoty, jež spočívá na ocelových táhlech, udržujících podpěry ve statické rovnováze. (Obr. nahoře a uprostřed.)

Jiným příkladem stadiónu budoucnosti je model arch. Raymonda a Rado. Je to stadión pro 99 000 diváků. (Obrázek dole.)

197 – 『ヴェダ・ア・テフニカ・ムラーデェジ』誌の複写。下の写真はA.レーモンドとL.L.ラドによるプロジェクト・モデル。

Facsimile of article from Věda a technika mláděži magazine (1960). The lower photograph shows a model of the project by A. Raymond and L. L. Rado

28 Zdeněk Thoma, „Antonín Raymond : český architekt v exotickém Japonsku". In: Technický magazín, 1978, XXI, No. 1, pp. 30〜31。

At that time considerations emerged concerning the necessity for a reconstruction and modernisation of the Strahov stadium. A brief magazine column was published with three images, concluded with the sentence: "Another example of a stadium of the future is the model by the architectural office Raymond and Rado. This is a stadium for 99 000 spectators."[25] In 1973 a short article was published, intended as a belated congratulation on the occasion of Raymond's eighty-fifth birthday.[26]

Two years later, in 1975, the aforementioned Zdeněk Thoma[27], a great lover of Japan, succeeded in establishing contact with Antonín Raymond. Despite the fact that by this time Antonín Raymond was now in failing health at the end of his life, he maintained a brief correspondence with this photograph, columnist and traveller. In a preserved letter, dictated in English, he provided a summary of the information regarding the Tokyo office, and attached a recommendation for its then head, Mr. Kimura. He was also perplexed by the fact that his work was practically unknown in Czechoslovakia, despite the fact that he was presented in publications such as *Who is Who in America* and *Who is Who in the World.*

Zdeněk Thoma's personal archive also contains a preserved short letter written in Czech, dated 10 October 1975, to which two photographs are attached. This letter documents not only how deeply rooted Raymond was in his native language, but also his great respect for the language, despite the fact that he had been living abroad since 1910.

Zdeněk Thoma was not able to make use of the information he had obtained about Antonín Raymond and his work abroad until 1978. At that time, after Raymond's death, at least basic information about this man forgotten in his homeland was made available to the wider public in the article "Antonín Raymond : a Czech architect in exotic Japan".[28] Among other images, *Technický magazín* (Technical magazine) also printed photographs sent by Raymond himself, which he had sent in a letter dated April 1975.

If we inquired at the beginning of this biographical article regarding the extent to which the architect Raymond was able to maintain contacts with his native land after 1945, we may state that these were occasional contacts with the embassy in Tokyo, and from the 1960s also his correspondence with František Sammer and Karel Neumann. It is therefore probable that post-war life in Czechoslovakia remained largely unknown to Antonín Raymond. Nevertheless, he never turned his back on his Czech roots, and considered it his duty to correspond with Czechs in his native language (mostly with apologies for his grammatical errors).

Antonín Raymond also merits our admiration because he managed to maintain his knowledge of his native language until the end of his days, thus after more than sixty years spent outside his native land. However, as a person living for so long on the other side of the Iron Curtain, he was never entirely able to understand the country's political development after the Second World War.

Irena Veverková

25 In: *Věda a technika mládeži*, 1960, no. 11, 26. 5. 1960, p. 331. – The fact that Raymond and Rado were architects of Czech and Slovak origin respectively was known only to experts at that time.

26 Prokop H. Toman, "Český architekt v Japonsku". *Lidová demokracie*, 1973, annual XXIX, no. 278, p. 6. (In the article the author erroneously states that A. Raymond was born in Řevničov).

27 Zdeněk Thoma (born 1938), photographer, columnist and traveller, originally a chemist by profession. After 1970 he systematically photographed in Asia.

28 Zdeněk Thoma, "Antonín Raymond : český architekt v exotickém Japonsku". In: *Technický magazín XXI*, 1978, no. 1, pp. 30–31.

写真提供者

五代 美子: 口絵、2～38、40、41、72～82

内藤恒方: 71

北澤 興一: 39、42～70、83～156

北澤 興一、小林 薫、小林 邦子、西嶋 泰親、西嶋 圭子: 157～195

個人所蔵: 1、197

Owners of illustrations

Godai Yoshiko: frontispiece, 2–38, 40, 41, 72–82
Naitō Tsunekata: 71
Kitazawa Kōichi: 39, 42–70, 83–156
Kitazawa Kōichi, Kobayashi Kaoru, Kobayashi Kuniko, Nishijima Yasuchika, Nishijima Keiko: 157–195
Private archive: 1, 197

チャプコヴァー・ヘレナ (1981) ロンドン芸術大学TrAIN研究センター修了。博士(芸術史) 立命館大学グローバル教養学部准教授。主な著作に、"Transnational networkers – Iwao and Michiko Yamawaki and the formation of Japanese Modernist Design" (Oxford Journal of Design History, 2014)、"'Believe in socialism…': Architect Bedřich Feuerstein and His Perspective on Modern Japan and Architecture" (Design and Society in Modern Japan, Vol. 28, 2016)、「アントニン・レーモンドとル・コルビュジエ、建築における海賊行為——形式ではなく精神性が与えた影響についての考察」(稲賀繁美編『海賊史観からみた世界史の再構築交易と情報流通の現在を問い直す』、思文閣、2017)、"'From Decorative Arts to Impressive Local Constructions and Materials' – On the New Japonisme for the Czechoslovak Republic (1918–1938)"、Studies in Japonisme/ジャポニスム研究、2018がある。

北澤 興一 (1937) 1 級建築士
1937 長野県生 現在、東京都渋谷区松涛(在住)。
1961 工学院大学建築学科卒 1962 同建築計画専攻課程修了。1962〜1971 レーモンド建築設計事務所 アントニン・レーモンドに師事。担当作品:南山大学・立教高校・立教大学・上智大学・CAJ 音楽堂・ハワイ国際会議センター他。1971〜株式会社北澤建築設計事務所設立・代表者 現在に至る。1972〜1977 工学院大学建築学科講師。1993〜2004 学校法人工学院大学監事。

ホリー・ペトル (1972) プラハ郊外のドブジーシュ生まれ。1990年プラハ・カレル大学文学部日本学科に入学し、語学短期留学で初来日。早稲田大学、東京学芸大学大学院、早稲田大学大学院にて歌舞伎を研究。2006年、駐日チェコ共和国大使館一等書記官として、同大使館内チェコセンター東京を新たに開設、2013年まで所長を務める。現在、チェコ文化・芸術の紹介と普及を目的にしたウェブサイト「チェコ蔵」を主宰。女子美術大学非常勤講師、早稲田大学演劇博物館招聘研究員、文化資源学会会員。

Helena Čapková (born 1981), following the completion of her Master's course in History of Art and Japanology at Charles University in Prague and SOAS in London, was awarded a doctorate in Transnational Visual Studies at the Chelsea College of Art and Design TrAIN Research Centre in London. Her key publications include the monograph Bedřich Feuerstein – Cesta do nejvýtvarnější země světa [Bedřich Feuerstein – A Journey to the Most Artistically Creative Country in the World] (Aula a KANT, 2014), "Marginální fenomén, nebo oběť orientalistického klišé? K vzájemným stykům japonských a evropských meziválečných avantgard" [A Marginal Phenomenon, or the Victim of an Orientalist Cliché? On the Mutual Contacts between the Japanese and European Inter-War Avant-Gardes] (Časopis Umění/Art, 2017), "Transnational networkers – Iwao and Michiko Yamawaki and the formation of Japanese Modernist Design" (Oxford Journal of Design History, 2014), "'Believe in socialism…' : Architect Bedřich Feuerstein and His Perspective on Modern Japan and Architecture" (Design and Society in Modern Japan, Vol. 28, 2016).

Kōichi Kitazawa (born 1937) completed his studies of architecture at Kōgakuin University in 1962, and during the years 1962–1971 worked in Antonín Raymond's studio, where he headed a number of prestigious projects: Nanzan University, Rikkyō University, the Congress Centre in Hawaii and others. In 1971 he established his own architecture office. He lectured at Kōgakuin University (1972–1977), where he also served on the university's administrative council (1993–2004).

Petr Holý (born 1972) commenced his studies of Japanology at Charles University in Prague in 1990. A sabbatical for the purpose of learning Japanese language brought him to Japan, where he studied at Tokyo Gakugei University and Waseda University, focusing primarily on the study of kabuki. In 2006 he entered the diplomatic services and became the director the Czech centre in Tokyo, which he headed until 2013. He is now engaged in the promotion of Czech culture in Japan, heading the Chekogura agency. He also lectures as an external speaker at a number of Japanese universities, and is a member of the Association for the Study of Cultural Resources (Bunka Shigen Gakkai).

チャプコヴァー・ヘレナ / 北澤興一 編
日本におけるアントニンレーモンド (1948〜1976)
知人たちの回想

文章: ヘレナ・チャプコヴァー、北澤 興一、五代美子、内藤恒方、小林薫、小林邦子、西嶋泰親、西嶋圭子、ペトル・ホリー、イレナ・ヴェヴェルコヴァー。
イラストレーション: 五代美子、北澤 興一、小林薫、小林邦子、西嶋泰親、西嶋圭子、個人所蔵。
日本語訳: 須藤輝彦、富重聡子、河上春香。
英語訳: エシュリ・デイヴィース
日本語監修: 長瀬海、須藤輝彦。
装丁、グラフィック加工、組版: Aula。
Karolinumが2023年にプラハで出版した。
xxx。
初版。

本著はチェコセンター東京、北澤アーカイブとの協力のもとで出版された。

helena čapková / kitazawa kōichi (eds.)
ANTONÍN RAYMOND IN JAPAN (1948–1976)
recollections of friends

Texts: Helena Čapková, Kitazawa Kōichi, Naitō Tsunekata, Kobayashi Kaoru, Kobayashi Kuniko, Nishijima Yasuchika, Nishijima Keiko, Petr Holý and Irena Veverková.
Illustrations: Godai Yoshiko, Kitazawa Kōichi, Kobayashi Kaoru, Kobayashi Kuniko, Nishijima Yasuchika, Nishijima Keiko and private archive.
Translation into Japanese: Sudo Teruhiko, Tomishegi Satoko and Kawakami Haruka.
Translation into English: Ashley Davies.
Editing of Japanese text: Nagase Kai and Sudo Teruhiko.
Cover, graphic layout and typesetting: Aula (Prague).
Published and printed by Karolinum Press, Prague, 2023.
First English edition.

The book is published in co-operation with the Kitazawa Archives.

ISBN 978-80-246-5330-3